BIOTECHNOLOGY

Recent Titles in
Contributions in Political Science

BIOTECHNOLOGY

Assessing Social Impacts and Policy Implications

EDITED BY
David J. Webber

Prepared under the auspices of the
Policy Studies Organization
Stuart S. Nagel, Series Advisor

Contributions in Political Science, Number 260

Greenwood Press
New York • Westport, Connecticut • London

Library of Congress Cataloging-in-Publication Data

Biotechnology : assessing social impacts and policy implications /
  edited by David J. Webber ; prepared under the auspices of the
  Policy Studies Organization.
      p. cm. — (Contributions in political science, ISSN 0147-1066;
  no. 260)
    Includes bibliographical references.
    ISBN 0-313-27454-1 (lib. bdg. : alk. paper)
    1. Biotechnology industries—Social aspects. I. Webber, David
  J., 1951– . II. Policy Studies Organization. III. Series.
  HD9999.B442B567 1990
  338.4′76606—dc20   90-2935

British Library Cataloguing in Publication Data is available.

Library of Congress Catalog Card Number: 90-2935
ISBN: 0-313-27454-1
ISSN: 0147-1066

First published in 1990

Greenwood Press, 88 Post Road West, Westport, CT 06881
An imprint of Greenwood Publishing Group, Inc.

Printed in the United States of America

The paper used in this book complies with the
Permanent Paper Standard issued by the National
Information Standards Organization (Z39.48-1984).

10 9 8 7 6 5 4 3 2 1

Contents

Tables

Preface

The project resulting in this volume began in 1986 when a number of my new social science colleagues at the University of Missouri-Columbia invited me to assist in forming a "social science cluster" of the University's "Food for the 21st Century" research program. Until that time this campus research effort was exclusively oriented towards the biological and food sciences. The challenge of focusing campus attention on the social, ethical, economic, and political aspects of biotechnology applications in agriculture was quite exciting. I was challenged also by the questions other social scientists asked of political scientists regarding the extent to which government institutions would be able to deal with certain projected economic and social impacts of some biotechnology applications. For example, an agriculture economist asked me how agriculture policy, specifically the milk marketing orders program, would withstand the estimated 40 percent increase in the milk supply due to the use of bovine growth hormone (or somatotropin). Believing that political scientists, and other social science-based policy analysts, would be able to provide insight into questions like this, I began a journey into several disciplinary literatures and identified several of the leading social science researchers on a variety of topics related to biotechnology. This volume and a set of articles published earlier in the *Policy Studies Journal* is the work of most of those researchers.

I am grateful for the support of the administrators of the University of Missouri's "Food for the 21st Century" project, especially Roger Mitchell, Dean of the College of Agriculture, and my former dean Milton Glick, now Provost at

Iowa State University, for financially supporting this project. I have enjoyed the intellectual challenges provided by the social science cluster of "Food for the 21st Century," particularly Bruce Bullock of Agriculture Economics, Rex Campbell of Rural Sociology, and Robin Remington of Political Science, and thank them for their encouragement and support. My thanks also go to Chris Plein, research assistant and collaborator, whose dissertation on "the evolution of the biotechnology policy issue" is keeping us both busy.

The views presented in this book reflect those of the authors and not the organizations, agencies, and affiliations to which they belong.

Introduction

Advancements in and applications of biotechnology present a range of technically and politically complex policy issues that need to be faced by local, state,
and national policymakers and a variety of academic, business, agriculture, and
medical institutions during the next decade. Biotechnology, usually defined as
any technique that uses living organisms or processes to make or modify products, to improve plants or animals, or to develop microorganisms, has some of
the same political characteristics that surround other technological advances
such as applications of artificial intelligence in manufacturing and new procedures in medicine. Biotechnology and other technological advances involve rapid
application of new scientific knowledge that challenges existing social values,
legal and political protections, and production processes. The wide use of biotechnology practices and procedures has potential environmental risks, a wide
range of economic repercussions, and international trade implications. Further,
biotechnology raises important ethical and legal considerations, including the
appropriateness of altering the genetic makeup of organisms and the stresses
placed on existing patent protection of intellectual property. The political process reacts to, and at times anticipates, the social, economic, and political impacts of these new technologies.

To some, biotechnology holds great promise for accelerating the reproduction
of limited enzymes and bacteria, like growth hormones, and in genetically altering plants and animals to "build in" what are seen as desirable characteristics like
improved production capacity or disease resistance. For others, biotechnology

raises the specter of environmental catastrophe due to accidental release of a genetically altered organism, economic dislocation as a result of a radically altered
agriculture industry, and human intervention in genetic decisions.

While biotechnology began to be of wide interest in the laboratory in the early
1970s, biotechnology as a policy issue has appeared on, and then disappeared
from, the public agenda. Between the significant event of the Asilomar Conference in 1975 and the preliminary announcement of the "proposal for a Coordinated Framework for Regulation of Biotechnology" in the Federal Register on
December 31, 1984, biotechnology and its regulation was of sporadic public concern. This lack of staying power in the public eye results from several factors:
uncertainty among policymakers how best to respond to the emerging issues, uncertainty from industrial investors about the commercial future of biotechnology, and unsustained public interest in biotechnology developments. Almost
certainly, the decade of the 1990s will see increased interest by policymakers, investors, and the American public.

The chapters in this volume are organized into four sections: social and political dimensions of biotechnology, institutional responses to biotechnology, assessing potential impacts of biotechnology, and public policy responses to this
new technology. Part I, "Social and Political Dimensions of Biotechnology," consists of three chapters examining three very different social and political aspects
of biotechnology. Paul Thompson, in "Biotechnology, Risk, and Political Values:
Philosophical Rhetoric and the Structure of Political Debate," explores the con-
trasting conceptions of societal risk presented by Burke and Bentham and shows
that the debate about biotechnology focuses on these competing views on risk
and its role in public policy. Thomas Wiegele's "Organized Religion and Biotechnology: Social Responsibility and the Role of Government" examines the
stated positions on biotechnology taken by major religious denominations.
Wiegele finds that most denominations' statements on biotechnology are quite
critical of scientists for their lack of ethical concern and do not address the social
value of biotechnology. William Browne and Larry Hamm, in "Political Choices,
Social Values, and the Economics of Biotechnology: A Lesson from the Dairy Industry," examine the technological innovation process by focusing on the availability of both economic and political incentives before technological change will
be widely adopted. Browne and Hamm argue that the scientific and commercial
development of bovine growth hormone for use in the dairy industry was not accompanied by the development of the requisite economic and political interests.

In Part II, "Institutional Responses to the Development of Biotechnology,"
Charles Johnson and Robin Moore examine "American Universities, Technology
Innovation, and Technological Transfer: Implications for Biotechnology Research" through a survey of how major universities encourage and structure
innovative work and technology transfer. Johnson and Moore document the importance of professional support staff in effecting the transfer of biotechnology
innovations. In "Biotechnology and Agricultural Cooperatives: Opportunities,
Challenges, and Strategies for the Future," William Lacy, Lawrence Busch, and

William Cole anticipate the response of one agricultural institution, cooperatives, to biotechnology developments affecting agriculture. They conclude that
while biotechnology offers cooperatives opportunities due to the potential to tailor crops and reduced purchased inputs, biotechnology could adversely affect
cooperatives if it results in greater monopolization of both the input and output
sectors of the agriculture industry. Robert Dixon, in "Plant Biotechnology Networking in Developing Countries," reviews the efforts of international organizations to increase the food supply of Third World countries and argues that
biotechnology's potential to increase food and fiber through improvements in nitrogen fixation, food fermentation, and microbial pesticides will not be achieved
unless the current networks focusing on science and commercial infrastructure
are expanded to include potential users of these biotechnological processes.

Part III, "Assessing Potential Impacts of Biotechnology," presents three perspectives on evaluating several of the expected impacts of biotechnology on agriculture and the food supply. Beverly Fleisher asks "Who Will Benefit from
Agricultural Biotechnology?" and examines the financial, legal, and regulatory
factors that are shaping the development and commercialization of biotechnology. Richard Sherlock and Amal Kawar contrast a market model with a social
model of regulation in "Regulating Genetically Engineered Organisms: The
Case of the Dairy Industry." They argue that regulatory concerns do not cover
all of the concerns that have been raised about the use of genetically engineered
organisms in food processing. Specifically, they urge that consumer choice be
considered as a regulatory mechanism for products of the dairy industry.

Fred Kuchler, John McClelland, and Susan Offutt, in "Regulatory Experience
with Food Safety: Social Choice Implications for Recombinant DNA Derived
Animal Growth Hormones," rely on three parallel controversies about food
safety, showing how they shaped the legal and regulatory definitions of product
safety. Kuchler et al. demonstrate not only the real cost of stalling the introduction of new technologies (demonstrated by their case study of milk pasteurization) but also the availability, after the fact, of nonregulatory mechanisms for
promoting food safety (demonstrated by a case study of DES used as a growth
promotant in cattle).

Part IV, "Public Policy Responses to Biotechnology," contains three chapters
that review how different aspects of the American policy process have responded
to the development of biotechnology. Christopher Plein presents a three-phased
evolution of public interest in genetic engineering. In "Biotechnology: Issue Development and Evolution," Plein argues that public concern with the scientific
development of biotechnology evolved from primarily a concern with ethics in
the early 1970s, to an interest in health and environmental safety in the late
1970s, to the present focus of the economic dimensions of biotechnology. Morris
Bosin offers policymakers a framework for thinking about their responsibilities
in regulating this new technology in "Policymakers Address Biotechnology: Issues and Responsibilities." Bosin argues that policymakers need to view their responsibilities as "risk management" and that the formulation and communica-

tion of national goals and risk acceptance relating to biotechnology are shaped by a variety of factors of which regulators need to be aware. Mack Shelley, William Woodman, Brian Reichel, and Paul Lasley examine the involvement of state governments and universities in encouraging biotechnology in "Economic Development and Public Policy: What is the Role for Biotechnology?" These authors review the activities of one state, Iowa, and examine the opinions and preferences of a sample of academicians, state policymakers, and clientele relating to a state economic development strategy focusing on biotechnology. Finally, in the concluding chapter, "Biotechnology Policy Knowledge: A Challenge for Congressional Policymakers and Policy Analysts," David Webber compares the types of policy concerns about biotechnology expressed by members of Congress and the themes examined by policy analysts studying a variety of aspects of biotechnology.

While this volume examines several aspects of the biotechnology debate, there are a variety of dimensions that are not addressed. For example, international trade and terrorism are not considered, while some aspects like patenting new life forms are mentioned but not fully developed. Taken together these chapters anticipate a variety of potential social, economic, and institutional consequences if biotechnology gains wide acceptance and use. In my judgment, the analyses contained in this volume are not alarmist, but rather can serve to assist policymakers in formulating effective policy strategies intended to minimize adverse impacts of this emerging technology.

I
Social and Political Dimensions of Biotechnology

1
Biotechnology, Risk, and Political Values: Philosophical Rhetoric and the Structure of Political Debate

Paul B. Thompson

Only a few years ago, new applications of recombinant DNA research and manufacturing techniques promised to spark political controversy on at least three independent fronts. First, and most prominently, since research and development of agricultural products would ultimately require field testing and release of engineered organisms into the environment, safety concerns that had largely become dormant for other uses of biotechnology (Cohen, 1977; Goodfield, 1978) were raised anew for agricultural applications (Baum, 1984; Thompson, 1987). Second, Edward Yoxen's 1983 book *The Gene Business: Who Should Control Biotechnology?* gave voice to a populist fear that biotechnology would increase corporate control over the economy. This fear was tied specifically to agriculture by Jack Kloppenburg (1984) and Martin Kenney (1985), but became most prominently associated with the impending introduction of bovine somatotropin or growth hormone (bGH) (Buttel, 1986a). Biotechnology reduces the cost of bGH, and bGH itself increases the productivity of dairy cows. The upshot is a projected shift in the economics of the U.S. dairy industry that was generalized to all of agriculture by economist Robert J. Kalter: "In sum, the introduction of biotechnology will probably accelerate the trend toward fewer and larger farms, and the structure of agriculture will tend more and more toward specialization" (1985:131). Finally, biotechnology became a new point in an old debate between those who see agricultural technology as a source of economic growth for Third World economies, and those who see it merely as a way of enforcing the Third World's dependency on the research and manufacturing capacities of developed capitalist nations (Buttel et al., 1984; Kenney and Buttel, 1985; Dembo et al., 1985).

There is an obvious sense in which all three problem areas involve interest groups. Corporate and scientific interests who stand to gain profits and research funding would prefer that biotechnology research be unimpeded by regulatory restrictions. Groups focused on environmental issues, farm protest, and international development might be losers if the preferences of biotechnology interests are allowed to hold sway, but they have largely failed to cooperate behind the scenes in a way that would enable them to play a decisive role in the development of a policy for biotechnology (Browne, 1987b). Advocates of aggressive research and commercial development nevertheless continue to express unease over agricultural biotechnology's vulnerability to political action (Moses and Hess, 1987; Brill, 1988). In 1984, interested parties predicted that the acrimonious atmosphere created by interest-group politics would militate against candor, and that public statements on biotechnology would increasingly reflect private rather than public interests (Webber, 1984). Despite years of action in the courts and in the executive branch (Thompson, 1987), the political issues underlying the future of biotechnology appear to be as volatile and indeterminate as they were in 1984.

In the following analysis, the interest-group politics of biotechnology will be largely ignored, and the contending parties will be examined with an eye to the way that their rhetoric expresses fundamental political values with respect to the social management of risk. All three issues deal with risk, though with different risks borne by different parties. The prospect of environmental release raises questions of public safety. The possibility of economic restructuring in the agricultural sector poses risks to firms most likely to be adversely affected. The development of biotechnology for the Third World poses risks to producers in both the developed and developing world, as the comparative advantages arising from climate and soils may be erased by genetically altered cultivars. This is not to suggest that philosophical attitudes toward risk are causally determinate in affecting biotechnology policy, nor even to suggest (as shall become clear below) that political values provide a definitive indicator for policy choice. Basic political values create a rhetorical space in which risk arguments can be advanced to make claims upon the public conscience. To the extent that basic political values are ideologically held, they may indeed influence an individual's policy preference, but it seems more reasonable to presume that such values have a greater influence in the way that they characterize the public interest, thus providing alternative visions of political legitimacy that can be selected by interest groups for their rhetorical advantages. The logic of these value systems is not, however, completely malleable; they provide both avenues for and constraints upon the advancement of interests and formation of political alliances.

The first section to follow outlines classical interpretations of conservative and liberal political values as they would be drawn from the philosophical writings of Edmund Burke and Jeremy Bentham. These philosophical statements do not readily translate into the contemporary political meanings of conservative and liberal; there are plenty of utilitarian conservatives in the United States today. As classic statements of alternative philosophical visions of political society, Burke and Bentham remain unsurpassed. In the second section, these statements are extended to provide alternative accounts of risk. A review of risk arguments on biotechnology follows in the third section. For the sake of simplicity, arguments on environmental release are discussed to the exclusion of arguments on farm structure and international development. The remaining two sections relate these arguments to political alliances and draw some speculative conclusions on biotechnology policy, respectively.

Burke and Bentham

Edmund Burke's *Reflections on the Revolution in France* is sometimes classified as an antitheoretical work, an opinion at least partially justified by Burke's persistent refusal to embrace theory as a map or guidepost for social reform. Jeremy Bentham, by contrast, outlines his theory of act utilitarianism in a few scant pages of his *Introduction to the Principles of Morals and Legislation*, and proceeds to advance it as the touchstone both for individuals and for public authorities. Utilitarianism is to guide public policy as a comprehensive theory of the law. It is in his mistrust of applied social theories, and not in any specific response to the consequential aspects of utilitarianism per se, that Burke provides a counterpoint to Bentham. Indeed, the *Reflections on the Revolution in France* devotes far more energy to critique of the "rights of man" theories of revolutionary Europe and America than to the specific form of utility maximization found in Bentham. While Bentham, however, rejects rights as "nonsense on stilts," Burke objects unilaterally to those who prefer theory to tradition.

This objection should not, however, be generalized too broadly. Burke has a theory of society; it is simply not one that lends itself to planned policy interventions. Perhaps the most enduring conservative insight of Burke's work is the idea that public policies are deeply embedded in the full institutional structure of society, including religion, the schools, the marketplace, and the home, and not simply in the statutes or administrative actions of government. The procedure for change in these embedded institutions is an evolutionary one in which the habits and attitudes of individuals are altered one by one as they become outmoded or are disproved through rational debate. Because government is only a single cog in this complex network of social institutions, it is dangerous to attempt sudden reform by adjusting its wheels and levers. One simply cannot know what accumulated wisdom, what adaptive functions, one threatens when one makes a seemingly innocuous adjustment of government practice. The conservative credo thus becomes one of evolutionary change rather than conscious manipulation. It is the institutions of society, after all, that must change as surely as the government.

As noted already, the approach to policy expressed in Jeremy Bentham's *Intro-*

duction to the Principles of Morals and Legislation could not have been more anti-thetical to Burke's distrust of theory. The utilitarian procedure for making law and policy is to project the consequences caused by the proposal and its alterna-tives. This done, one applies a decision rule (for Bentham it was, of course, to produce the greatest good) to identify the optimal choice. Since Bentham there have been two centuries of debate over the utilitarian maxim, but remarkably lit-tle alteration in the basic procedure. Policy is to be decided by a two-stage pro-cess. The first utilizes the best available method for anticipating the expected outcome. As the techniques of social and natural sciences have matured, the best available method has made increasing use of scientific theory as a predictive tool. The second stage is the application of a decision rule that evaluates the predicted consequences of each option. Philosophical debate has questioned whether this rule should be a maximizing one, a libertarian one, a game-theoretic one, a dis-tributive one, or some combination of rules; but all these debates take place within the policy framework advocated by Bentham, and rejected by Burke.

Where Burke is reticent, Bentham is intervening. Where Burke defines proce-dure by the evolving set of social institutions, Bentham defines it as a conscious projection and evaluation of expected outcomes. It is a dispute that goes to the very logic of public action, and it is not surprising that it has reached its bicen-tennial. In contemporary debate, the conservatism of Burke continues to be ech-oed by conservative opposition to government interventions of all kinds. Today, however, this opposition frequently has a classically liberal rationale, as neoclas-sical economics is often cited to demonstrate the inefficiency of government programs. A Burkean conservative should have no more faith in the theoretical projections of the Chicago School than the *philosophes'* proclamation of the rights of man. It is the classical Burkean and Benthamite definitions of conserva-tive and liberal political values that will be presupposed in this analysis.

Political Values and the Concept of Risk

Although the concept of risk does not figure explicitly in Burke and Bentham (as it does, for example, in Rawls and Nozick), it is fairly easy to sketch the im-plications of their views. For a true conservative, simply to call an act "risky" is to introduce some prejudice against it. Our traditions and institutions help us sort acts into two categories: those acts that are ordinary and unexceptional sim-ply by virtue of their utterly prosaic character, and those acts which deviate from pattern, custom, and conventional practice, and which threaten the stability of life's commonplace regime by doing so. There may be some such acts (risks) that are excusable either because they cannot be avoided or because desperate cir-cumstances dictate unusual measures, but none of that is to deny the irreducible suspicion and distaste with which they are to be regarded.

For the Benthamite, all acts have consequences and most will have some bad that must be weighed against the good. Risks are not fundamentally different from negative outcomes, aside from the fact that their probabilistic character complicates our decision rule for weighing good and bad. Indeed, it is the consequentialist followers of Bentham in contemporary utility theory and rational choice who have given us the elaborate definitions of risk as a function of probability and utility of outcome. This means that there is no bias against risk per se (aside from the obvious fact that risks are counted on the "cost" side of a policy evaluation). The acceptance or rejection of a risk can only be made after a predictive analysis that identifies (however roughly) the expected consequences, and assigns a probability to them. This assessment of an action's risk does not introduce a prejudice against the act, for it is only after the decision rule has been applied that a risk is determined to be acceptable or unacceptable.

The notion of weighing an action's probable negative outcomes against its benefits has become so thoroughly entrenched in policy analysis that many seem to have difficulty thinking of risk in any other terms. The difference between the two views harks back to the radically different views of policy procedure. For the Benthamite liberal, procedure consists in the examination and evaluation of options, candidates for action, and risk emerges as a property or trait that applies to every option, just as the general outcome-oriented properties of benefit or cost apply to every possible choice. For the Burkean conservative, procedure is the accretion of traditions and institutions that reinforce or sanction one pattern of behavior, while obstructing and thwarting unhealthy deviates. Here risk is a category of action, rather than a trait that might be applied across the board to any action. It is not as if Benthamite liberals and Burkean conservatives apply different moral standards to the evaluation of a commonly understood notion of risk; the different approaches to procedure entail different definitions for the word, definitions operating at logically incompatible levels of grammar.

In common speech we accomplish the logically impossible almost routinely, so one should not make too much of this grammatical anomaly. If the implications of these alternative views are followed out strictly, however, two telling points of tension become conspicuous. First, because the Burkean procedure sorts actions according to their consistency with traditional practice, for the Burkean conservative ordinary behavior is not risky at all. A traditional practice cannot be a "risk" simply because it is so ordinary, the sort of thing that everyone does all the time, and for which no one could be held to blame. For the purposes of assessing consequences, however, traditional practices are no different from any others, save for the fact that we may know better what their outcome will be. A true Burkean will thus, on occasion, express conservative values by denying that a proposed action is risky, while to a Benthamite utilitarian such a view is just logically absurd. The second tension is procedural. The Burkean procedure involves drawing analogies to traditions and precedents, much as is done in the common law. For the Benthamite, each case is new and to be decided by evaluating expected consequences. The procedure is to deduce the outcome by hypothesizing our proposed action, and combining it with our (scientific or commonsensical) knowledge of causal regularities. The Burkean logic is one of classification by analogy, while the Benthamite is using a version of the hypothetico-deductive method. The Benthamite may thus express liberal values by calling for scientific assessment of risks, while the Burkean may find this an elaborate waste of time. In the next section we shall examine how these tensions animate the debate on biotechnology.

Biotechnology: The Rhetoric of Debate

There are three groups of contending parties in the public debate on biotechnology. First are the advocates of relatively unencumbered research and development, representing both public and private research ventures, mostly focused on microbiology. Second are the critics of biotechnology, prominently led by Jeremy Rifkin and the Foundation on Economic Trends (FET). These two groups have been antagonists over biomedical applications of recombinant DNA research for over a decade. The appearance of agricultural applications of genetic engineering techniques has given rise to the third group, led mainly by ecologists and environmental scientists. Since it is impossible to duplicate the level of containment that exists in laboratory conditions when testing organisms in the field, the possibility of agricultural research using engineered organisms has added environmental issues to the agenda of political and regulatory debate. It will be useful to examine a few examples of the rhetoric that typifies each of these three perspectives.

One of the leading spokesmen for biotechnology is Winston Brill, a corporate officer of Agracetus and adjunct professor of bacteriology at the University of Wisconsin. Brill's seminal article in *Science* (1985) describes potential benefits to agricultural production and takes up safety concerns by drawing an analogy between recombinant DNA techniques and traditional plant breeding practices. His logic is that genetic engineering will, in comparison to plant breeding, make "well-characterized and specific modifications," hence the environmental dangers of biotechnology should not be regarded as different in kind from those of plant breeding (Brill, 1985: 384). Writing more recently, Brill continues to stress the analogy between engineered organisms and unexceptional varieties produced by routine plant breeding:

Given the limited changes that are possible, a recombinant organism will be readily recognized as the same organism it was before foreign genes were added. A useful organism, therefore, will not inadvertently be converted into a pest, pathogen, or entirely new species (Brill, 1988: 45).

In a 1987 address to an audience of agricultural economists, Brill adds that reaction against biotechnology threatens the traditions of scientific and commercial practices by introducing regulatory roadblocks in the path of well-functioning and long established research practices (Brill, 1987). Brill repeats this theme in his 1988 paper by raising the specter of competition from unregulated foreign scientists (Brill, 1988: 49). The total argument thus classifies biotechnology as non-risky by virtue of its close analogy to the products of traditional plant breeding, and then ties these traditional practices to the smooth functioning of a successful economy. Brill's argument by analogy is echoed in the scientific press in articles by Harvard microbiologist Bernard D. Davis (1987a, 1987b) and by private-sector scientists such as Ralph W. Hardy and David J. Glass (1985).

Environmental scientists became active participants in the debate in 1983 when a group of ecologists joined an FET lawsuit against the National Institutes of Health (NIH) Recombinant DNA Advisory Committee (RAC), which had become the primary review group for biotechnology research (Norman, 1983). Daniel Simberloff, a biologist from Florida State University, and Robert K. Colwell, a zoologist from the University of California, issued an explicit call for risk assessment of engineered organisms in a 1984 issue of *Genetic Engineering News*. Colwell and Simberloff were joined by three distinguished coauthors in a letter responding to Brill's 1985 article in *Science*, where they criticized Brill's reasoning as a "firm *a priori* prediction of the modified organism's performance when it is released in the environment" and rejected Brill's advocacy of light regulation. The letter questioned Brill's neglect of unintended environmental consequences that follow the introduction of new varieties, regardless of whether they are produced by genetic engineering or traditional plant breeding. The authors concluded by calling for "thoughtful case-by-case experimental studies of the potential effects of recombinant organisms" (Colwell et al., 1985).

A more systematic argument was made by bacterial ecologist Martin Alexander, who outlined a rough and ready methodology for quantifying the risks of deliberate release as a combination of events in the six discrete categories of release, survival, multiplication, dissemination, transfer, and harm. Alexander (1985) suggests that benefit-risk criteria should be used as a decision rule applied to the quantified projection of unwanted outcomes that would follow a risk assessment using these categories. Taking up the case in 1987, Francis A. Sharples argued in *Science* for a regulatory approach that would require assessment of probability and outcome for both experimental and commercial procedures involving environmental release of genetically engineered products. Sharples does not advocate any decision rule, but is clear in indicating that correct policy can only be devised after some attempt has been made to systematically predict the probability with which outcomes can be expected to occur (Sharples, 1987). The environmentalist case for regulation of biotechnology is stated most eloquently by Jack Doyle, who also considers impacts on farm structure and international development in his 1985 book *Altered Harvest*. Doyle's basic approach to the issue is encapsulated in the conclusion to a 1985 article in *Issues in Science and Technology*:

Today we can clearly see the costs and risks associated with modern high-yield agricultural systems: high-energy costs, pesticide toxicity, increasing rates of pest resistance, fertilizer runoff, genetic uniformity, overspecialization, and market volatility. We know, however, that biotechnology—as well as conventional agricultural research—may help us reduce or eliminate some of these costs and risks. We would do well to apply the best of these technologies to our most pressing problems. With biotechnology, however, we must move cautiously to avoid creating new risks of perhaps a more difficult order. . . . At this juncture the wisest course is to look carefully at all the alternatives and choices we now have before us with this new "agrigenetic" technology and chart a course to maximize economic and biological diversity in the very broadest sense of these terms (Doyle, 1985b).

Brill and the defenders of biotechnology fall into classically Burkean analogies, while Doyle and the environmentalist critics appeal to a classically Benthamite quantification of consequences. Brill and Davis for the microbiologists and Colwell, Alexander, and Sharples for the ecologists have couched the issue as a dispute over scientific prediction, each group implying that the other has failed to grasp some fundamental principle of biology, but it seems unlikely that it could be resolved on empirical grounds. The mere fact that engineered organisms are "like" organisms that are not currently regulated is, if one takes the ecologists' view, simply a reason to regulate conventionally produced organisms too (Simberloff and Colwell, 1984). The call for assessment of risks does not necessarily entail extended or exhaustive testing (a point made clear by Alexander), but it does entail a specific role for science in the formation of environmental policy. The microbiologists reject that role, and in doing so reject the Benthamite values that underlie environmental impact assessment generally.

The third group is less readily classified. FET lawsuits have sought to place biotechnology research under very much the type of regulatory authority advocated by Sharples. It is not clear, however, that FET's litigation indicates a Benthamite philosophy. As typified in the writings of Jeremy Rifkin, the more radical opponents of biotechnology appeal to both consequentialist and traditionalist reasoning. For example, in *Declaration of a Heretic*, Rifkin cites Colwell, and describes potentially catastrophic consequences (such as a total disruption of climatic rainfall patterns) that might follow the environmental release of a genetically engineered organism such as the "ice-minus" bacteria (Rifkin, 1985: 49-50). Rifkin makes no attempt to quantify or cite probabilities for such outcomes, however, and in fact devotes considerably more effort in his books to an altogether different kind of argument. Starting with *Who Should Play God?* Rifkin has argued that biotechnology in all forms is morally equivalent to eugenics experiments conducted by Nazi doctors in World War II. This theme in Rifkin's thinking can be best recognized by following the development of his argument over the past decade.

In *Algeny*, perhaps Rifkin's most sophisticated book, recombinant DNA technology is related to the intellectual movement that has Bacon and Descartes as its founders, and continues through Locke, Newton, Adam Smith, Malthus, and Darwin. Rifkin portrays these thinkers as revolutionary figures who systematically reinforce reductionist and mechanistic ideas of nature and humanity. They rationalize materialist consumption and competition, and mystify wholeness, integrity, and purpose. Over the past decade, Rifkin's rhetoric in mounting this argument has moved increasingly toward traditionalist, even fundamentalist, suspicion of scientific models. For example, in 1977 he describes the creation story in physicalist and evolutionary terms (Rifkin and Howard, 1977: 19). By 1985, his choice of words is somewhat different:

The story of the bomb begins with the story of our species and that story begins back in the garden of Eden on the sixth day. On that day God created Adam and Eve from the dust and ashen debris of the great cosmic firestorm. . . . God only asked that they not eat from the tree of knowledge, because to do so would be to claim their earthly independence of God. Armed with knowledge they could assert their authority over God's and begin to wrest from him power over the rest of creation (Rifkin, 1985: 13).

Rifkin goes on to link the fall from grace in the Garden of Eden explicitly to the ideas of the European Enlightenment. The rhetoric makes an identification between genetic engineering, with its attempt to decipher and control life's most hidden secrets, and the moral equivalent (if not literal instance) of original sin. This may be little more than a crass attempt to bring conservative Christians into accord with FET's political goals, but Rifkin's extended use of metaphor and analogy throughout his books and public speeches suggests that it is not.

Both groups of scientists are able to agree that the method of manufacture for these organisms is irrelevant to the issues of risk, though there is continuing ambiguity as to how the risks of releasing any organism ought to be handled as a matter of policy (Miller, 1987; National Academy of Sciences, 1987; Young and Miller, 1987). The microbiologists cite analogies to classify the organisms as "non-risky," while this category is meaningless to the ecologists, who may still admit that a perfunctory risk analysis would show the risks to be negligible. The method of manufacture is crucial to Rifkin's argument, however, since it is the new approach to manipulation of nature that classifies biotechnology as an act of supreme risk. As such, there is no need for Rifkin to look to its consequences to determine its moral character. It is wrong no matter what benefits may tempt us, and no matter what kind of utilitarian calculations might be cited in rationalization.

Political Alliances in the Biotechnology Debate

It seems reasonable to presume that the political goals of each group are fairly transparent. The microbiologists want subsidies for biotechnology research, but their main goal is to avoid regulatory entanglements that might slow research and commercial development of the products of genetic engineering. The ecologists want a formal regulatory procedure to assess, then accept or reject, the risks of both research and development. Although these two groups of scientists have contradictory goals with regard to regulation, they have a common goal in supporting the research and development of biotechnology as a matter of principle.

Rifkin and the FET would prefer that research and development of recombinant DNA products would cease altogether. The creation of regulatory entanglements is a way of slowing the pace of investment in biotechnology, hence it is instrumentally valuable to the long-term goal.

This picture of the political agenda places environmentalists in a middle position between laissez faire biotechnology entrepreneurs and activists unalterably opposed to all forms of recombinant DNA research. To date, environmentalists have been aligned with FET in attempting to establish a regulatory procedure for review of environmental risks associated with field testing and commercial release of engineered organisms. As noted above, scientists associated with environmental criticisms have testified in behalf of FET lawsuits against NIH and against University of California microbiologist Steven Lindow. Environmentalists and the FET are critics of biotechnology, and they have a clear common interest in opposing its most aggressive advocates and in slowing the pace of research and development. This alliance is, however, a marriage of convenience to the extent that Rifkin has committed FET to a posture of opposing evolutionary paradigms in biology. In *Algeny* (1983) and in his most recent book, *Time Wars* (1987), Rifkin advocates a philosophy of science that rejects the reductionism and competitive individualism that he finds inherent in the line of scientific thinkers that stretches from Bacon and Descartes to Charles Darwin. Although Rifkin would reject the suggestion that his view is antiscientific, it is nonetheless fair to classify it as requiring a substantial departure from the methodological and metaphysical presuppositions shared by the majority of microbiologists and ecologists alike. What is more, ecology-oriented scientists such as Colwell and Alexander have taken some pains to indicate that they do not object to biotechnology in principle or unilaterally; their goal is the establishment of a risk-assessment regulatory procedure for approving experimental and commercial release. It is easy to imagine scenarios in which Rifkin and FET might advocate a restructuring of science policy that would be opposed univocally by the science community, and which would pit both biotechnologists and environmentalists against the FET and other traditional critics.

Natural alliances among the parties in this triangle are inherently unstable, however, since there are significant political aspects of the biotechnology debate in which any two are aligned against the third. While it is relatively easy to see how environmental scientists occupy a middle ground in the biotechnology debates, it is more difficult to see how avid supporters of genetic engineering have anything in common with their sworn enemies in groups such as FET. It is this point that brings us back to the question of broader political values and the preceding discussion of Burke and Bentham. The analogy-based reasoning of Winston Brill contrasts with the consequence-anticipation reasoning of Frances Sharples or Jack Doyle. This contrast echoes the procedural contrast between the political philosophies of Edmund Burke and Jeremy Bentham. Brill's use of analogies to sort activities into categories of "traditional or time-honored" vs. "untried or risky" appeals to the conservative political values advanced in Burke's

Reflections on the Revolution in France. The environmentalists' insistence upon a procedure that first quantifies the expected consequences of an act, then applies a decision rule to determine its acceptability, appeals to the classically liberal values voiced by Bentham in *The Principles of Morals and Legislation.*

Rifkin's arguments link genetic engineering with crass materialism, with a failure to acknowledge spiritual qualities in nature generally, and particularly in regard to human beings. The microbiologist is portrayed as the henchman of dark forces that desanctify nature by substituting a mechanistic philosophy for the richer religious and teleological visions of times past. Once stripped of the sacred, nature can be put to any use as determined by utility; once stripped of the soul, human beings become raw materials for similar manipulations, paving the way for abortion, surrogate pregnancy, and human fetal tissue technologies. In Rifkin's argument, the potential consequences of biotechnology are really little more than a way of teasing the audience into his more fully elaborated position, where the new biology is portrayed as categorically wrong, as a risk to the traditional and fundamental values of Judeo-Christian civilization. In mounting their arguments, both Brill and Rifkin categorize biotechnology by drawing analogies to paradigm cases. Brill's analogy is to plant breeding; Rifkin's is to eugenics and to nuclear weapons. Both are classically Burkean arguments, though they differ radically in how the final classification is made. In terms of underlying political philosophy Brill and Rifkin are closer to each other than is either with the Benthamite calculators representing the environmentalist camp.

Needless to say, reconciliation between Brill and Rifkin is unlikely despite the ground they share philosophically, but two political points can be drawn from their shared Burkean conservatism. First, to the extent that a Burkean vision does undergird contemporary conservative political values, Brill and Rifkin are competing for the same audience, and this can only strengthen the hand of the environmentalist critics. Although many American conservatives would find little resonance with Burke, Burke's appeal to tradition, to the tried and true, remains a theme in recent conservative thought. Russell Kirk's (1982) anthology of conservative thought emphasizes Burkean themes to the virtual exclusion of libertarian ideas or neoclassical utilitarian defenses of unfettered capitalism. Brill and Rifkin could be expected to split this segment of conservatives, and such a split would make mobilization of political power more difficult.

The second point is, perhaps, the more important one. The conservative rhetoric of Brill and Rifkin precludes any logically consistent reconciliation, and hence any permanent alliance between either of these groups and the environmentalist critics. Since the microbiologist advocates of light regulation and the activist opponents of all recombinant DNA research are so unalterably opposed to one another at the level of self-interest, the additional opposition of both against the environmentally oriented ecologists at the political level virtually assures that political opinion will be split three ways. This triangular standoff undoubtedly has multiple consequences for policy. One is that the issue becomes rather difficult to understand for an American electorate conditioned to thinking in bipolar terms. A corollary outcome may be the relatively inert character of public debate on biotechnology risks since 1984.

Biotechnology and the Future Politics of Risk

There is an occasional tendency among philosophers to assume that philosophical values are the determining factor in human action, that traditionalism or utilitarianism represent creeds that people apply in deciding how to act. Such an assumption has not guided the preceding analysis, nor is there any presumption that it would be valid for policy analysis generally. In this case, such an assumption would be tantamount to the ridiculous idea that my characterization of developers of biotechnology from microbiological disciplines as Burkean conservatives, and of environmental scientists advocating risk assessment as Benthamite liberals, extends across the spectrum of political opinion for members of these groups. If ideological considerations have determined political opinion in this case, they would almost certainly have to be found in the disciplinary orientations of the scientists, and not in any alleged fealty to conservative or liberal political values.

It is as rhetorical strategies that these political values attain whatever policy significance they might have. Policy dialogue is almost always conducted in language that appeals to alternative philosophical conceptions of justice, liberty, or the foundations for the state. Although interests and affiliations may frequently have more to do with the way that individuals and groups coalesce in support or opposition to particular policy proposals, the appeal to underlying political values is crucial to legitimation. The logic of political values entails tensions, contradictions, and inconsistencies that place a limit on the malleability of political argument. This chapter has been an attempt to sketch some key limitations on the political rhetoric of risk arguments as they are applied to biotechnology. To the extent that these limitations remain in force, it is possible to project the tripartite structure of the current debate into the future. The alliance between the environmental scientists and Rifkin is forced to make a divided appeal in the public debate, one that must not delve too deeply into basic goals and values lest the inconsistencies emerge in embarrassing fashion. Similarly, a unification of the scientific community would require one of the two groups to abandon the basic structure of their rhetoric. The risk-assessment orientation of environmental scientists represents a deep commitment to consequence anticipation, one that could not be abandoned without sacrificing the basic goals of the environmentalists entirely. Given the risk-assessment orientation of environmental scientists, it seems unlikely that they could abandon the Benthamite values that underlie their position.

It is more likely, therefore, that the scientific community can only be politically unified when microbiologists interested in the commercial potential of biotechnology accept the legitimacy of the regulatory paradigm. Although many scientists speaking for this group have proposed analogies intended to show that environmental release of genetically engineered organisms is "not risky," their true interests do not necessarily depend upon a strong, Burkean interpretation of this claim. Recent statements by David Glass (1988) and Ralph Hardy (1988) acknowledge that government risk assessment could help secure public acceptance of the new technology, a goal strongly desired by proponents of commercial use. If the industry's fear of entanglement in bureaucratic disputes can be assuaged (Crawford, 1986), there is little reason why proponents of biotechnology cannot accept the principle of assessing risk and deciding case by case. If Brill and the pro-biotechnology group accept the legitimacy of the regulatory paradigm, they might still maintain strong opposition to excessively expensive review procedures on traditional cost-benefit grounds.

A political unification of scientists would leave Rifkin and FET without the support of many scientifically based environmentalists. This would place them in somewhat the same position as the antinuclear movement prior to Three Mile Island. During the late 1970s, scientists generally accepted the validity of nuclear power risk assessment, and opposition to nuclear power embraced a general attack upon the limitations of scientific method (Thompson, 1984). For the time being, risk assessment is a way of opposing and slowing new applications of recombinant DNA, but when regulatory procedures are in place it would become a way of making the ultimate release of many products inevitable. At that time, one would expect anti-biotechnology rhetoric to reverse its field, and to decry risk assessment and environmental impact analysis as bogus and methodologically flawed. Rifkin is already poised to make his case as a blanket indictment of science, as the recent book *Time Wars* (1987) makes clear.

Finally, it must be noted that the impact of recombinant DNA techniques upon the agriculture of developing countries and upon the economic structure of the U.S. farm sector complicate the analysis of biotechnology policy. Closely related to the economic issue is the question of biotechnology research at public institutions; some have questioned whether land grant university and USDA researchers should do work that benefits big business more than the farm community (Buttel, 1986b). If FET and other opponents of biotechnology can join these issues to the risks of environmental release, they may find the "policy window" that William Browne (1988) says such groups need to influence political leaders. At present, environmental release has failed to generate much public interest outside the California communities where "ice minus" experiments were proposed (Sun, 1986), so it would appear that, bereft of his scientific allies, Rifkin would have great difficulty in achieving his political goals. On the other hand, it may turn out that, relieved of the arcane and technical baggage of risk-assessment projections, Rifkin can make a more effective case to the public. In either instance, the policy debate can be seen in broader scope than the pros and cons of biotechnology.

The issues were similarly complex for nuclear power, but when public safety became a political issue in the late seventies, the rhetoric of debate was strikingly similar (Thompson, 1984). If the environmental dangers of biotechnology become a broad public concern, we can expect political values to be reflected less in whether partisans are pro or con than in the conceptual approach they take to the problem of risk. These values are apparent even in the more technically informed debates of the scientific community. Although they do not determine the political positions taken by contending groups, they do constrain the shape of their arguments, and, hence, of their alliances.

2

Organized Religion and Biotechnology: Social Responsibility and the Role of Government

Thomas C. Wiegele

Science and technology have always had an impact on human social relationships, politics, and culture. As Phillips (1988: 18) has observed, "social systems are functions of technologies; and philosophies express technological forces and reflect social systems." As we move into the final decade of the twentieth century, science and technology more than ever shape human life. As one of those shaping forces, biotechnology must be considered among the major scientific developments of our era.

Today we are living on the threshold of the age of biology in which new scientific knowledge will be applied through biotechnology to a broad range of human concerns. Many of these applications will have therapeutic benefits for individuals and for society generally. However, because some developments in biotechnology raise ethical and moral issues when applied to human beings, various religions have expressed concern about the implications of continued scientific progress in this area. Along with these concerns, religions have made demands for public policies, requesting that government play an active role in examining and determining future social impacts of biotechnology. This chapter will investigate and synthesize the positions and demands of organized religions with regard to future public policies. It will accomplish this by examining the now extensive literature which has been produced by official religious study groups and issued as doctrinal statements. This analysis will not explore the ethical and moral issues related to specific elements of biotechnology; that has been done frequently and there is no need to revisit that work (see, for example, Angus,

1981; Eibach, 1981; Englehardt, 1984; Gafo, 1980; McCormick, 1985; Miller, 1984; and Reiter, 1986).

This chapter first briefly looks at religion and public policy and the context of government regulation. Then an outline of the research design used in this chapter is followed by a consideration of early demands by religious leaders, but not organized religions, for some type of public policy action or regulation. The central sections of this analysis then address three principal questions: (1) why do religions want government regulation of biotechnology, (2) how should government regulate biotechnology, and (3) what do religions want government to do, substantively, about biotechnology? The chapter concludes with a general assessment of the posture of organized religion toward biotechnology.

Religion and Public Policy

Numerous writers have reflected on the importance of various religions and the influence of clergy on questions of public policy. For example, Fowler (1985: 168) has posited four factors which can be used to appraise the interest-group activity of religions. First, the character of the belief is relevant to influence. Second, the internal strength and organization of religious groups is related to their effectiveness. Third, the access that religions have to political elites clearly relates to eventual impact. And fourth, having minimal political opposition allows for more efficient advancement of a religion's positions. These factors are probably as important in industrialized societies as they are in developing nations (see, for example, Smith 1970: 128 and 1974).

In the United States the positions taken by religious bodies on public policies for biotechnology are important. Religions have great influence in our society, and that influence, especially in the public sector, appears to be growing. Religious leaders command the attention of the press and the executive branch of government, as well as the U.S. Congress. Moreover, on questions involving scientific expertise, religious elites appear able to acquire, through their positions and staffs, a considerable amount of knowledge which laypersons do not command. Thus, laypeople frequently acquiesce or defer to the positions taken by their religious leaders, although the empirical evidence on this question is not clear (Greenawalt, 1988: 33, 210). As a result, religious elites often exercise considerable political influence. On questions related to public policies for biotechnology, organized religion, as we shall see, has articulated a number of positions which now lay on the public table. These positions could play a strong role in shaping the future of biotechnology policies.

The Regulatory Context

This paper will take what Nader and Nader (1981) refer to as a "wide angle on regulation," that is, a broad holistic conceptualization. In this view, the regulatory process consists not only of government agencies but also of politicians in elective offices, public opinion, individual firms, trade associations, professional organizations, voluntary associations, individuals, and organized religion. Membership in churches represents the most common form of voluntary association in the United States, approximating two-thirds of the population (Wald et al., 1988: 532, 546). U.S. government agencies involved in regulation include the National Institutes of Health, the Environmental Protection Agency, the Food and Drug Administration, and the Department of Agriculture. Moreover, various pieces of legislation provide competing regulatory regimes. Beyond this, local and state governments are currently engaged in an uneven process of establishing a variety of regulatory postures which could conflict with or expand upon federal requirements. Hundreds of commercial biotechnology firms now operate in the United States and many university-based researchers contribute to the development of marketable genetically engineered products. Biotechnology trade associations have also been formed.

A holistic view of the regulatory environment entails a number of factors that are developing into a regulatory process. These factors, however, have yet to reach a stable and predictable state. Thus, in the presently evolving regulatory context, the positions taken by organized religions are likely to be important. Recent work by Wald et al. (1988) supports this contention. They argue that most studies of the contextual influences on the formation of political attitudes are based upon data that are organized geographically. Although an areal orientation is important, they further demonstrate that individuals bound by strong affective connections with their churches are influenced in their political attitudes by this social milieu. Moreover, churches have become active in developing the national political agenda in which biotechnology is emerging slowly as an item of major public importance, especially as seen by religious leaders. Miller (1985: 20) has found in a survey of leaders in science and environmental policy as well as religious leaders that 42 percent of religious leaders indicated major social problems in the conduct of recombinant DNA experiments while only 17 percent and 27 percent of science and environmental policy leaders, respectively, held this opinion. This concern extends to the general electorate across all demographic subpopulations as shown in Table 2.1 below.

When asked specifically about regulation of biotechnology, U.S. citizens display mixed feelings, as Table 2.2 illustrates. Noteworthy in this table is that 43 percent of respondents preferred strict government regulation of biotechnology. The implication of these attitudes, when combined with the views of religious leaders, is that religions and their adherents may project biotechnology as a significant political issue in the immediate future.

Research Design

Data for this paper were collected during the spring and fall of 1987. Letters requesting official documents on genetic engineering and public policy were sent

Table 2.1
Concern About Science Policy

Question: How concerned are you about government policy concerning science and
             technology--are you very concerned, somewhat concerned, not very concerned, or
             not concerned at all?

		Very concerned	Somewhat concerned	Not very concerned	Not concerned at all	Not Sure
Total 1986	(1,273)	32%	50%	11%	7%	1%
Sex:						
Male	(635)	35	49	9	6	<1
Female	(638)	29	50	13	7	1
Age:						
18 to 34	(546)	26	52	13	9	-
35 to 49	(343)	30	58	8	4	<1
50 to 64	(252)	34	46	11	6	2
65 and over	(127)	44	36	12	6	2
Education:						
Less than high school	(165)	32	42	17	8	1
High school graduate	(458)	24	56	11	9	1
Some college	(300)	36	53	8	3	1
College graduate	(347)	44	45	8	2	<1
Science understanding:						
Very good	(236)	46	46	4	3	1
Adequate	(707)	34	52	10	4	1
Poor	(316)	19	50	18	13	<1

Source: Office of Technology Assessment (1987a:19).

to over 30 mainline U.S. religions, producing 13 usable responses. Some data,
such as the Vatican document, were available in complete textual form in the
public press. Many religions have given questions of biotechnology considerable
attention, and their published statements are quite elaborate. On the other hand,
quite a few religions have chosen not to develop positions on biotechnology.
These include the American Baptist Churches, the Assemblies of God, the
Christian Reformed Church in North America, and First Church of Christ Scientist, the Independent Fundamental Churches of America, the International
Church of the Foursquare Gospel, the Mennonite Church, the Orthodox Greek
Catholic Church, and the Seventh Day Adventists. Individual authors represent-

Table 2.2
General Opinions About Biotechnology

Question: I will now read you a few statements. For each, please tell me whether you agree
              strongly, agree somewhat, disagree somewhat, or disagree strongly.

	Agree strongly	Agree somewhat	Disagree somewhat	Disagree strongly	Not sure
The potential danger from genetically altered cells and microbes is so great that strict regulations are necessary	43%	34%	14%	6%	3%
The risks of genetic engineering have been greatly exaggerated	15	40	27	10	8
It would be better if we did not know how to genetically alter cells at all	13	20	34	31	2
The unjustified fears of genetic engineering have seriously impeded the development of valuable new drugs and therapies	20	38	26	9	8
We have no business meddling with nature	26	20	31	21	2

Source: Office of Technology Assessment (1987a:81).

ing Conservative, Orthodox, Reconstructionist, and Reform Judaism have addressed the challenges to traditional Jewish law raised by developments in
biotechnology (for example, Green, 1985; Rosenfeld, 1979; Rosner, 1979 and
1981; and Troster, 1984). However, there is no officially agreed upon Jewish position on biotechnology.

   Those churches that have addressed issues of biotechnology include major denominations and religious organizations. Among the religions that have produced statements are the Episcopal Church, the Lutheran Church in America,
the Roman Catholic Church, and the United Church of Christ. In addition, two
cooperative religious groups, the National Council of Churches and the World

Council of Churches, have developed extensive documents on this topic. It is conceivable, although there is minimal evidence for this, that denominations that have not developed positions on public policies for biotechnology simply endorse either or both the National Council of Churches or the World Council of Churches biotechnology statements.

Once aggregated, these statements then became the information which was examined comparatively for each of the research questions posed. This examination was necessarily qualitative, because each document was a subjective and uniquely structured statement and because the universe of religious documents is quite small, thus allowing no meaningful quantitative analysis.

The Prelude to the Positions of Organized Religions

Prior to the development of official position statements on biotechnology, some individual religious leaders were active in calling attention to the emergence of potential social problems and in making their views known to Congress. In a sense, the opening religious call for government regulatory activity was sounded by three prominent religious leaders in a letter to then President Jimmy Carter on June 20, 1980. The signatories of the letter, Dr. Claire Randall, General Secretary of the National Council of Churches, Rabbi Bernard Mandelbaum, General Secretary of the Synagogue Council of America, and Bishop Thomas Kelly, General Secretary of the U.S. Catholic Conference, made an impassioned plea for the involvement of all branches of the federal government in developing regulatory policies for biotechnology. The basis for their appeal to the president was their perception that "we are rapidly moving into a new era of fundamental danger triggered by the rapid growth of genetic engineering." They asked several rhetorical questions that led directly to reflections on government control: "Who shall determine how human good is best served when new life forms are being engineered? Who shall control genetic experimentation and its results which could have untold implications for human survival? Who will benefit and who will bear any adverse consequences, directly or indirectly?" (Randall et al., 1980: 47). These questions were followed by still another: "Given all the responsibility to God and our fellow human beings, do we have the right to let experimentation and ownership of new life forms move ahead without public regulation?" (Randall et al., 1980: 48).

These questions were answered in the concluding paragraphs of the letter. The signatories demanded that the public interest must be represented in these matters by individuals and groups, an interest that supercedes the interests of the commercial, medical, and broader scientific communities. Arguing that no agency is exercising oversight or control, the signatories demanded a comprehensive government (presumably executive) investigation of genetic engineering issues. Beyond this, the signatories requested that the U.S. Congress investigate judicial decisions allowing the patenting of new life forms. The letter concluded with a demand that the U.S. government explore the development of international guidelines for biotechnology with other nations as well as appropriate international organizations.

Interestingly, there was nothing particularly religious about this letter to the president from the three clerics. It was virtually a straightforward plea to begin the process of federal investigation and lawmaking on behalf of the public interest. Although it did allude to the temptation to "play God," it did not in any way emphasize a religious orientation.

Public reactions to this letter were not especially positive. Most informed observers felt that the clerics had overreacted to presumed fears, and that the regulatory environment was unfolding in a rational manner (Kaiser, 1980: A16). However, in response to the letter of the three clergy, President Carter appointed a Commission for the Study of Ethical Problems in Medicine and Biomedical and Behavioral Research to examine questions raised by developments in biotechnology. On November 16, 1982, the commission transmitted its report to President Reagan. The commission's report was comprehensive, exploring a range of issues associated with biotechnology and its social impacts. Regarding the distribution of political power over biotechnology, the commission asked: "Who should decide which lines of genetic engineering research ought to be pursued and which applications of the technology ought to be promoted?" (President's Commission, 1982: 73). Recognizing that this was an unusual question to ask of the scientific research community, the commission pointed out that biotechnology has such broad implications that the normal units of government were ill-equipped to handle its challenges. The commission hinted that new institutional arrangements might be necessary.

One year later the House Subcommittee on Investigations and Oversight of the Committee on Science and Technology held hearings on human genetic engineering. Clergy of the Jewish, Catholic, and Protestant faiths were called to testify. Dr. Seymour Siegel of the Jewish Theological Seminary in New York argued that "it is quite clear that public policy must take steps both to encourage and to monitor the achievements and projects of the genetic engineers" (U.S. Congress, 1983: 313). Dr. Richard McCormack, a Catholic priest, insisted that genetic engineering was "too important to be left to the ordinary political dynamic"; and he called for "some public mechanism of ongoing deliberation and assessment" in the area of biotechnology (U.S. Congress, 1983: 307). Arguing that the Congress cannot legislate reverence, Dr. Roger L. Shinn, a Protestant, stated that "legislative regulation may be appropriate when a public interest is involved." He went on to argue that "scientists themselves should have a voice in the formulation of regulations, but they should not have the sole voice; the public interest is not always identical with the professional interest of experimentors" (U.S. Congress, 1983: 302).

On balance, these three religious representatives were in strong agreement. All saw the need to serve the public interest by creating some mechanism at the federal level to regulate research in biotechnology. But a somewhat different religious view emerged from the activities of Jeremy Rifkin, leader of the

Foundation on Economic Trends. In the spring of 1983, Rifkin circulated a letter among a broad range of religious leaders and some scientists asking their approval of the resolution "that efforts to engineer specific genetic traits into the germline of the human species should not be attempted" (Norman, 1983: 1360; Briggs, 1983: 1). Many clergy endorsed the letter as a way of bringing ethical issues in biotechnology into the public domain. Some signatories felt that the resolution might have led to formation of a governmental commission to deal with such issues. Although Rifkin was willing to support the cessation of germline research, he did not endorse the idea of a commission. Such a commission, according to Rifkin, by limiting certain kinds of research might have endorsed others, thereby legitimizing some forms of genetic engineering (Norman, 1983: 1361). This exercise of a circular letter illustrated that it might be possible to build a broad-based public interest coalition composed of liberal and fundamentalist clergy as well as scientists. Such a coalition could attract considerable media attention.

These activities represent a prelude to the sectarian statements that emerged later. The letter to President Carter, the report of the president's commission, the congressional testimony of clerics, and the Rifkin resolution were all very public acts which were widely reported in the press. It is likely that they created an atmosphere of some urgency which encouraged individual religions to develop position statements on public policy for biotechnology.

Why Religions Want Government Regulation of Biotechnology

For the most part, religions prefer to maintain as autonomous a posture as possible with regard to moral issues. Rarely will they request governmental intervention into what they consider their special domain of interest. However, in the case of biotechnology many religions have virtually demanded government regulatory activity.

In 1982 the World Council of Churches (WCC) published the earliest comprehensive religious document on biotechnology. It explored a broad range of issues associated with human genetic engineering, and it also spelled out a case for government regulation. "Many of the social and ethical issues that arise in debates about genetic engineering have less to do with genetics," the WCC argued, "than with broader questions of human good. . . . Because genetic engineering brings new human power, it raises to new importance many old questions about the use and direction of power" (WCC, 1982: 5). Building on this observation, the statement went on to argue that "too often, membership of review bodies has been dominated by those with interests in the promotion of the techniques under consideration. The best protection of the rights of human subjects of genetic engineering will be to ensure adequate participation in decisions by those affected" (WCC, 1982: 11). In its recommendation to national church groups, the WCC stated that "the WCC Central Committee . . . invites the churches to examine how they can contribute to this human subjects' review process and to the work of national regulatory committees with respect to genetic engineering" (WCC, 1982: 11). The WCC called for women and minorities to be represented on review bodies when questions of eugenics or reproduction were the subject matter. Thus, as seen from the perspective of the World Council of Churches, the emerging expertise in biotechnology would lead inevitably to questions of social power. Individual churches, therefore, should attempt to influence national regulatory bodies in order to allow involvement of "those" affected. The implication here is that scientists need to be checked or balanced by laypersons who presumably will be more objective in their judgments.

In 1984 the National Council of Churches' Panel on Bioethical Concerns (NCC/PBC) published a comprehensive study guide on genetic engineering. After reviewing many ethical and moral concerns and strongly urging continued research and innovation in biotechnology, the panel wrote that "voluntary self-regulation of genetic engineering is not sufficient. Reassurances of scientists notwithstanding, the field of genetic research is still new enough, and the potential harm great enough, that we advocate some form of explicit governmental regulation of all parties engaging in genetic research" (NCC/PBC, 1984: 37). The argument of the panel was essentially one of distrust of those involved in the genetic research process.

Recognizing that elements of the U.S. regulatory process were already in place, the National Council of Churches' (NCC) Governing Board nevertheless has expressed skepticism as to whether the community of scientists could regulate itself (NCC, 1986: 10). As a result, the NCC recommended some type of government oversight mechanism to represent the public interest. Presumably such a mechanism would be a federal responsibility, although this issue was not discussed.

The Episcopal Church has carefully examined numerous ethical issues related to biotechnology, but has paid relatively little attention to the role of government in the evolution of public policy questions. At its 1985 General Convention the House of Bishops of the Episcopal Church considered a resolution encouraging continued research in biotechnology, "provided that through action of Congress authorization is given to the Food and Drug Administration or some other appropriate agency which includes those competent in the necessary scientific disciplines and also persons with training in ethics and representatives of the general population, to assure an ethically acceptable use" of the products of biotechnology (House of Bishops, 1985). Rather than expressing distrust of scientific expertise, as the World Council of Churches had done, the Episcopal Church insisted that regulatory bodies must include scientific specialists. Despite this reasoning, the Episcopal position encouraging government intervention into aspects of the research process appears to be based on apprehension about the rapidly unfolding advances in biotechnology. Indeed, a report (1985: 145-146) of the Standing Commission on Human Affairs of Health to the 1985 General Convention contained a section entitled "The Historic Basis for Fear of Scientific Advances."

A study commissioned by the American Lutheran Church, the Association of Evangelical Lutheran Churches, and the Lutheran Church in America (Burtness, 1986), although technically not representing an "official" position, takes an unusual view of developments in biotechnology. Asserting that "participation in the management of the creation is something which Christians accept as both gift and responsibility" (Burtness, 1986: 11), the study then expresses a curious lack of trust in the wisdom of future developments in genetic engineering. Arguing that biotechnology regulation is possible, the study goes on to observe that "because of its awareness of the demonic potential of human activity, the church . . . will insist that regulation is necessary" (Burtness, 1986: 11). No reference is made to the expected agent of regulation, but the study implies that the church ought to play a role.

Two major religious documents were issued during 1987: one by the United Church of Christ (UCC), the other by the Roman Catholic Church. Recognizing that knowledge of biotechnology has developed more rapidly than the "general understanding" of its social implications, the United Church of Christ advocated that its members read and study the documents of the World Council of Churches and the National Council of Churches on this topic (General Synod, UCC, 1987: 31). However, the UCC, while acknowledging that "genetic engineering and therapies have the potential to affect all creation for good or for harm," accepted the WCC exhortation for pastors and laypersons to participate on institutional review boards (IRB's) of health care institutions (General Synod, UCC, 1987: 31). Although this represents less than full government involvement, it does indicate a certain lack of trust in currently existing organized processes for reviewing the application of biotechnologies to human beings. Thus, because the "theological and societal implications are quite profound," the church must insert itself into the public dialogue on biotechnology (General Synod, UCC, 1987: 29).

As with the statement by the World Council of Churches, the document of the Roman Catholic Church (RCC) released on March 10, 1987, speaks to a universal audience rather than to the U.S. regulatory context. However, the implications for American society are quite clear in this comprehensive document. "Basic scientific research and applied research constitute a significant expression of . . . the dominion of man over creation," the Vatican argues, and science and technology have value when they serve general human needs. But it goes on to say "It would . . . be illusory to claim that scientific research and its applications are morally neutral." Indeed, "science without conscience can only lead to man's ruin" (RCC, 1987: A14).

With this distrust of developments in applied science as a foundation, the Vatican argues that "fundamental moral values . . . are constitutive elements of civil society and its order. For this reason, the new technological possibilities which have opened up the field of biomedicine require the intervention of political authorities and of the legislator [sic], since an uncontrolled application of such techniques could lead to unforeseeable and damaging consequences for civil society" (RCC, 1987: A17). Thus, a regulatory role for legislators and presumably the executive branch of government ("political authorities") is required to maintain moral values in civil society.

As a group, these statements express a considerable amount of sympathy for enhanced government regulation of biotechnology. Running through most of the statements is a strong distrust of the scientific and, to some extent, commercial communities. The protection of human subjects is a concern, with some sensitivity to having multiple constituencies represented on review bodies when the public interest is involved. Definitions of the public interest are not offered; nor is there a sensitivity to specific levels of government or to their individual units.

Positions on Government Regulation

Having established that organized religions want government to intervene in the regulation of biotechnology, the important question of precisely how this regulation should take place comes forward. In general, it is safe to assert that most religious statements have paid little attention to the actual mechanics of government regulation. Of course, regulation of biotechnology is a complex area which is not yet fully stabilized within the American polity. Moreover, conflicting perceptions exist within the regulatory community itself over questions of agency responsibilities and specific pieces of legislation.

As a general statement directed toward all nations, the World Council of Churches (WCC, 1982: 16) calls for regulation "at all institutional levels with special emphasis on the commercial sector and large scale operations." Although it does not deal with specific national regulatory postures, the WCC statement does call upon churches to explore ways they might become involved in the work of regulatory agencies (WCC, 1982: 11). This is the only document that is minimally sensitive to the multiplicity of governance levels and the large-scale nature of commercial enterprise in biotechnology.

The National Council of Churches takes a somewhat different position than the WCC, but it too declines to examine specific regulatory requirements. Rather, the NCC adopts a grass-roots approach, arguing that the public must be "educated and well informed," and that local churches have a responsibility to sharpen the public's awareness of political issues associated with bioengineering. With proper church activity, the public will become informed about the ethical values involved, and presumably it will express its concerns to a broad range of regulatory agencies (NCC/PBC, 1984: 44-45). The assumption is that the public has a major role to play in the regulation of biotechnology by exerting political pressure on regulatory bodies.

The NCC/PBC statement was later amplified by the NCC Governing Board. Recognizing that a cadre of instructors was needed to stimulate grass-roots involvement, the NCC (1986: 16) recommended that "theological seminaries in particular should provide basic education in genetic counseling and its pastoral implications." These clergy, then, would assist their congregations in examining a broad range of genetic issues. So important is biotechnology, the NCC argued (1986:16), that collaboration on the issue is required across numerous religious bodies in a manner similar to the collaboration of the "world's scientific community." This latter point was not elaborated, but it certainly is politically significant. Again, though not providing detail, the NCC called for an unspecified "federal regulatory commission, consisting of members drawn from a variety of scientific and non-scientific fields" to establish guidelines in the public interest (NCC, 1986: 15).

The Episcopal Church apparently has adopted a position similar to that of the National Council of Churches, focusing its attention at the grass-roots level. The House of Bishops considered a resolution requesting seminary deans to establish a study group with appropriate scientific and theological knowledge to examine the implications of biotechnology for the Church's teaching and to include basic training in human genetics for all seminarians (House of Bishops, 1985). Trained clergy would then work with congregations to develop a sensitivity to issues in biotechnology.

Lutheran documentation on how biotechnology should be regulated is apparently nonexistent, or perhaps Lutherans have chosen not to become involved with this issue. However, Lutherans are aware that research in biotechnology will proceed and that questions of regulation will inevitably unfold. In such a situation that embodies a technology full of promise, "the tendency of human activity ought to be toward investigating its possibilities" (Burtness, 1986: 10). Indeed, "the Christian is inclined, therefore, to underscore the promise rather than the peril of new discoveries" (Burtness, 1986: 10). Moreover, argues this study, regulation of research procedures and the control of potential hazards have worked reasonably well, and therefore enlightened Christians have a responsibility to at least not oppose progress in biotechnology.

The United Church of Christ in its 1987 General Synod also adopted a grass-roots approach to regulation, much like that of the National Council of Churches. Clergy and laity were encouraged to participate on institutional review panels that grapple with genetic issues, and the creation of education forums that deal with genetic engineering was recommended. In a political sense, these activities seem far removed from the sources of regulatory authority in American society.

The Vatican, again speaking to a universal audience, has argued that regulation must come through laws enacted, presumably, at the national level. This faith in legislators appears to be based upon a strong distrust of scientific expertise: "No biologist or doctor can reasonably claim, by virtue of his scientific competence, to be able to decide on people's origin and destiny" (RCC, 1987: A14). Thus, "if the legislator responsible for the common good were not watchful, he could be deprived of his prerogatives by researchers claiming to govern humanity in the name of the biological discoveries and the alleged 'improvement' processes which they would draw from those discoveries" (RCC, 1987: A17). Although the position of the Vatican is not clearly spelled out, it comes down strongly for central government regulation through national legislation, and it emphasizes the personal morality of the legislators themselves.

Clearly, religious positions on the manner in which biotechnology should be regulated are not well-developed. Little, if any, sensitivity to the process of regulation is in evidence. Most religions are focused solely at the sublocal level of government in institutional review boards and nongovernmental discussion groups. One religion, the Roman Catholic Church, looks to the highest level of government. How levels of government might be interrelated is not even approached. Some interest-group thinking is in evidence with the view that individual citizens can exert pressure on regulatory agencies. There is a hint in the statement from the National Council of Churches that the development of cooperative religious initiatives in public policy might be a potentially useful strategy for religious organizations. Given the fact that religions are apparently eager for governmental regulation of biotechnology, it is surprising how little attention they have devoted to the mechanics of how this should be accomplished.

What Religions Want Government to Do Substantively with Regard to Biotechnology

We come now to the question of precisely what religions want to regulate. Substantively, what should government do about the issues raised by biotechnology? The World Council of Churches has developed the most comprehensive and well-organized set of recommendations among all the religions examined for this chapter. The WCC (1982: 16) called for the "establishment of appropriate health monitoring procedures for the facilities and communities" where research in biotechnology takes place or is used. The World Council of Churches is one of the few religious organizations that is concerned with the local level of government. Moreover, the WCC is sensitive to activities in the Third World. It argues that "therapies or products produced must fit the local, cultural, economic, and social needs" of nations as well as "protect against social impacts that tend to promote dependency rather than self-reliance" (WCC, 1982: 17). Although the WCC was aware of patenting questions in biotechnology, it made no specific regulatory recommendations here; instead it suggested that its own organization study the matter.

On issues related to the use of biotechnology in warfare, the WCC endorsed the Biological Weapons Convention of 1972 and called for its broad international adoption. The WCC also urged all nations to endorse the 1925 Geneva Protocol and extend its coverage to prohibit the stockpiling of toxic substances created through genetic engineering (WCC, 1982: 25). Although not requiring direct government action, the World Council of Churches' request that scientists not take part in biological or chemical weapons research could ultimately have an effect on government policy in this area. It should be pointed out that well over 100 nations have signed the Biological Weapons Convention, and the request that scientists not engage in weapons research is a complex question involving aspects of offense and defense unresolved by the current international regime on biological weapons.

The National Council of Churches' document closely follows the philosophical spirit of the WCC, but does not provide the kind of specificity regarding subject matter to be regulated. The one exception is its exhortation that a regulatory commission be established at the federal level to "be responsible to public comment as well as professional proposals" (NCC, 1986: 15). Presumably this means that government actors should develop policies that take not only government's interests into account, but also the interests of the public and the scientific community as well. This regulatory body "should keep in mind the protection of individuals, various groupings of people, and the environment." Moreover, "it should foster the free flow of information derived from genetic research, while advocating the continuing funding by the government of needed research" (NCC, 1986: 15).

Although the NCC recommendations regarding regulatory policy seem general and innocuous, they could be interpreted quite differently. For example, the exhortation that the federal regulatory body protect "various groupings of people" could cause the federal government to become deeply involved in genetic-based regulatory questions associated with race and sex. "Fostering the free flow of information derived from genetic research" could imply, ironically, the imposing of significant restrictions on what is patentable for academic as well as commercial biotechnology operations. These restrictive interpretations are not unreasonable, given the tone of the NCC statement, which is quite negative regarding the social impacts of biotechnology.

The draft Episcopal statement is undeveloped and fragmentary regarding the subject matter of political regulation. The statement asserts that it "encourages genetic engineering research to increase human understanding of vital processes," and it recognizes "that human DNA is a great gift of God lying at the center of life and directing our development, growth, and functioning" (House of Bishops, 1985). Certainly, this is an endorsement of the research process in biotechnology, but it provides little in the way of guidance to regulatory bodies.

Lutherans too have been quite general and have not considered the specifics of regulation. Declaring that Christians are a hopeful people, Lutherans argue that hope "excludes naivete, invites participation, and encourages the thoughtful directing of those social and scientific processes over which we have some control" (Burtness, 1986: 10). Indeed, "if a new procedure such as genetic manipulation appears to be full of promise, the tendency ought to be toward investigating its possibilities. A negative judgment ought not to be made prematurely" (Burtness, 1986: 10). Consistent with this reasoning, "the drive toward the future redemption of all things would seem to suggest that those who oppose the genetic engineering procedure be asked to present solid reasons for that opposition" (Burtness, 1986: 10). The Lutheran statement provides little guidance to the public policymaker in biotechnology. However, it is a positive statement in the sense that regulators are being instructed to look upon biotechnology as a worthwhile human activity that deserves responsible control. Precisely what is to be controlled is not specified.

The United Church of Christ (UCC) also avoids specifying a set of direct instructions to government regulatory bodies. Rather, as noted above, it prefers to work through lower level institutional review boards (IRBs), its own hospitals, and religious constituencies with which it is organizationally related. Interactions with IRBs, however, do create opportunities for the intertwining of government policies and the positions taken by an organized religion such as the United Church of Christ.

On the other hand, the UCC, although recognizing that human beings have a responsibility to relieve pain and suffering through interventions into the human body, argues that intervention must have some limits. "Having dominion over the created order is not a license for exploitation and abuse; rather, it is a covenantal responsibility to care for the created order and to enhance the use of its gifts for the healing of humanity and creation." Our temptation is to see promise and to "distort it to our designs." Indeed, "is not the Creator's design of unbelievable variety produced through the amazing capability of the genetic structure more desirable in the long run? If the technology becomes possible for positive eugenics, then who decides?" (General Synod, UCC, 1987: 30–31).

Recognizing that the societal implications of biotechnology are not well-understood, the United Church of Christ has adopted a low-key position with regard to the substance of regulation. Although the UCC exhorts its membership to study the position papers of the World and National Councils of Churches, papers which are often very ambitious, it specifically suggests only limited involvement at the lowest levels of governance for its own constituencies. The instruction here is to be healing but cautious in maintaining genetic diversity.

The statement of the Roman Catholic Church, although directed to moral issues associated with essentially reproductive technologies, has broad applicability to other biomedical technologies and to biotechnologies in general. The statement argues that reliance on individual conscience is inadequate for regulation: "Recourse to the conscience of each individual and to the self-regulation of researchers cannot be sufficient for insuring respect for personal rights and public order" (RCC, 1987: A17). Moreover, it would "be illusory to claim that scientific research and its applications are morally neutral. . . . One cannot derive criteria for guidance from mere technical efficiency, from research's possible usefulness to some at the expense of others or, worse still, from prevailing ideologies" (RCC, 1987: A14). Thus, researchers' consciences are inadequate to regulate biotechnology. As a result, government action is required: "the task of the civil law is to insure the common good of people through the recognition of and defense of fundamental rights and through the promotion of peace and public morality" (RCC, 1987: A17).

As in the statements of other religious bodies, that by the Roman Catholic Church is not enlightening due to the lack of specific positions taken on the substantive issues regarding regulation of biotechnology. General guidelines for policymakers are presented and several moral principles are articulated, but a digging into the regulatory specifics is avoided. As with the WCC statement, this is to some extent understandable because both the WCC and the RCC are not speaking to specific individual governments.

Taking all of these statements as a group, careful moral and ethical argumentation is exhibited by virtually all religious bodies, but a set of substantive regulatory observations is not provided. Specific regulatory recommendations are, of course, difficult to generate. Nevertheless, given the importance of biotechnology to organized religions, the virtual avoidance of the substantive regulatory context is difficult to justify.

Findings

It is somewhat confusing to look at a multiplicity of religious positions as a group because, as explained above, religions have taken a variety of positions on questions of biotechnology. However, regardless of nuances, emphases, and shadings of language, the statements just described do have a reasonably strong resemblance to each other. Several findings are in evidence.

First, all of the statements recognize biotechnology as an issue of momentous importance, and clearly a major scientific challenge to religious thinking and public policy. All emphasize the moral, ethical, and philosophical questions that have been brought into focus by biotechnology. What religions basically have seen, however, is a challenge at the level of the individual person; the wide-angle regulatory concerns have been ignored.

Second, the position papers of organized religions are in place and available to be activated politically. This is by no means insignificant, because these positions can be linked with and amplified by the mass media should a genetic engineering issue be forthcoming on which the media choose to exert political pressure. Should the contentiousness of biotechnology issues increase, the position papers of organized religions might play a larger role in any potential policy debate.

Third, little attention is directed at the social dimensions of biotechnology. It is, of course, quite logical to focus primarily on biotechnology. Its benefits are discussed in virtually all documents, but individual-level shortcomings are singled out for special attention. Unfortunately, attention to broader social concerns such as agriculture, nutrition, terrorism and conflict, international decisional structures, and legal regimes, especially patent policies, is not in evidence. This is a serious omission because the social aspects of biotechnology entail issues most likely to be addressed by legislative bodies, and therefore these aspects should have been explored by religious documents, especially if government regulation is being encouraged. In a very real sense, the religious statements are focused almost exclusively at the individual level.

Fourth, a disheartening dimension of these statements is their almost universal criticism of the scientific community for its lack of moral sensitivity. This condition is simply asserted as a truism without offering convincing evidence, and empirical evidence may be difficult to locate. A perusal of scientific journals reveals a rather profound awareness of moral issues and attempts to resolve them despite the difficulties in doing so. Although many of these vexing issues remain unresolved, the scientific community has addressed them in publications and scholarly conferences. Indeed, it would not be incorrect to assert that there has been a persistent interest in the moral aspects of questions arising from biotechnology over the past decade.

Fifth, the statements display an almost complete lack of appreciation for what it means to be a professional scientist. The religious documents show little sensitivity to the continuously unfolding process of expanding knowledge which is at the heart of the practice of science. Rather, most religions have argued, in effect, that biologists are making them "uncomfortable" by their discoveries and the application of those discoveries in technology. The momentum of discovery is unappreciated, as is the thirst for knowledge which is an intimate part of being human.

Sixth, no appreciation of the value of commercial biotechnology firms is in evidence in the documents. Many of the documents are strongly critical of the role of commercial biotechnology firms and generally suspicious of their motives. Virtually no appreciation of the value of these firms is in evidence. For example, the statements do not display an awareness of the frequent large investments required to develop a new genetically engineered product, the scale-up processes needed to produce it, and the acumen and persistence in bringing such a product to market. By no means can this be considered an insignificant role, yet it is neglected by the religious statements. Moreover, a question of moral equity for commercial firms relates to intellectual property rights and patents (Daus, 1986; Casey and Moss, 1987; and Bent et al., 1987). These issues too remain untouched, despite their central importance to industrial competitiveness.

Seventh, the documents display a lack of understanding of the regulatory process itself. In calling for government regulation, the word "government" is used crudely and without an appreciation of its complexity. There is virtually no sensitivity to the levels of government—local, state, or national—or to their interrelationships, which are often quite complicated. This is not an unimportant point, because some of the most bitter debates over biotechnology have taken place at the local level and local communities have enacted some of the most stringent laws. Furthermore, the relationships between, for example, local/state government and the federal government over questions of biotechnology are emerging as increasingly complex and confusing (Blank, 1981; Huber, 1987). Indeed, some scientists have claimed that there is already too much government interference in the research and marketing of biotechnology products (Strobel, 1987). Beyond this is the important point that the very process of regulation in biotechnology is one of the most complex in the federal government, to say nothing of regulation at the local and state levels. The religious documents do not recognize this fact when calling for "government regulation of biotechnology." Numerous laws are already in place, various federal agencies have seized their corners of the regulatory turf, and some thought has been given to an over- arching regulatory framework. No understanding of the decade-old evolution of this regulatory context is in evidence in the religious statements.

And eighth, little appreciation is displayed for the fact that the "public" has been involved on various review bodies, institutional biosafety committees, and congressional hearings. Questions involving environmental release of genetically engineered organisms have attracted considerable attention from various groups (Abramson, 1986), but are not dealt with in the documents. This is not to argue that public participation in questions in biotechnology has been ideal or even sat- isfactory (Goldberg, 1987), rather that the religious statements do not define or adequately dig into this very important question. This is, of course, ironic given that these religious papers are strongly oriented toward the public's side of the political spectrum. It is even more ironic because the church's authority extends into the public domain, and yet the public dimensions of these problems remain quite underdeveloped.

Finally, some general comments are in order. Without question, these reli- gious writings display what C. P. Snow called the "two cultures" problem of the separate worlds of the natural sciences and the humanities (Singer, 1985). Those who produce religious documents are essentially humanists who in all likelihood lack a comprehensive and intimate understanding of the multiplicity of issues in science and technology. As indicated above, the reverse is not nec- essarily true. However, the documents cannot be used to make a complete case. Indeed, the mere fact that many religions recognize developments in genetic engineering as worthy of their attention certainly speaks to the breaking down of at least some barriers to interdisciplinary cooperation. To that extent, these documents surpass much of what has been done in the traditional social science disciplines.

On balance, then, the public policy aspects of these documents should be viewed as initial attempts to grapple with some of the social issues raised by biotechnology. As new knowledge unfolds in biotechnology, these religious docu- ments will require significant rethinking and revision. As part of this process, life scientists, especially those involved in biotechnology, will have to work with humanists if credible religious positions are to be developed. Biosocial and biotheological concerns are emerging into the public domain so rapidly that any- thing less than an intimate collaboration will fall short of political needs. Most certainly, as Markle and Robin (1989) indicate, the far-reaching commercial as- pects of biotechnology will have to be integrated into the broader social and po- litical landscape. Thus, the wide-angle concerns alluded to earlier in this paper remain before us waiting to be addressed. Until these broader social and political concerns are integrated into our view of individual-level issues, we will have an incomplete and ineffective understanding of the impact of biotechnology on human society.

Note

Thanks to Craig Koukol for his research assistance and to Robert H. Blank and Odelia Funke for their helpful comments.

3
Political Choices, Social Values, and the Economics of Biotechnology: A Lesson from the Dairy Industry

William P. Browne and
Larry G. Hamm

Americans, perhaps through cultural belief, hold on to the almost deterministic view that technological innovation will prevail, or roll-on, over any and all obstacles to introduction. As long as a new technology works, Americans maintain a troubling tendency to believe that adoption is inevitable.[1] This might be best termed roll-on theory, the widespread belief that technical advancement rolls on and over any obstacles getting in the way. Roll-on theory is blessed by its simplicity, a condition that Don K. Price (1969: 135) summed up two decades ago by agreeing with the platitude "knowledge is power."

Price, however, was not of the opinion that technology prevails because it makes winners of all society. Rather, as he suggests, technology wins because the institutions that provide it are involved with "the centers of political and economic decision" (Price, 1969: 136). This chapter, based on careful analysis of a single production innovation, is in fundamental agreement with that view; but it also suggests a changing context that calls into question whether or not specific technological adoption will take place with the same likelihood as in the past. Our analysis contends that there can be very little that is simple in the adoption of present and future technology, especially in agriculture. On the contrary, the following seems increasingly true: technological innovation will be accepted only when supporters possess strong economic incentives to promote their good and when they generate equally strong political incentives to accompany adoption.

After setting the stage for analysis by discussing issues regarding agricultural research, the chapter proceeds in three parts. We first introduce bovine somatotropin technology and examine the market complexities of the dairy industry. Parts two and three focus, respectively, on economics and politics. Market forces, the analysis shows, clearly place the final burden of economic risk on firms introducing the new technology. Their's is not an easy task of successfully gaining product acceptance. Nor, given redistributive concerns with the product, do bovine somatotropin producers find the political environment more hospitable than the marketplace.

Our analysis suggests that societal beliefs about the inevitability of technology led the developers of bovine somatotropin to ignore, through false confidence, many identifiable political variables that influenced the marketability of their product. But politics is complex and its effects spill over from the regulatory and legislative arenas into the marketplace. This happens both accidentally and by design as proponents and opponents of a product escalate the level of conflict. In seeking advantage, these diverse interests create a situation where they bring forth numerous issues associated with a single product. The interplay of those issues, in turn, determines much about the acceptability of the new technology that the product represents. Biotechnology firms, especially because of the importance of this product in setting regulatory precedents for future biotechnologies, should have been as careful in assessing its political feasibility as they were in judging the economy and efficiency of its use. This would have avoided the surprising emergence of new issues that confronted and proved costly to producing firms.

Agricultural Research: Its Current Problem

If economics and politics are major factors in the diffusion of technology, the explanation lies in the imprecision with which society understands what it wants in relation to what science can provide. New products and techniques can work, that is, satisfy certain functional requirements, but still not satisfy social wants. Likewise, innovations may produce unwanted consequences that, despite major contributions, call new things into question. As a result, it becomes quite unclear as to who will win—and lose—if technology should roll on. In the absence of certain answers, other factors become persuasive.

The history of agricultural research reveals that there have long been difficulties in gaining acceptance for technological change (Marcus, 1985). More immediately, that history indicates that political allies, such as the National Grange, have been invaluable in converting farmer opinions toward scientific innovation. There has never been a consensus among potential recipients of agricultural research that new service institutions, arrangements for diffusion of knowledge, techniques, applications, and products were beneficial.

To that extent, the present uncertainty as to whether or not agricultural technology will satisfy basic wants, and be widely accepted, is nothing new. As Marcus (1985: 221) points out, there have been round after round of attacks on research institutions for their failure to solve whatever farmers see as their greatest farm problems, almost all of which have been caused by low prices and oversupply. These recurring attacks take place because the inability to manage oversupply has inexorably pushed the farm sector toward financial stress, generating fewer but larger farms as survivors were required to become larger and more specialized in order to lower costs.

There are several features of the U.S. food system that are new with regard to the present lack of consensus over proper directions for agricultural research and technology. First, biological technology—especially biotechnology—no longer emanates only from a research establishment of federally supported land grant colleges and research stations (Doyle, 1985a; Kenney, 1986; Buttel and Kenney, 1987). Non-land grant institutions, especially those related to human medical research, have become important players. So too have private and other public universities. The private business sector is an increasingly active participant and vested interest, both in doing and financing research. Second, there exists a resourceful and politically legitimate set of nonfarm critic organizations (externalities/alternatives interests) whose representatives are, in terms of their agricultural concerns, mostly involved with the externalities of and alternatives to technology (Hadwiger, 1982; Browne, 1988). Agricultural policymaking is the active domain of a large number of organized interests, from consumers to environmentalists, that call attention to and challenge the third-party or publicly assigned effects of farm and food production practices. Third, opposition to present research activities and arrangements are broadening beyond these externalities/alternatives interests and now encompass a wide range of nonallied critics: including farmers who see a better use of federal funds, family farm advocates, and numerous market-oriented agribusinesses (Browne, 1987a). Each of these new features brings forth new motives for opposing the products of agriculture research. This combination represents a significant departure from past patterns of opposition to agricultural technology, primarily because both the institutional conditions of policymaking and the market conditions that influence them are increasingly complex.

A fourth feature, and an even greater point of departure from past concerns, is no less important. Agricultural technology always benefited from the prevailing Malthusian fear that the world, burdened by an exploding population, would run out of food. While in the short term American farmers were chronically plagued by overproduction, their long-term salvation was always to be that eventual day of reckoning when agriculture would be called upon to make an heroic effort to feed a universally food-short world (Ruttan, 1982a). This contextual advantage for those who promote agriculture research has changed. As Lipman-Blumen and Schrom (1984) contend, research goals and priorities are unclear. For many reasons of increasing agricultural productivity, massive food shortages are no longer feared.[2]

In that sense, agricultural technology has, through its successes, become more susceptible to challenge because it no longer represents social values that mandate acceptance. The political discourse surrounding conflicting interests in ag-

riculture portrays several alternative production routes, all leading to a sufficiently sustainable agriculture. From that perspective, no single innovation has
compelling support. With alternatives available, massive efforts are often required to mobilize support for adoption and to overcome the wide range of potential opponents for any single one of them.

In reality, changes in packaging or preparation technology are eminently more
important to the perceived well-being of most consumers than are agricultural
innovations. With only around 30 percent of the consumer food bill being for the
actual agricultural commodity, food buyers generally see no direct benefit to
them from any particular technological innovation. Increasingly the benefits of
agricultural research are diluted and diffused to the point where they are unrec-
ognizable by their ultimate users. Likewise, with over 15,000 items in a typical
grocery store, consumers most often have many alternatives if they believe that
the new technological innovation generates any actual or perceived risk to them.
Only if the innovation does affect a product or class of products with few substitutes or alternatives will consumers consciously applaud the appropriateness of
that innovation's use. Since consumers are both the final users and the majority
of the taxpayers who fund agricultural technology, their longer-term wishes may
well prevail. In essence, the dynamics of the modern U.S. food system act to di-
lute and diffuse the benefits of the successes of agricultural research and make
opposition to new technology both compelling and virtually without cost to
many individuals. This brings forth an important observation which we, in a preliminary sense, test and confirm with this interview-based research: the risks of
technological product failure in agriculture will continue to increase as political
and economic support fragments in an increasingly complex arena.[3]

The Case of bGH, bST

A growth hormone (bGH), found to increase the milk production of lactating
cows and extractable from bovine pituitary glands, was first reported in the early
1930s (Baldwin and Middleton, 1987). Until recently, bGH had to be extracted
from the pituitary glands of slaughtered bovine animals. The extraction methods
and limited natural supply made commercial application of this known technology impossible. Genetic engineering research changed that possibility in the
1980s as scientists reproduced large amounts of bGH genes from bacterial hosts
to which extracted genes has been linked. For scientists, the bGH technology was
another application of the general gene splicing-fermentation extraction technology being used in human medical research (Longworth, 1987: 188).

The product, now more widely called bovine somatotropin (bST), has the potential to increase milk production by an average of 10-20 percent per cow, perhaps slightly more. Recombinant DNA procedures have been employed by four
U.S. firms to develop bST for farm use. American Cyanamid, Elanco Products,
Monsanto, and Upjohn are all working with university agricultural scientists to

perfect the product and establish the parameters for its use (Browne, 1987b; Rauch, 1987: 820).

Since bST is a substance naturally produced by a dairy cow and occurs in her milk output, the federal Food and Drug Administration (FDA) has ruled milk treated with bST to be safe for human consumption. But as yet, the FDA has not ruled it safe for dairy cows; nor have FDA mandatory determinations of "environmental safety" been addressed (Teske, 1987: 31). Therefore, at the earliest, bST will not be commercially available to most dairy farmers until 1990, perhaps not before 1991.

Not a great deal is known about what will happen to dairy production when, and if, bST becomes available. Both the competitive secrecy surrounding product development and the likely variability among farm user skills create this uncertainty (Buttel, 1986a). We do know, however, that there will be escalating political controversy. Uncertainty, as we shall demonstrate in the following sections, is magnified when the probable productivity increases are factored, as they must be, into an agricultural sector with some unique economic and political conditions.

Characteristics of the U.S. Dairy Industry: Market Complexity

The market issues affecting the dairy industry are complex beyond the simple questions of supply and demand for fluid milk. In addition to the market itself, federal price support policy, cooperative marketing arrangements, the national political strength of the milk lobby, and the industry's dependence on good relationships with grocers all influence farm profits. Moreover, technology-driven productivity increases are nothing new for a constantly evolving dairy industry that encompasses many market issues. Mechanical milking machines, artificial insemination, nutrition research, and many other innovations have helped push average annual production per cow from 5,314 pounds in 1950 to 13,786 pounds in 1987 (United States Department of Agriculture [USDA], 1950-1987). Productivity increases for the U.S. dairy industry have averaged about two percent a year for most of this period. Increases have accelerated in recent years to a point where serious surpluses developed in the dairy industry. In 1983, the USDA purchased 16.8 billion pounds of surplus milk equivalent to about 11 percent of U.S. production. Since that peak, federal dairy policy has been revised several times and two forms of voluntary supply management have been used. All this has been accompanied by serious political controversies over the cost and tactics of dairy programs (Hamm, 1987: 7-11).

Amid this controversy, existing in the throes of national budget concerns, dairy price supports have declined 20 percent since 1983 and have caused severe financial stress to many dairy farmers. The current dairy legislation contained in the 1985 Food Security Act, including 1988-89 drought relief, assures that milk prices will fall another $1.00 per hundredweight if surplus continues (Glaser, 1986: 2).

If bST is adopted and only increases production 15 percent over a five-year period, productivity increases from bST alone could be three percent a year; or higher than the historic trend. Given the current dairy income environment, bST technology will become part of ongoing federal policy debates over dairy pricing. Three sets of attitudes toward bST, ranging from steadfast opposition to great enthusiasm, have already developed among our respondents and other dairy farmers (Stanfield, 1987; Schneider, 1988). Recognizing that bST will, in practice, probably be large-farm biased, many small and limited-resource dairy farmers view bST as a livelihood-threatening technology and argue against it on the basis of social values of the family farm. Another group of highly progressive producers actively seeks the technology in order to be ahead of the pending price impacts of future adoption. A third large segment of the industry, perhaps the majority of producers, recognizes the need to adopt bST, but these farmers are uneasy about the technology. Because dairying is a proportionately higher fixed-cost industry than other farm commodities, bST will have to be used to spread the fixed overhead of the operation if it becomes available to anyone. These producers feel economic trends will soon force them to jump on a rapidly moving technological treadmill.

The attitude of dairy producers is also conditioned by another unique characteristic of the U.S. dairy subsector, one that transforms most individual preferences into a collective choice. The initial market for milk is controlled by dairy farmer-owned and -controlled marketing cooperatives. Dairy cooperatives market about 78 percent of all producer milk in the United States. In addition, cooperative dairy farmers own nearly 90 percent of the butter/dry milk powder processing plants, about 55 percent of the cheese manufacturing plants, and around 15 percent of the fluid milk processing plants (USDA, 1984). Therefore, most producers must evaluate, as did our respondents, the impact of bST on their own collective marketing/processing investments as well as on their individual farming investments.

For most past agricultural research innovations, only the individual farm or microimpacts drove producers' conscious economic and political actions. In the dairy industry, however, the broader macroeconomic impacts are now well-understood because of past production increases; and they are within the purview of dairy producers for control. For this reason, respondents expressed hostility to bST because they saw it as a threat to their collectively maintained dairy industry marketing and governing institutions. They saw check-offs, marketing trade councils, dairy policy provisions, and even the cooperative structure itself all at risk.

This attitudinal posture has been important because it reached into national politics. Most of the dairy cooperatives in the United States are linked together in an umbrella cooperative, the National Milk Producers Federation (NMPF). NMPF, recently rated as Washington's fourth most effective lobby (Solomon, 1987: 1706), effectively oversees the industry-wide perspective on issues affecting dairying. After dairy leader opposition to bST was expressed as a collective choice problem, the organization moved quickly in refusing to endorse the adoption of bST technology until after market uncertainty is determined.

Another critical dairy sector participant, one of great importance to attaining the goals of NMPF, is the retail-wholesale grocery store industry. Most fluid milk is sold through retail grocery stores. Therefore, the most lucrative segment of the dairy industry is directly influenced by the actions and marketing practices of food retailers, a factor that brings compatibility in goals between producers and those who market dairy products.

In the food inflation years of the early 1970s, news reports showed consumers picketing their local markets to protest high food prices. To prevent themselves from being on the wrong side of the consumers again, the food retailing industry has positioned itself on public relations matters to be the defenders of consumer interests rather than champions of what farmers want to sell (Browne, 1988: 110). If any agricultural technology is deemed not to be in the consumer's best interest (that is, acceptable), the retail sector uses its procurement powers to resist the implementation of that technology. The most recent example includes removal of Alar-treated apples from produce departments. This gatekeeper role is so significant that food processors and manufacturers also follow with a similar posture.

The modern food system operates in ways which shift the costs of economic change and financial risk up and down the vertical food chain (Hamm, 1981). If consumers decide not to bear any food safety risk (real or perceived) and reward economic risk takers, food chains will transfer their financial risks to processors and manufacturers. If the processors have sufficient power, they will shift their financial risk to producers. The producers have sufficient power to either shift the cost back up to processors or down to bST suppliers. The preferred shift is obviously downwards; one that rewards old allies, minimizes uncertainty, and restrains threatening technological innovation.

As agricultural technology confronts this vertical farm-to-market chain and becomes entangled in health and safety regulation, the political economy facing the new innovation becomes the unit of analysis. Regulation and risk shifting are fundamentally done by defining property rights of "who gets to do what to whom?" It is, therefore, left to the interplay of political issues to determine the ultimate legitimacy of a new technology such as bST. As shall be demonstrated below, this political interplay is not much kinder to technological innovators than is the market economy of the dairy industry.

Creating Political Issues: Institutional Complexity

To the surprise of many, especially bST developers, the introduction of bovine somatotropin generated considerable political controversy both within and apart from the dairy program. This should not have been a surprise, nor would it have been one except that obvious issues of conflict were ignored by those steeped in the comforting reassurances of roll-on theory. There were always many institutional implications to provoke controversy. First, bST would set regulatory precedents that would advantage the introduction of future products and make challenges to them much harder. Future regulatory standards, procedures, and questions of property would all be influenced by the way bST was treated in the policy process. Second, as noted earlier, an extensive array of newly institutionalized externality interests have recently raised policy questions about the agricultural sciences and they were important challengers on bST issues. Third, as stated above, the new product was not likely to be scale-neutral in its effect on dairy producers. Rather, as an imperfectly received collective good (Guttman, 1978), bST was likely to be adopted by the most efficient and generally the largest producers, lead to production and price disadvantages for non-adopters, and through their attrition, reinforce structural trends toward fewer and larger dairy farms (USDA, 1987a). Also, technology will likely lead to less gross income to the dairy sector as a whole and a threat to the U.S. basic dairy policy.

As explained in an article on the emergence of the bST controversy (Browne, 1987b), three rather independent but related issues focused wider policy attention on FDA deliberations over the growth hormone. From the perspective of proponents, who wanted to market bST, the issue was simply one of protecting property rights and investor profits through government regulation. They only wanted to stabilize the industry by going to government, not develop a defense of their product or its worth. But opponents, their attention focused on social rather than economic values, first defined the issue as one of opposing technology. Later they bolstered their opposition to bST by infusing technology into the broader issue of the declining family farm. Because the intensity of the disagreements resulted from the likely importance of bST as a precedent-setting genetic engineering product, instigators of these policy debates—unlike many of the allies who joined the fray—were less interested in bST on its own marketplace merits. The presence of both immediate and long-term policy implications created an especially cantankerous and often clouded controversy, one where an increasing range of social values were touched.

Biotechnology Proponents

Given a choice, proponents of genetic engineering research would have preferred that bST was never addressed in any contentious issue. Indeed, executives of the four producing firms, in varying degrees given the differing attention to politics within the corporations, worked toward a consensus of support for their innovation. Their efforts paid off in quick FDA acceptance of milk from bST-treated cows as fit for human consumption (Browne, 1987b: 78). Compelling research demonstrated that biologically inert bST residues are digestively destroyed, leaving no trace in consumers. No evidence to the contrary has yet to surface (Teske, 1987: 31).

This success notwithstanding, farm and business leaders agree that consensus tactics have accomplished little more than the hoped-for assembly of a lobbying infrastructure and a reputational expertise for addressing pending policy decisions about biotechnology in general and bST in particular. To this end, firms worked quietly on several matters: they lobbied collectively on what were first thought to be the obscure policies of patenting intellectual property and developing internationally agreed upon regulatory standards; Monsanto sought added agricultural credibility by participating in farm bill debates during 1985; the Industrial Biotechnology Association (IBA) was created in 1981 and efforts were made to expand its member base; massive education efforts to inform diverse dairy policy participants were cooperatively initiated; opinion polls were commissioned; and very unusually, the FDA was urged to discuss publicly the human safety aspects of bST while the product was still under investigation.

No quiet campaign of information-based lobbying was sufficient to keep policymakers in the USDA and the Congress from becoming wary, rather than supportive, of bST as the FDA prepared its ruling, however. For one thing, critical regulatory agencies such as the FDA and the Environmental Protection Agency were not well prepared to address the impact of biotechnological innovations (Stanfield, 1987). Industry complaints were made to Congress and the administration about bureaucratic ineptitude and the negative affects of delays on new and costly product lines. Second, these went to a Congress already made wary of biotech firms by earlier complaints of member states of the Organization for Economic Cooperation and Development (OECD) in 1985. Several OECD officials accused United States corporations of both delaying proceedings and coopting U.S. participants to an OECD report on the safety and regulation of biotechnology. Complaints from corporate officials about the FDA and EPA only heightened congressional suspicions of what bST innovators really wanted. Congressional staff respondents to this study noted that their attitudes about bGH went from neutral to extremely cautious during this period.

While such problems might well have been overcome by the formidable array of information and lobbying resources of bST proponents, other domestic interests were not allowing biotechnology advocates time to do so effectively. Even as the IBA was expanding and while participating firms were making commitments to work together in providing information (Rauch, 1987: 820), opponents were popularizing a negative view of bST that had little to do with the lobbying initiatives set forth by its proponents. As a result, neither international nor domestic issues of biotechnology standards have been resolvable.

Biotechnology Opponents

The catalyst for domestic opposition to bST was Jeremy Rifkin, the persona behind the Foundation on Economic Trends (FET). As one of the many externalities/alternatives organizations with a policy interest, FET directed its earliest and greatest efforts against biotechnology (Rifkin, 1983). At the onset, Rifkin carried on a dispute with biotech corporations, including Monsanto and American Cyanamid, over plant and seed technology. At issue was the release of genetically engineered bacteria into the environment and the likelihood of genetic collapse should these bacteria spread.

Foundation tactics embraced judicial litigation as a means of delay, public confrontation with genetic engineering proponents, cultivating support—both active and passive—from other externalities/alternatives interests, using the media to communicate its message, and depicting worst-case scenarios to elicit public attention. Rifkin also benefited from two specific sources of support: the Humane Society of the United States attracted the attention of animal rights activists to what were not obviously animal issues; and the Agricultural Resources Project under Jack Doyle (1985a) of the Environmental Policy Institute asked questions about whether science could remain neutral in the face of the concentrations of wealth found in research-sponsoring genetic engineering firms. The former became an active ally against bST, and Doyle's research, even during its early stages, was widely cited as a reason for skepticism about the claims of bST-producing firms.

The issue of technological dissent, while not ignored, was not met with the approval that many critics hoped for. While the Humane Society aided FET in litigating against using bST on cows in 1986, basing its case on the stress of increased milk production, other externalities/alternatives interests provided little support.[4] Many consumer and environmental activists, interested in food prices and land use problems, found biotechnology potentially important to those concerns. In particular, reductions in farm acreage and animals could: limit use of fertilizers and pesticides, lower irrigation use of water, and remove fragile lands from production. In some instances, our scientist and public interest group respondents hoped genetics could replace chemicals and reduce the water consumption needs of plants.

The impact of this division among environmental and conservation activists, in addition to further confusing policymakers about the acceptability of environmental risk factors, meant that bST gained greater attention as a farm policy issue than an environmental one. An unusual alliance between externalities/alternatives opponents of bST and the Wisconsin Family Farm Defense Fund generated national publicity. Media and public attention was directed to the farm structure consequences of large farmers being the most able and likely to adopt bST. Wisconsin contacts with other state farm protest groups through the National Save the Family Farm Coalition spread farmer dissatisfaction with bST. Our respondents emphasized that many of these state activists, especially those working together on both farm bill and farm credit legislation, found the anticorporate warnings of Rifkin and Doyle quite compatible with their own neopopulist and antiagribusiness rhetoric. Through their efforts, bST became a grass-roots issue within the American Agriculture Movement (AAM), National Farmers Organization (NFO), National Farmers Union (NFU), and some regional dairy cooperatives. An exceedingly vocal minority, using communication tactics similar to Rifkin's, trumpeted bST as another vehicle for destroying the family farm. Most of our farm respondents voiced more practical concerns, though. Many farmers who shared the skepticism and who came to be seen as moderates on bST were more restrained in their opposition, reserving their hostility to the likelihood of an increase in milk supplies overburdening and thus collapsing the federal dairy support program.

Public Opinion: The Hormone Question

The opponents of bST could have been dismissed as sadly resourceless in comparison to corporate proponents. The opponents after all were just those natural casualties of scientific progress whose outcries were predictable and whose proposed solutions were un-American and anti-free market. The externalities lobby, under the most favorable circumstances, has major problems in winning on agricultural issues (Berry, 1977: 216; Browne, 1988: Chapter 7). Divisions over the benefits of bST create less than favorable conditions for a Washington-based assault on policymakers. The grass-roots farm lobby has little visibility inside Washington, and so can do little by way of adding support. Membership divisions within the AAM, NFU, and NFO precluded their lobbyists from working against bST. Even if they did lobby, representatives of these organizations have little legitimacy and credibility as the most effective voices of agriculture (Browne, 1988: Chapter 5). So their assistance would not have been formidable.

If roll-on theory were operative, few would have questioned whether major bST opponents had created a burden-of-proof question. But because the new technology was perceived to present a food safety risk, the question for producing firms of who must bear that risk was still able to be brought to the political arena. Societal experience with past broken promises from technology (the safety of nuclear energy, for example) and the advent of better understanding of indirect consequences of technology have shifted the burden of proof to the advocates of technology, at least in the eyes of an attentive public that regularly scans the news for symbols of risks and hazard.

So the playing fields of public policy are not level, to be tilted toward a victory for one side or another on the basis of somewhat superior institutional and lobbying resources. In the case of those with a new technology, there are numerous legislative and administrative hurdles that may be raised and need to be overcome. Opponents, on the contrary, need only one effectively blocked hurdle to doom a product or halt a proposal. This, compounded with the burden of proof that falls on the advocate, is the major defensive advantage held by opponents of innovations that require government intervention before rolling on.

One such hurdle, raised by the media-conscious and public-directed opposition to bST, is the image of the product. The label "hormone," in the course of this controversy became identified with the product. In becoming important, an already addressed (at least by the FDA) subset of food safety risk factors came to life just as the main set of environmental risk discussions bogged down. No amount of emphasis on using the phrase bST rather than bGH could keep opponents from reminding consumers that the inert residue they ingest remains that of a hormone, a substance of great scientific mystery and health uncertainty for many. Even chemical company respondents acknowledged that fact in our interviews.

By late 1986, a few California consumers discovered they were drinking milk from bST-treated cows being used for safety experiments to generate data required by the FDA. These consumers complained to their grocery stores and, in essence, said they would not bear any of the risks associated with this new technology. Coop milk suppliers became visibly worried for one simple reason. Food retailers, given their protector of the consumer posture, immediately demanded assurances that their milk supplies contained nothing from bST-treated cows. The processors (some of whom are vertically integrated food chains) requested formal written assurances from raw milk suppliers (mostly producer-controlled cooperatives) that they would be receiving no bST-treated milk. When the California experience was reported in the national dairy press, processors from Florida to Minnesota asked for and received similar assurances from their cooperative suppliers. The market demand risks by then rested clearly on the shoulders of dairy cooperatives and their dairy farmer owners. Producers were exposed to the supply risk (What will bST do to our cows? To industry? And to government policy?) and the demand risk (What will bST do to the image of the purity of milk?).

This situation intensified over the next three years, becoming a "marketers nightmare" (Richards, 1989: B1). Minnesota and Wisconsin legislators considered bills to ban bST before rejecting them amid considerable public attention. After five large national food market chains banned test-market bST milk from their stores, the Michigan legislature was faced with a product-labeling bill in which milk from hormone-treated cows had to be identified on the carton. Internationally, where public pressure was often more intense than in the United States, the European Economic Community, following a ban on growth-hormone treated cattle, considered a ban on bST dairy products. This became a matter of contention in negotiations over the General Agreement on Trade and Tariffs (GATT), fueling further controversy here and abroad.

As can be seen in the character of the U.S. dairy industry, supplier/producers had no choice but to comply with bST opponents and then to continue to hedge their bets. Dairy farmers currently spend, from funds collected from themselves, about $200 million a year just to promote the image and sale of milk and in extensive health and nutrition education. They must do so because of oversupply and their weak market position. As the bST controversy played out, commercial dairy farmers saw themselves exposed to the costly consequences of an experimental biotechnology they perceived was primarily in the interest of four business firms.

In much of agricultural technology, the market risks would have stayed on the producers. However, the dairy industry is unique in distributing market risks.

The NMPF, representing the vast majority of producers, decided to take a neutral stance on the value of bST (Rauch, 1987: 820). This action, because it withheld support for a potentially important dairy industry tool, was widely viewed as a negative for the new technology. Milk producer leadership, farm group respondents claim, then went even further to demand that their neutrality would be removed only if the biotech firms would undertake a nationwide effort to successfully educate all segments of society about the nature of bST. The joint public relations efforts are funded through the Animal Health Institute (AHI). The AHI was charged with, among other things, the immense task of communicating with all opinion leaders in the food industry, universities, extension services, and media. It also, according to industry and coop sources, is undertaking a plan to establish bST advisory groups of key leaders in all major dairy states in the United States.

The dairy industry has also funded, through their own marketing organizations their officials note, independent consumer attitude studies to determine for themselves how damaging the "hormone issue" might be to the basic consumer demand for their products. Through their actions, dairy producers have shifted the burden of proof and its associated costs back to the technology's advocates and founders. All this may be little more than the first stage in saying "no" to technology as a means of avoiding the treadmill.

Conclusion: Tapping Social Values

Our analysis is not meant to be unfriendly to bST. Rather it demonstrates that a product that performs as its developers intended may well not succeed. As we outlined, there exist many problems that get in the way of technological "roll-on." In the process of shifting the burden of costs associated with bST's technological risk and uncertainty, a major portion of the food system has been exposed to many core issues surrounding the emergence of genetic engineering technology. The technology of bST became burdened by the yoke of normal resistance plus the increasing policy uncertainty created when both the affected institutional and market forces are so complex.

Moreover, policy controversies, prompted by business needs and by policy opposition, have brought forth and reinforced important symbols associated with bST: corporate control, hardship for family farmers, government ineptitude, and food safety. These symbols have been linked by opponents, and to an important extent by the public, to develop a powerful rhetoric against bST.

As our analysis shows, biotechnology firms shared too much faith in roll-on theory as they prepared to introduce bST. Typical of the agricultural lobby, these interests initially carried on a low-key campaign of addressing narrow regulatory and standards issues (Browne, 1988: Chapter 11). But bST as a policy issue came to be defined in other, more encompassing ways, ones not compatible with the public affairs and relations approach of the producer firms. As E. E.

Schattschneider (1960) might suggest: "things got out of hand" in an extended policy controversy.

The faith in roll-on theory also seems misplaced in the degree to which producer firms were willing but seemingly unprepared to take on farm and grocer uncertainty over inherently unstable markets. In effect, introduction challenged the specifics of the dairy program, the highly regulated structure of the dairy industry, and farm leaders' commitment to government price intervention in agriculture. So market risks as well as political risks now work to the disadvantage of the innovators behind bST.

The litany of statements, premises, and postulates of biotechnology's opponents—no matter how flawed or fallacious—do serve to intensify the debate. American society and its belief in environmentally riskless innovation assures the potential for tight political control of biotechnology and, resultingly, market risk avoidance by industries that are skeptical of political conflict. Increasingly the burden of proof will be on the producers of technology, adding to the up-front and documentable costs of technological change.

That process may well move technological acceptance procedures further toward state control, where only the most economically viable biotechnologies with the most widely appreciated societal benefit-cost equations can be successfully introduced. The introduction of bST would not have been expected to elicit policy debate only a few short years ago. But in the late 1980s, these are responses that politically stressed regulators speak of as necessary in determining acceptable risk. Already there have been stringent demands for Congress and the FDA to revise the standards and procedures that led FDA to declare bST individually and environmentally safe. Release of the product was still somewhat in question in early 1990.

In the face of such trends, if they should develop, the American belief in the inevitable roll-on of new technology may become another unfortunate relic of the folklore of American history. The kinds of controversy associated with bST have inspired numerous externalities/alternatives interests to demand totally risk-free procedures as a prerequisite to regulatory approval. These demands, merged with general scientific skepticism, have gained a measure of popular support in both newsprint and citizen attitudes. Many now expect risk-free food consumption when they have no such expectations about such everyday actions as driving home or going for a neighborhood walk. We hope, because of technology's promise for the future, that our previous faith in science and technology is not lost. Rather we prefer another scenario than the confused policy debate that exists for bST. We hope that the developers of future biotechnology products will expend as much effort on careful studies of political feasibility (Webber, 1986) as they do on research into economic and efficient use. Only then can scientists and investors bring forth safe products that really will be judged in the economic marketplace rather than a political market that operates off rhetoric and public policy paranoia.

Notes

1. Those in the physical sciences are certainly exceptions to that belief. Most fully comprehend how much politics matters to their work.

2. Critics, nonetheless, do exist; and they raise questions about sustainability (Cornucopia Project, 1981; Doyle, 1985a).

3. This research is based on over 100 extensive interviews with dairy industry leaders and farmers as well as congressional, administrative, and private interest participants in the policy process. We have also made considerable use of generally available data on the dairy industry and dairy program.

4. These allies, in a related display of dairy interest, also co-litigated the facial branding provisions of the whole herd buy-out program of the 1985 Food Security Act.

II
Institutional Responses to the Development of Biotechnology

4

American Universities, Technology Innovation, and Technology Transfer: Implications for Biotechnology Research

Charles Johnson and Robin Moore

Biotechnology is one of the most rapidly expanding areas of university research today. Because some of the products of this research have tremendous commercial potential, the transfer of this technology is an issue of interest to both public and private users of the technology. How universities manage this technology transfer profoundly affects whether university-based innovation is rewarded, whether state and local economies benefit from the research, and whether technology is successfully transferred to the appropriate external users. Researchers and research administrators are increasingly aware of the importance of technology transfer; unfortunately, the transfer process and the results of varied choices within the process are poorly understood. The research reported here has the overall objective of shedding light on the early stages of the technology transfer process. We identify a number of strategies and processes by which different universities promote the transfer of research and assess factors associated with the development of these strategies.

In 1980, two government actions significantly altered the university biotechnology research environment. The United States Supreme Court ruled in *Diamond v. Chakrabarty* (447 US: 303) that, under some circumstances, new life forms resulting from such research could be considered inventions and thus be entitled to patent protection (Saliwanchik, 1982). Public Law 96-517, enacted by Congress on December 12, 1980, amended Title 35 of the U.S. Code to allow universities and small businesses to patent and retain title to inventions resulting from government-sponsored research (Dickson, 1984: 94). These changes allowed universities three product protection avenues: (1) patents, which require substantial disclosure of information (Epstein, 1983; Kintner and Lahr, 1982; Daus, 1986), (2) licensing without a patent, which is faster than patenting but offers less protection from infringement, and (3) trade secrets, which involves no disclosure, thereby keeping the development as secret as possible (McCurdy, 1985; Unkovic, 1985; Epstein, 1983; University of North Carolina, 1983).

We focus on the first of these strategies since it is the most widely used by American universities. Studies of university patent policies (Palmer, 1948; National Association of College and University Business Officers [NACUBO], 1978; National Council of University Research Administrators [NACURA], 1984) and reports in other related literature (Kenney, 1986; Twentieth Century Fund, 1984; Dickson, 1984; Omenn, 1983: 25) tend to discuss institutions such as MIT, Harvard, and Stanford, which have unique or particularly large funding in biotechnology fields. As a result, universities active in biotechnology but without especially notable industry-research relationships receive little attention. The research reported here seeks to fill that gap in the empirical record.

Overview of Methodology

This study investigates a varied sample of universities doing biotechnology research. A sample of 34 universities was devised using data from the National Science Foundation (NSF) on research funding (1985a: 43-46, 104-105; 1985b: 42-43, 65-66, 88-91). The various NSF rankings were averaged and a sample of 34 universities was chosen from this population in an effort to be representative in geography, research funding level, and university type. A survey questionnaire was developed for use in telephone interviews with university administrators. Using approaches recommended by Dexter (1970), the telephone interviews were conducted between mid-November 1987 and mid-March 1988 with technology transfer specialists and research administrators at the universities in the sample. At our request, all universities in the sample sent copies of their intellectual property protection policies. The response rate for our telephone interviews is 78 percent, which means that our analysis will involve 26 universities. A few of those surveyed indicated that their current policy was either under revision or was to be revised in the near future. Two areas were perceived as needing the most revision: the specific addressing of biotechnology products and processes and the manner in which royalties are divided among the inventor, the inventor's department, and the institution. Our basic finding is that two dimensions of activities are important: (1) the extent to which institutions encourage faculty with incentives to promote innovation and transfer of research, and (2) the extent to which institutions provide professional staff to support innovative work and technology transfer.

Strategies for Technology Transfer

Review of patent policies and responses in interviews suggests that strategies for technology transfer can be arrayed along at least two dimensions. The first dimension is *Institutional Approach*, which is comprised of the individual universities' intellectual property policy and their philosophy regarding how to reward innovation. The second dimension is *Institutional Support*, which indicates the level of centralized support universities give the technology transfer process.

Institutional Approach

This dimension was measured using responses to questions concerning with whom the title to an invention rests, the level of royalty payments to the inventor, whether royalty payments are a percentage of the gross or net royalty revenues, and whether or not the university encourages and the state allows start-up companies as a form of economic development. There was great variation along this dimension. Universities such as Stanford and Wisconsin are the ones most willing to allow inventors to retain title to their inventions. The majority of other universities in our sample release title to inventions back to the inventor only if no (or "no significant") university time, money, or resources were used, and, in the case of the University of Alabama at Birmingham, if the invention is outside the inventor's normal field of work.

All of the universities in our sample (except the University of Wisconsin) give the inventor a percentage of the net revenues the institution receives—that is, the university first recovers its direct expenses associated with patenting or licensing the invention before the inventor receives any royalties. While this seems very reasonable, Janet Trubatch (1988), Associate Vice-President at the University of Chicago, suggests that inventors could be encouraged more if they received a percentage of the gross revenues from their inventions—that is, if the institution was more willing to take some risk and pay the inventor a portion of even the initial revenue. The Universities of Wisconsin and Chicago, and North Carolina State University are examples of institutions which follow the "percentage of gross" philosophy (only Wisconsin is in the current sample). The actual percentage of revenues that inventors receive varies from a flat 15 percent at Iowa State to 60 percent of the first $100,000 at Oklahoma State. While the University of Washington recovers expenses before distributing royalties, the inventor receives all of the first $10,000 net royalties and graduated percentages thereafter. The majority of universities have some form of graduated system in which the inventor receives a higher percentage of early royalties than of later aggregate royalties.

A final aspect of the Institutional Approach dimension concerns economic development and start-up companies. The University of Michigan and the University of Missouri at Columbia both encourage start-up companies while inventors at Virginia Commonwealth University are prohibited by state statute from this sort of entrepreneurial activity (Chermside, 1987: 11). A number of states, including Missouri, North Carolina, Florida, New York, Oklahoma, and Virginia, have some sort of state-sponsored initiative to facilitate technology transfer. In the case of North Carolina, it is the North Carolina Biotechnology Center; in New York, Cornell hosts the biotechnology and agriculture portions of the Center for Advanced Technology, while the bioprocesses segment of the Center is at SUNY-Stony Brook.

Combining these characteristics of Institutional Approach results in three models along this dimension: the Entrepreneurial Professor Model (EPM), the Encouraging Institution Model (EIM), and the Conservative Institution Model (CIM). Criteria for inclusion in the Entrepreneurial Professor Model were that the inventor could retain title fairly easily or that the institution encouraged start-up companies and there was no prohibition against start-up companies through a conflict-of-interest statute or policy. Criteria for inclusion in the Encouraging Institution Model were that the institution provided the inventor with rapid monetary benefit (through using a "percentage of gross" philosophy, a payment at the time of disclosure, or all of a set percentage of initial net proceeds) or more than 40 percent of the first $50,000 net royalties. Additionally, the university or its research foundation generally holds title and any conflict-of-interest statute or policy does not effectively prohibit start-up companies. Criteria for inclusion in the Conservative Institution Model were that payments to the inventor were based on net royalties after patenting costs were paid, were less than 40 percent of that net, and that state statute or university policy might effectively prohibit start-up companies.

Institutional Support

This dimension involves the centralized support that an institution gives the process of technology transfer. Centralized support is measured by the staffing of the office which handles technology transfer. The variation which emerged in the staffing of technology transfer offices (using the office name generically to indicate the office which takes care of patenting, licensing, and marketing of university technology) was based on the number of professionals in the office and the ratio of professional staff to clerical staff. The first of the two models along this dimension is characterized as the Professionally Supportive Institution (PSI), which has two or more full-time equivalent (FTE) professionals in the office and a professional to clerical ratio generally of more than one staff member to each clerical person. The Clerically Supportive Institution (CSI), which has less than two FTE professionals and a professional to clerical ratio of less than one staff person to each clerical person is the second model along this dimension. This measure does not capture any decentralized support that deans, department heads, or others may give the technology transfer process.

In the PSI technology transfer offices, the professional personnel tend to be individuals with training and experience in marketing, finance, general business, or law. The professionals in CSI offices are more likely to be professors from engineering or one of the physical or life science fields, many of whom also have teaching responsibilities, who wear the part-time hat of technology transfer or patent officer.

Findings

Using the criteria articulated above, the universities in the telephone sample fall as seen in Table 4.1. For simplicity's sake, we will refer to the different models as Categories I, II, III, IV, V, and VI. Having identified five technology transfer models (the cell for Category IV is empty), we turn to the issue of whether there are systematic similarities among universities within categories and systematic differences between categories.

Type of University

Universities in this sample are classified as a private, land-grant, or public institution in Table 4.2. This classification is based on the NSF (1985b: 88-91) categorization of public and private institutions and the *Encyclopedia of Education* (1971: 321-22) list of land-grant universities.

In this sample of universities, more private and land-grant institutions fall in the Conservative model while public universities are most prevalent in the Encouraging model. This seems both reasonable and not unexpected since private universities might retain a larger portion of royalties to help fund university research endowments which are not supplemented by governmental appropriations. Land-grant institutions are generally thought of, with the possible exception of the University of California-Berkeley, as being the more conservative segment of the academic community. Finding that most such institutions are in the Conservative categories is in keeping with that line of thought.

Interestingly, most private and land-grant universities (80 percent and 75 percent, respectively) are again similar in their provision of professional support for the technology transfer offices at their institutions. It is possible that this level of professionalism is a function of the length of time these institutions have been pursuing patentable research or their level of experience with technology transfer.

There is no such consensus regarding institutional support in our sample of public universities. They are split almost evenly between the Professionally Supportive and Clerically Supportive models. Some of the universities listed as Clerically Supportive indicated in our interviews that they were in the process of, or soon would be, reevaluating their policies and program. It is possible that such a reevaluation would include adjustments to staffing of the technology transfer offices.

Finally, the summary figures suggest that institutions which have professionally staffed technology transfer offices are not always encouraging to the inventor. Note that Category III, the largest single category, is the Conservative Pro-

Table 4.1
Classification of Universities by Institutional Approach and Institutional Support

Institutional Support	Institutional Approach		
	Entrepreneurial Professor Model	Encouraging Institution Model	Conservative Institution Model
	Category I	Category II	Category III
Professional	Stanford U. of Wisconsin U. of Michigan U. of Missouri-Columbia	U. of Washington U. of Florida U. of Pennsylvania U. of California-Berkeley[1] Wayne State U.	Boston University U. of Georgia Cornell University U. of Kentucky-Lexington U. of Utah U. of Minnesota Iowa State Colorado State
	Category IV	Category V	Category VI
Clerical	(No universities in this category)	Mississippi State Oklahoma State Oregon State U. of N. Carolina-Chapel Hill[2] Virginia Commonwealth	U. of Arizona U. of Oklahoma U. of Alabama-Birmingham Northwestern U.

1   Technology Transfer is done centrally for the entire UL system; the centralized office is categorized as "professional".
2   UNC does not use their technology transfer office for licensing -- they use Triangle Universities Licensing Consortium (TULCO).

fessionally Supportive Institution in which there are few encouragements provided to individual researchers.

Federal Funding

The level of total federal funding to each institution in the sample (NSF 1985b: 88-91) is indicated in Table 4.3. The most striking difference among the various categories occurs between the Professional and the Clerical models. Mean funding for Professionally Supportive Institutions is more than twice that of the Clerically Supportive Institutions. While this relationship should not be viewed as causal, it is evident that some sort of association exists. Within the Professional group, greater incentives to inventors are also associated with higher levels of funding.

Table 4.2
Institutional Classification by Type of Institution

Category	Institutions	Private	Public	Land Grant
			Type of University	
I	Stanford	X		
	U. of Wisconsin			X
	U. of Missouri			X
	U. of Michigan		X	
II	U. of Washington		X	
	U. of Florida			X
	U. of Pennsylvania	X		
	Wayne State Univ.		X	
	U. of California-Berkeley			X
III	Boston University	X		
	U. of Georgia			X
	Cornell University	X		
	U. of Kentucky-Lexington			X
	U. of Utah			X
	U. of Minnesota			X
	Iowa State			X
	Colorado State		X	
IV	(None)			
V	Mississippi State			X
	Oklahoma State			X
	Oregon State		X	
	U. of NC-Chapel Hill		X	
	Virginia Commonwealth		X	
VI	U. of Arizona			X
	U. of Oklahoma		X	
	U. of Alabama-Birmingham		X	
	Northwestern U.	X		

Summary by Categories

	Private	Public	Land Grant
Entrepreneurial Professor (I + IV)	1	1	2
Encouraging Institution (II + V)	1	5	4
Conservative Institution (III + VI)	3	3	6
Professional Support (I, II, III)	4	4	9
Clerical Support (IV, V, VI)	1	5	3

Table 4.3
Total Federal Funding for FY 1983 by Classification and Institution[1]

Category	Institution	Funding (Thousands $'s)
I	Stanford	$152,906
	U. of Wisconsin	111,709
	U. of Missouri-Columbia	28,725
	U. of Michigan	95,902
II	U. of Washington	134,929
	U. of Florida	50,675
	U. of Pennsylvania	95,787
	Wayne State University	21,548
	U. of California-Berkeley	87,570
III	Boston University	45,251
	U. of Georgia	36,977
	Cornell University	112,868
	U. of Kentucky-Lexington	30,216
	U. of Utah	48,766
	U. of Minnesota	99,709
	Iowa State	25,270
	Colorado State	31,163
IV	(none)	
V	Mississippi State	19,317
	Oklahoma State	21,654
	Oregon State	38,814
	U. of North Carolina-Chapel Hill	57,949
	Virginia Commonwealth	28,841
VI	U. of Arizona	52,738
	U. of Oklahoma	15,271
	U. of Alabama-Birmingham	41,625
	Northwestern University	42,540

Summary Table

Category	Avg. Funding per Institution	Standard Deviation	n
Entrepreneurial Professor (I)	97,310.5	44,732.9	4
Encouraging Institution (II + V)	55,308.4	37,168.9	10
Conservative Institution (III + VI)	48,532.8	27,821.5	12
Professional (I, II, III)	71,174.8	41,188.7	17
Clerical (V, VI)	34,972.1	14,426.4	9

1 Source: National Science Foundation. 1985. Federal Support to Universities, Colleges, and Selected Nonprofit Institutions, Fiscal Year 1983. (Detailed Statistical Tables) (NSF 85-381) pp. 88-91. Washington, DC; U.S. Government Printing Office.

The mean funding levels for each category seem to bear out the intuitive assumption that institutions most renowned for research receive significantly higher research funding than those not as renowned. This may be a function of long-established research programs, different prioritizations of the traditional university goals of teaching and research, prestige of individual researchers, or other factors not addressed in this study. As Linnell (1982: 106) observes, "investigators *without* an established background *in the area of their proposed research* will find funding hard to come by" (emphasis in the original).

The dynamic produced by funding for research may drive a maturational process within the university leading to our association between funding levels and institutional support for technology transfer. First, inventions occur naturally as a result of research and thus occur more frequently at institutions with higher research funding. Second, the higher frequency of discoveries then leads to a high frequency with which the technology transfer offices are utilized. And third, the more the offices are used, the more familiar they become with the process of technology transfer, thereby increasing their level of sophistication in the field. Higher levels of professionalization seem a reasonable outgrowth of the increased sophistication. As indicated by the funding levels, being an Encouraging or a Conservative institution (Professional or Clerical model) makes little difference in funding received.

Patents

The relationship between the provision of incentives and support for innovation on the one hand, and the potential transfer of those innovations on the other, can be explored by considering the production of patents by higher educational institutions. Two indicators are considered here: the total number of patents awarded to universities in our sample and the ratio of number of patents to federal research dollars received by the institutions. The number of patents is the actual number of patents awarded to the universities in our sample during 1987—the most recent year for which data were available. The ratio of the number of patents to the level of federal funding (in millions of dollars in 1987) gives some indication of the "efficiency" of patent production. It must be recognized that these data are not unproblematic since they only involve a single year and because the ratio assumes a linkage between federal dollars and patents that may in fact be suspect. Nevertheless, these data are useful in providing tentative information on the impact of different approaches to technology transfer and the outcomes of those approaches are presented in Table 4.4.

Several observations can be made from this table. First, the number and cost of patents varied greatly in the Entrepreneurial Professor Model. Unfortunately, we do not know the number of patents from these institutions that are in private hands. Second, institutions in the Encouraging Institution Model had the lowest patent rate and the highest costs. This was particularly true for the institutions in Category V, which had virtually no patents issued to them in 1987. Third, the

Table 4.4
Number and Cost of Patents by Category and Institution

Category	Institution	# 1987 Patents (a)	Cost Per Patent (b)
I	Stanford	42	3.6
	U. of Wisconsin	11	10.2
	U. of Missouri	7	4.1
	U. of Michigan	1	95.9
II	U. of Washington	1	134.9
	U. of Florida	13	3.9
	U. of Pennsylvania	1	95.8
	Wayne State	6	3.6
	U. of California-Berkeley	- (c)	--
III	Boston University	9	5.0
	U. of Georgia	5 (d)	7.4
	Cornell University	29 (d)	3.9
	U. of Kentucky	3 (d)	10.1
	U. of Utah	12	4.1
	U. of Minnesota	28	3.6
	Iowa State	15	1.7
	Colorado State	4 (d)	7.8
IV	(none)		
V	Mississippi State	- (e)	19.3
	Oklahoma State	- (e)	21.6
	Oregon State	- (e)	38.8
	U. of North Carolina-Chapel Hill	2	28.95
	Virginia Commonwealth	- (e)	24.8
VI	U. of Arizona	2	26.4
	U. of Oklahoma	2	7.6
	U. of Alabama-Birmingham	1	41.6
	Northwestern University	11	3.9

a   Source: Stokes, Claire Z. 1988. University Patents Issued 1987. Presented at the annual meeting of the Society of University Patent Administrators.
b   Total federal funding FY 83 divided by number of 1987 patents
c   Not included - number of 1987 patents shown only for UC system
d   Patents received by university research foundation
e   No patents listed on source document

	Summary Table	
Category	Average Number of Patents	Average Cost per Patent
Entrepreneurial Professor (I)	15.25	6.38
Encouraging Institution (II, V)	2.55	24.05
Conservative Institution (III, VI)	10.08	4.81
Professional (I, II, III)	11.68	6.47
Clerical (V, VI)	2.00	17.49

Conservative institutions had a healthy number of patents and also had the lowest average cost per patent. The fact that this model is the mode for land-grant institutions may have a bearing on these figures. Fourth, Professionally Supportive Institutions produced more than five times the patents of Clerically Supportive Institutions and did so at one third of the federal funding cost. Finally, the number of patents issued in 1987 to the private and land-grant institutions in this survey greatly exceeded those issued to the public institutions (188 vs. 16, or means of 11 vs. 1.7).

The results of this survey indicate that the greatest differentiation of universities lies along the Institutional Support axis. The Professionally Supportive Institutions model contains the modes for both private and land-grant institutions and has higher mean federal funding, 1987 patents, and lower mean cost per patent than the Clerically Supportive Institutions model. The distinctions among the Entrepreneurial Professor, Encouraging Institution and Conservative Institution models are evident, but are not as consistent as the Professional/Clerical distinctions.

Implications for Biotechnology Research

Without exception, all the universities in the survey indicated that research in biotechnology fields was increasing. As a relatively new research area, this is not unexpected. Universities such as the University of Florida indicate that conscious decisions were made within the institution to expand within the biotech fields. Other institutions, such as the University of North Carolina-Chapel Hill, indicate that they were working in biotech "all along."

The rapid progress in biotechnology is evidenced by the backlog of biotechnology patent applications at the U.S. Patent Office. Michael Richards (National Public Radio, 1988) testified before a Senate Subcommittee hearing that the number of biotechnology disclosures had doubled in the last two and one-half years. Additionally, he testified that these inventions were taking four to five years to patent, which is "much longer" than other types of inventions. Table 4.5 indicates the number of biotech-related inventions disclosed during the past two years at the surveyed institutions.

Disclosures at the Entrepreneurial Professor institutions remain the highest, but, unlike the differences in numbers of patents, the number of disclosures at Encouraging and Conservative Institutions are very similar. This may indicate that recent changes made by Encouraging Institutions are "paying off"—the encouragement is resulting in the filing of more invention disclosures, which could lead to receiving increased numbers of patents in the future.

Differences continue between the Professionally Supportive and Clerically Supportive Institutions. The mean number of disclosures through the Professional technology transfer offices is slightly over twice that of the Clerical offices; for all patents, by way of comparison, the Professional offices had five times as many as the Clerical offices. One could expect that increased disclo-

Table 4.5
Biotechnological Invention Disclosures by Category and Institution

Category	Institution	Number of Disclosures 1986-87
I	Stanford	100
	U. of Wisconsin	36
	U. of Missouri - Columbia	12
	U. of Michigan[1]	--
II	U. of Washington	85
	U. of Florida	22
	U. of Pennsylvania	75
	Wayne State	5
	U. of California - Berkeley	20
III	Boston University	40
	U. of Georgia	16
	Cornell University	30
	U. of Kentucky	20
	U. of Utah	17
	U. of Minnesota	30
	Iowa State[1]	--
	Colorado State[1]	--
IV	(none)	
V	Mississippi State	5
	Oklahoma State	10
	Oregon State	3
	U. of North Carolina-Chapel Hill	29
	Virginia Commonwealth	14
VI	U. of Arizona	9
	U. of Oklahoma	15
	U. of Alabama-Birmingham	28
	Northwestern	34

[1]Number of disclosures presently unavailable

Summary Table

Category	Total Number of Disclosures	Average Number of Disclosures
Entrepreneurial Professor (I)	148	49.3
Encouraging Institution (II, V)	268	26.8
Conservative Institution (III, VI)	239	23.9
Professional (I, II, III)	508	36.28
Clerical (V, VI)	147	16.33

sures to the clerical offices would increase their workload, hence, their expertise, and could lead to restructuring of offices if the trend continues. At the present time, however, it appears that higher levels of Professional support seem to indicate a university's willingness to "beat the bushes" for disclosures and more actively pursue patenting and licensing than would logically be possible under the Clerical model.

Conclusion

Developing models of university transfer systems will be helpful in trying to ascertain how universities carry out this function. The two-dimensional model proposed here provides an initial framework for that analysis which focuses on the incentives universities use to encourage innovation and technology transfer and on the structures universities develop to support these activities. The analysis suggests that universities within some of the categories share many similarities and that collectively they differ from universities in other categories. The issue to be addressed now is whether those differences will affect the development of biotechnological research capabilities and the transfer of those technologies. Our preliminary analysis suggests that some differences will emerge in terms of the number of disclosures in the biotechnology areas.

While the classification of schools into the six categories resulted in a degree of uniformity within categories, there were a few notable exceptions. Stanford has consistently been the highest in the survey in funding, patents, and biotechnology disclosures. The University of North Carolina-Chapel Hill stands out as differing consistently from the other institutions in its category—it is much more like a Professionally Supportive Institution. These exceptions need further study to determine the reasons for their variance with similarly classified schools.

The most striking result of this analysis is the importance of professional staffing in technology transfer offices. Although the nature of the relationship between staffing, research funding, and patent production is unclear at this point, the high correlation among these factors suggests that greater attention needs to be paid to their role in technology transfer. In the area of biotechnology, it suggests that universities will be more likely to succeed with a professional staff working on technology transfer.

The analysis gives mixed results on the impact of incentive structures for individual faculty on technology innovation and transfer. We found, for example, that institutions taking an entrepreneurial approach had the highest average number of patents, but the number ranged from 1 to 42 patents in 1987. On the other hand, the conservative institutions, those providing the lowest level of incentives to faculty for technology innovations and transfer, consistently had a significant number of patents, with an average that was only slightly less than the entrepreneurial average. Institutions that were encouraging, with such policies as rapid monetary payoffs for patents, had the smallest number of patents. What these findings seem to suggest is that providing an extra 10 or 20 percent more in royalties or quicker paybacks to faculty for transferable technology will not necessarily increase technology transfer. The difference between conservative and encouraging institutional politics may be significant on paper, but of little consequence in the real academic world.

The implications of this study for biotechnology research, innovation, and transfer in American universities must be tentatively drawn because of limitations associated with the data. Nevertheless, two consequences can be noted. First, the investment of resources in developing a professional staff familiar with biotechnology and the technology transfer process would appear to be critical for universities interested in succeeding financially in this area. Without a professional staff, researchers are left to their own counsel and their own initiative to realize the potential of their inventions. Given the reward structure in most academic institutions, professional publications are far more important than patents and commercial developments, and therefore, professors on their own are not likely to become major players in the technology development and transfer process. Secondly, the success of many land-grant institutions should not go unnoticed. Although we could not measure it or assess its impact directly, there may be an ethic associated with land-grant institutions which emphasizes the applied side of research, which, in turn, encourages technology development and transfer. Establishing this innovation and transfer ethic among the faculty may be critical for bringing research results to the market place. This ethic may not be incompatible with the basic research ethic found at many major universities, but the acceptance of both applied and basic research will likely be necessary for successful technology transfer programs.

5
Biotechnology and Agricultural Cooperatives: Opportunities, Challenges, and Strategies for the Future

*William B. Lacy, Lawrence
Busch, and William D. Cole*

Since its inception, the American capitalistic economy has undergone a series of structural changes which have affected every sphere of the economy. One of these spheres is the institution of agriculture. The nature of American agriculture has shifted from its original form of subsistence and family farming to the large corporate and commodity farming of modern times. Its changing nature and structure has forced farmers to examine closely all of their agricultural and economic alternatives. One such alternative has long been the farmer cooperative system.

Farmer cooperatives are a structured, organized alternative to the more traditional capitalistic form of agricultural business. Instead of operating in and through a conventional market structure, the farmer may elect to operate within a cooperative. Cooperatives facilitate the business of buying and selling both farm supplies and products by providing member farmers items at a price lower than conventional retail and by providing them markets at slightly higher than conventional wholesale rates. Since cooperatives are nonprofit, all profits are returned to the members after legitimate expenses are paid. At present, cooperatives function to supply farmers with the seeds, tools, machinery, and chemicals they need to produce a crop as well as to provide a purchasing alternative once that crop is produced. In addition to the more conventional crop cooperatives (such as grains or nuts), the modern cooperative system deals with meat, poultry, and dairy products; the newest emergent form of cooperatives deals with petroleum products. The American cooperative system, essentially evolutionary in nature, has reached out to encompass the many diverse needs of American farmers. The farmer cooperatives' total business volume of $66.7 billion in 1983 was approximately 30 percent of the total volume of American agriculture (Ingalsbe, 1984). The result of this evolution is that the cooperative has remained a viable institution in the constantly changing structure of American agriculture.

Today, however, agriculture and agricultural cooperatives are facing new opportunities and challenges. The application of certain new biotechnologies to agriculture is likely to precipitate a series of technical and related social and economic changes of far-reaching significance. Recently, the president of a large U.S. public university noted that "biotechnology, genetic manipulation, and engineering research will have tremendous impact on the crops and animals we grow for food, affecting agriculture in ways never before dreamed possible" (personal interview, 1986). In a recent issue of *Science*, Monsanto, a leading agricultural chemical and biotechnology company, proclaimed:

Biotechnology will revolutionize farming. . . Plants will be given the built-in ability to fend off insects and disease, and to resist stress. Animals will be born vaccinated. Pigs will grow faster and produce leaner meat. Cows will produce milk more economically. And, food crops will be more nutritious and easier to process. . . The products of biotechnology will be based on nature's own methods, making farming more efficient, more reliable, more environmentally friendly and, important for the farmer, more profitable (1988: 1384).

The potential revolution in biological research also promises to transform the agricultural research community and industries that serve agriculture, and thus eventually agricultural cooperatives and farming. Dr. Howard Schneiderman, Senior Vice-President for Life Sciences Research at Monsanto Corporation, indicates that this new biotechnology is "absolutely a global market" and one some experts believe will reach $100 billion in sales by the 21st century (Schrage and Henderson, 1984: 5). The public land-grant universities that have traditionally conducted agricultural research have already instituted major changes in an effort to participate in the technical and economic opportunities in biotechnology and to provide support for new clients in the private sector. In addition, other universities are playing an increasingly important and central research role in plant and animal molecular biology (Kenney, 1986). Furthermore, biotechnology is serving as the technical impetus for increasing concentration in the agricultural inputs sector, with the chemical-pharmaceutical industry mobilizing to participate in the new agricultural biorevolution. Finally, by 1988 over 40 new high-technology biotechnology firms specializing in plant and animal agricultural applications had emerged to take advantage of the new market opportunities in agriculture (Office of Technology Assessment [OTA], 1988). To date, U.S. agricultural cooperatives have been minimal or nonexistent participants in these developments (Lacy and Busch, 1988a; Kenney, 1986).

Simultaneously, changes have been occurring in patent laws and court interpretations which have facilitated, if not stimulated, development of agricultural biotechnology and heavy investment by the private sector. Some examples of these include: the Plant Variety Protection Act (PVPA) passed by Congress in 1970 to provide patent-like protection to new, distinct, uniform, and stable varieties of plants that were reproduced sexually; the U.S. Supreme Court case *Diamond v. Chakrabarty* (1980), providing utility patent protection for genetically engineered microorganisms; the 1985 Patent Office ruling that utility patents could be granted for novel plants; and the 1988 Patent and Trademark Office patent issued for genetically altered mammals that can be used to detect cancer-causing substances (Wheeler, 1988). In contrast to the PVPA, these recent decisions provide exclusive patent protection for higher life forms as long as the organism results from ingenuity and intervention (Buttel and Belsky, 1987). Applicants for plant utility patents have grown from 73 in 1986 to an estimated 400 in 1988 (Naj, 1989). Cooperatives are unlikely to participate in the development of patentable agricultural products. Access to these products by cooperatives will probably come only upon payment of large royalties.

In this chapter we examine the diverse trends and impacts in the development of agricultural biotechnology. First, we briefly trace the development of biotechnology and examine some recent products and future prospects which will likely dramatically affect the economic context in which cooperatives function. Then we review the rapidly increasing federal and state government and industrial investment in biotechnology, with particular focus on agricultural biotechnology and the role of cooperatives in these developments. Next we note the possible consequences for cooperatives. These may include loss of their competitive position in major markets, reduced access to inputs at reasonable prices, reduced access to public-sector information and research findings, and a public-sector research agenda which doesn't serve their needs. Finally, we propose alternative strategies that cooperatives can employ in the face of biotechnology.

Technological Developments and Future Prospects

Developments in agricultural biotechnology may entail improvements and modifications in traditional means of production of animals, plants, and food products as well as increasing convergence of agriculture and industrial practice. There will likely be a reorientation in relationships between and among agro-suppliers (for example, cooperatives and the agrichemical industry), farmers, and the food-processing industry. This section briefly traces biotechnology developments from their initial beginnings in human health and pharmaceuticals, through animal health and animal reproduction and growth, to perhaps the most promising long-term potential in plant biotechnology. It concludes with a discussion of the possible restructuring of global agriculture production.

Following the successful directed insertion of foreign DNA into a host microorganism in 1973, researchers have recognized the knowledge opportunities for basic molecular biology and the commercial potential of this technique in such areas as pharmaceuticals, animal and plant agriculture, specialty chemicals and food additives, commodity specific chemicals, energy production, and bio-electronics. Initial efforts were devoted to developments in pharmaceuticals and chemicals, with large funding provided by the National Institutes of Health. In the mid-1970s, Genentech, the first firm completely devoted to genetic engineering, was established. Its initial project was to induce bacteria to produce a small human brain hormone, somatostatin. By 1982, government approval had been obtained for the first rDNA pharmaceutical product (human insulin) for use in the U.S. (OTA, 1984a).

With the heavy research investments in human health biotechnology in the late 1970s and early 1980s, it is not surprising that animal agriculture has been the first area in agricultural biotechnology to receive major attention and to produce viable commercial products. By 1984, animal health sales reached $2.3 billion in the United States (Kenney, 1986), with large mammals receiving the greatest attention. Early genetically engineered products included a vaccine against scours, a yearly killer of millions of newborn calves and piglets, and a sub-unit vaccine to prevent hoof-and-mouth disease, by Molecular Genetics. A pseudorabies vaccine is close to being marketed and bovine interferon is being tested for efficacy against shipping fever.

Other promising areas in animal biotechnology include animal reproduction (for example, embryo manipulation), genetics, lactation, and growth (for example, growth hormone or somatotropin in swine and beef and dairy cattle). The genetically engineered microbial production of bovine growth hormone (bGH) has been shown to increase milk yields in dairy cattle by as much as 10-20 percent. Genentech has estimated the global market for bGH to be approximately $500 million (Baumgardt, 1988).

Despite the more advanced developments in biotechnology for mammals, plant biotechnology may offer the greatest long-term agricultural potential. One area of importance is the use of genetically engineered microorganisms such as the altered bacteria which confers crop tolerance to sub-freezing temperatures (Frostban), and a recombinant bacteria for improved nitrogen fixation in alfalfa. These two biotechnology products moved closer to market with recent EPA approvals for new field tests. Field tests for Frostban were conducted in California in December 1987 and tests of the nitrogen-fixing bacteria were conducted in Wisconsin in summer of 1988 (Orton, 1988; Sterling, 1988).

Another promising area is in the use of plant genes from existing species which were previously difficult or impossible to access. Through several techniques such as protoplast fusion, clonal propagation, and direct transformation, several important genes have been transferred to commercially valuable crops. Significant progress has also been made in developing several food crops which have enhanced resistance to diseases, insects, and herbicides. For example, a gene has been identified that produces a protein that kills the larvae of certain lepidopteran pests (for example, tobacco hornworm, bollworm) but is not toxic to humans or beneficial insects such as honeybees and ladybugs. Its potential market in cotton to control bollworm is estimated at \$550 million (Hebblethwaite, 1988).

Furthermore, the techniques of growth and fermentation of bacteria, already well-known to certain segments of the food processing industry, will be important in the future. These processes, combined with new techniques of cell culture, could be used to transform the production of certain agricultural commodities into industrial processes (Harlander, 1988). In principle, any commodity that is consumed in an undifferentiated or highly processed form could be produced in this manner. Similarly, although with greater difficulty, tissue culture techniques could be used to produce edible plant parts *in vitro*. In short, agricultural production in the field could be supplanted by cell and tissue culture factories (Rogoff and Rawlins, 1986).

Markets for certain tropical commodities have already been restructured. Sugar, once an extremely important tropical commodity, has already been hard-hit by the development of corn sweeteners and sugar substitutes such as aspartame (Nutrasweet), a genetically engineered amino acid which had sales in excess of \$400 million in 1985 (Busch and Lacy, 1988). Moreover, work is currently underway to produce the flavor components of expensive fragrances, spices, and flavoring agents through tissue culture. As one proponent puts it, "the research and development effort required is well worth the effort to achieve the *in vitro* production of not only specialty biochemicals, but potentially, food, spices, and industrial commodities" (Staba, 1985: 203). In addition, work is apparently in progress to produce coffee, cocoa, rubber, and tea *in vitro* (Orton, 1988).

Countries, particularly in the Third World, who are dependent on the production and sale of these products for the viability of their economy could be greatly affected by *in vitro* production. Indeed, these developments have the potential for not only restructuring agricultural production in our country and overseas, but of reordering the entire global economy, with major social and political consequences.

Government and Industry Investments

With these new developments on the horizon combined with enormous commercial potential, many old and new organizations and institutions are being attracted to biotechnology. This section briefly reviews the increasing substantial investments in biotechnology and agricultural biotechnology by federal and state governments, universities, multinational private corporations, new U.S. venture capital firms, and foreign governments. The magnitude of the investments and the collaborations being formed through these investments raises important questions for the role of cooperatives.

The federal government, and to a lesser extent state governments, began investing heavily in research on genetic engineering and agricultural biotechnology in the 1980s. By 1987, the federal government spent approximately \$2.7 billion to support research and development in biotechnology, with $150 million targeted for agricultural biotechnology (OTA, 1988). Moreover, the National Research Council's Board on Agriculture has recommended that the amount for federal funding in agricultural biotechnology be increased to $500 million annually by 1990 (Moses et al., 1988).

Similarly, 33 states are actively engaged in promoting biotechnology research and development, with total appropriations in 1987 amounting to nearly $150 million (OTA, 1988). A substantial portion of these funds is being devoted to agriculture. The purpose is to establish research and development (R&D) centers linking industry to universities with a view to promote economic development. In many states, university-industry collaboration is a condition for qualifying for research funds.

The private sector has been equally active with substantial investments in R&D in agricultural biotechnology. A recent report by the Office of Technology Assessment (1988) identified 403 American companies dedicated to biotechnology and 70 established corporations with significant investments in biotechnology. The report estimated the combined annual expenditures in biotechnology research and development to be $1.5 to $2.0 billion. Moreover, several hundred million dollars in venture capital have been generated to fund the start-up of more than 100 new biotechnology firms (Miller, 1985). Despite agriculture's third-place rank in industrial applications of biotechnology, a 1985 survey indicated that over 100 firms in the U.S. are engaged in agricultural biotechnology with investments exceeding $200 million annually (Blumenthal et al., 1986b). The large, established multinational companies specializing in oil, chemicals, food, and pharmaceuticals (for example, American Cyanamid, DuPont, Monsanto, Rohm and Haas, Sohio, and ARCO) are being joined by a number of smaller, newly established, venture capital firms (for example, Agrigenetics, Calgene, Cetus, DNA Plant Technology Corporation, and Molecular Genetics) engaged exclusively in the field of biotechnology and agricultural bioengineering.

In addition to in-house R&D, the biotechnology industry has invested heavily in university research. In 1984, biotechnology companies provided about $120 million in grants and contracts to universities (Blumenthal et al., 1986c). Corporate investments have helped to establish a variety of comprehensive and often exclusive arrangements with individual faculty, departments, and institutes.

Concomitant with these developments is the emphasis being placed on biotechnology in foreign countries. As Philip Abelson, Deputy Editor of *Science* points out, "virtually every developed country and many developing countries have targeted leadership in biotechnology as a national goal" (1988: 701). For example, as early as 1983, Japan's Ministry of International Trade and Industry provided $100 million in biotechnology research and development support to Japanese firms (OTA, 1984a). Interestingly, despite a general lead in biotechnology, Abelson (1988) points out that the U.S. could become second-rate in agricultural biotechnology because of the relative neglect of basic research in plant biology. Furthermore, foreign countries such as Japan and Germany are developing exclusive arrangements and partnerships with U.S. venture capital firms (Wysocki, 1987).

Despite the infancy of the development of agricultural biotechnology, a multibillion-dollar market has been projected to develop products in the near future. Several impacts are anticipated. The processes by which these products are developed will affect the structure of the public and private agricultural research communities, changing the nature of their agendas and who they serve. The way in which these products are developed and marketed will likely favor the large-scale companies and producers and significantly affect the cooperatives. The products themselves may affect the structure of agriculture and the nature of the food system in this country and around the world (Kenney, 1986; Lacy and Busch, 1988a).

Agricultural Cooperatives: An Alternative

It is important to briefly trace the history of the cooperatives before turning attention to the potential consequences for cooperatives of the products and organizational structures emerging from biotechnology. Agricultural cooperatives have offered an important alternative to U.S. farmers for production supplies, inputs, marketing services, and other farmer needs for over 200 years. The cooperatives are voluntary, democratically controlled contractual organizations of persons having a mutual ownership interest in providing themselves needed services on a nonprofit basis. Historically, farm members have formed cooperatives to develop self-help methods, to obtain needed services, and to improve their farm's earnings rather than to realize a high return on their investments. Where monetary gains have arisen, they were allocated and distributed in proportion to farmers' use of service (Kirkman, 1980).

The first efforts to organize U.S. farmers on a formal basis occurred in 1785. One hundred years later there were cooperatives for purchase of fertilizers, for grain, tobacco, fruit, and livestock (hogs and poultry) marketing, and for processing and marketing of dairy products (over 400 cooperatives were engaged in this activity). By 1956 the number of farmer cooperatives (10,179) and number of members (7,732,000) had reached its peak (Ingalsbe, 1984). In the 1980s, cooperatives are characterized by economic integration, consolidations, and mergers, with membership loss paralleling the drop in farm population and business service expansion. Today, roughly 1.4 million of the nation's 2.4 million resident farm operators are members or nonmember patrons of cooperatives. Cooperative membership is particularly high for the larger farmers and specific groups such as dairy farmers. Through widespread consolidation and mergers, several cooperatives have emerged as very large regional and national organizations. The 14 largest cooperatives (primarily dairy and grain marketing) have sales in excess of one billion dollars and constitute over one third of the farmer cooperatives' $95.1 billion annual gross business volume in 1982 (Richardson, 1984).

This pattern of increasing concentration in cooperatives, although complicated by emotional ties to traditional organizations, is likely to continue. Indeed, one cooperative leader noted that the diminishing number of farmers can't support the present number of cooperatives and predicted that by the 1990s "there may be less than ten large agricultural cooperatives down from an estimated fifty now" (personal interview, 1986).

Biotechnology's Consequences for Cooperatives

Despite their historical significance, size, and resources, agricultural cooperatives are facing serious challenges to their long-term viability. Biotechnology and other changes that are occurring in the U.S. and worldwide are generating new competition and may significantly affect the ways cooperatives function. The ultimate configuration of commercialized agricultural biotechnology will represent choices among a broad range of alternatives. The nature and impact of biotechnology on the structure of agriculture and agricultural research is just beginning to emerge. Among the possible impacts with consequences for agricultural cooperatives discussed here are: (1) increased concentration in the agricultural inputs sector and the industrialization of the food system with a concomitant loss of the cooperatives' competitive position in major farm input markets; (2) a shift in public-sector research and technology development to basic molecular biology, which does not meet cooperatives' needs for applied research; (3) increased concentration of research funds at a small number of public and private institutions, with the research needs of regional or local cooperatives very likely ignored; (4) increased collaboration between industry, government, and universities, with restriction of scientific communication particularly for cooperatives and a potential for conflict of interest, favoritism, and increased scientific misconduct; and (5) a shift of the emphasis and agenda of the public-sector research community from serving farmers, cooperatives, and rural communities to the multinational agrichemical and food-processing corporations.

One of the most significant consequences of the new biotechnologies for agricultural cooperatives may be its effect on the structure of the agribusiness community. As noted earlier, biotechnology is also providing the impetus toward increased concentration in the agricultural inputs sector, the unique development of high-technology biotechnology firms specializing in agricultural applications, and the increasing interest of foreign corporations in U.S. agriculture. Biotechnology is also providing the technical base on which the chemical, pharmaceutical, oil, agricultural, and food-processing industries can be fused. Large multinational corporations view biotechnology as another tool in their efforts to diversify away from bulk commodities and to integrate their operations. Commercial opportunities abound in agriculture considering farmers' operating costs for fuel, oil, and fertilizer. The chemical and pharmaceutical industries with existing agricultural input activities are consolidating their positions by purchasing other agribusinesses such as seed, bioinsecticide, and innoculent companies (Makulowich, 1988a, 1988b). They view the seed as the vehicle for conveying the variety of products of biotechnological research to the farmer and the means for realizing a significant market share (Kloppenburg, 1988).

These developments could place agricultural cooperatives at a distinct disadvantage. Although biotechnology is currently more of a promise than a product, it has already led to a number of new proprietary agricultural products which will likely increase in number and importance in the future. Furthermore, these products are most likely to be developed in the areas with the largest markets. Access to these products will probably come only upon payment of a large royalty, which will affect the cooperatives' competitive position. Biotechnology's first impacts are already being felt among dairy and beef cattle farmers and cooperatives. Moreover, if cooperatives lose their competitive position in major markets they may be relegated to the minor and regional crops which do not have a sufficient market to make them economically attractive for the large corporations. Large chemical, pharmaceutical, and oil corporations have pursued with renewed interest their efforts at both horizontal and vertical integration in agriculture and food production. Given their integration, these corporations are likely to develop input packages to sell directly to their own distributors. These trends may undermine cooperatives' access to inputs at reasonable prices and ultimately their very capacity to provide an alternative force in the marketplace.

A second consequence concerns the relevance and usefulness of the new research findings for agricultural cooperatives, which have long recognized the importance and need for research and technology. Historically, cooperatives have relied primarily on publicly funded research for their research needs. These public institutions are undergoing major changes which may make the research programs irrelevant or inaccessible to cooperatives. There is strong pressure being exerted on public-sector scientists from the large multinational corporations and research administrators to abandon varietal breeding and applied research for basic molecular biology and biotechnology research (Lacy and Busch, 1988a). This parallels the shift in emphasis in the agricultural inputs industry from an applied routinized technology such as fertilizer to the new biotechnologies that produce patentable materials. While farmers, small independent seed companies, and most agricultural cooperatives have depended on the state agricultural universities to meet their applied research needs, the large integrated multinational corporations believe they can accomplish these tasks and want to end competition from the public sector as well as the small operators. Furthermore, they recognize that plant molecular biology requires a large amount of basic research that is unprofitable in the short run before commercial products can be developed. Finally, they believe that the basic science capacity of the public sector is in need of revitalization and have joined with key national science policymakers to attempt to push public-sector agricultural research towards a more basic science thrust (see, for example, Rockefeller Foundation, 1982 and American Seed Trade Association, 1984).

This effort has resulted in the acceleration of changes in the relative distribution of disciplines in the U.S. State Agricultural Experiment Stations (SAES). Over 200 scientists have been added to the biotechnology disciplines in the last few years, with 430 full-time equivalent (FTE) faculty positions being devoted to biotechnology by 1986 (NASULGC 1985, 1987). Concomitantly, between 1982 and 1984 there was a decline of 17 percent among U.S. plant breeders and 21 percent among U.S. animal breeders for a loss of 80 plant-breeding positions and 35 animal-breeding positions (NASULGC 1983, 1985, 1987). The new public-research basic science orientation may be directly useful only for those large multinational organizations with sophisticated R&D facilities who can build upon the molecular biological research and develop the proprietary products for major markets.

A third consequence of biotechnology is an increase in the concentration of research funds and scientific talent at a small number of public and private institutions. For example, every U.S. state can afford and has had a conventional plant breeding program. Every state cannot afford and will not be able to have a comprehensive plant biotechnology program. This should lead to concentration of scientific talent in a few states. For example, six states (California, Michigan, New York, Texas, Washington, and Wisconsin) account for 42 percent of all U.S. Experiment Station FTEs for biotechnological research (NASULGC, 1985). As one cooperative leader observed, agricultural cooperatives in the past have relied heavily on public research institutions for their research needs. Many of those institutions may simply not be active participants in the new biotechnologies (Hansen et al., 1986).

Several cooperatives have continued to recognize the importance of research and have banded together to form Farmers Forage Research (FFR) and Cooperative Research Farms. For example, one midwestern cooperative executive observed that through FFR, cooperatives had access to international research and hybrid development that enabled them to introduce five new hybrids suited for farmers in Michigan in 1986 (personal interview, 1986). However, the total annual funding for these research cooperatives may be less than one month's funding of one large private R&D program. Furthermore, while seed and supply cooperatives are researching and developing cooperative lines, the character of this work tends to be primarily traditional plant breeding and experimentation with existing technology. This will probably not be enough to keep pace with the speed and efficiency of testing and evaluating germplasm provided by the new biotechnologies. An executive of a large northeastern cooperative noted that even the very largest cooperatives that are already spending several million dollars on research generally conclude that financial requirements are too great to proceed with a research consortium in agricultural biotechnology (personal interview, 1986).

A fourth consequence of biotechnology for cooperatives may be the inadequate access to information. The scientific and commercial potential of biotechnology, and decreasing federal funds for research, have led to increasing university-industry ties. While partnerships between universities and industries have existed for several decades, the new types of university-industry relationships in biotechnology (for example, centers, institutes, research parks, and public corporations) are more varied, more aggressive, and more experimental. They include: large grants and contracts between companies and universities in exchange for patent rights and exclusive licenses to discoveries; programs and centers organized at major universities with industrial funds that give participating firms privileged access to university resources and a role in shaping research agendas; professors, particularly in the biomedical sciences, serving in extensive consulting capacities on scientific advisory boards or in managerial positions of biotechnology firms; faculty receiving research funding from private corporations in which they hold significant equity; faculty setting up their own biotechnology firms; and public universities establishing for-profit corporations such as Neogen at Michigan State to develop and market innovations arising from research.

Proprietary concerns have begun to inhibit the flow of information among biotechnology scientists. This is particularly true with private-sector grants. Scientists often must delay public discussion of such work, or its results, until it has been reviewed by the sponsoring company. In Blumenthal et al.'s study (1986b, 1986c), 25 percent of industrially supported biotechnology faculty reported that they have conducted research that belongs to the firm and cannot be published without prior consent, while 40 percent of faculty with industrial support report that their collaboration resulted in unreasonable delays in publishing.

The investment of venture capital in the SAES, often tied to exclusive release of technology via patent rights or exclusive licensing, is viewed by many scientists as an even more disturbing development than decreased communication. In interviews, both public and private-sector scientists stressed the potential detrimental effects of granting private patents for work done in the public sector. These include potential favoritism, unwarranted financial advantage through privileged use of information or technology partly derived from research using public funds, constraints on sharing of germplasm, and shelving of research which may be of interest to the public but not to the corporation. Even if cooperatives are able to improve their capacity to utilize the new research findings, they may find inadequate access to the information.

A fifth consequence of biotechnological developments may be the relative emphasis of the research. Traditionally, much public-sector research has been oriented toward farmers and farm cooperatives. However, with the increasing interest and investments of multinational agrichemical and food-processing corporations in the products of agricultural research, the primary clients for the research may change. These large companies tend to have the money needed for biotechnology research; thus they influence the kind of research performed. Agricultural cooperatives and farmers need biotechnology and other research programs in the public sector to help them become low-cost, environmentally safe producers in a highly competitive world market. Conceivably, the new biotechnologies would be used to do just that. Much of the evidence, however, suggests that just the reverse is happening. An associate dean of a U.S. college of agriculture illustrated this conflict when he related the following, "In speaking to a group of state agribusiness leaders recently, I observed that in the distant future I could foresee a perennial corn crop which fixes nitrogen, performs photosynthesis more efficiently and is weed and pest resistant." With that one statement he alienated nearly every sector of the agribusiness community (personal interview, 1986).

Sixth and finally, the new biotechnologies underline the contradictions inherent in the cooperative form. The fact that cooperative members are land-based limits the use of certain business strategies; in contrast, corporations can move from one location to the next with few regrets. The principles of one member, one vote, and the same price to all make good cooperative practice, but they may make competition more difficult in the future. Cooperatives can be seen as a form of vertical integration for farmers. Yet the extent of their vertical and horizontal integration is limited by their commitment to farming regardless of its returns to investment. Finally, their financial structure often makes it difficult to accumulate the necessary capital for long-term investment strategies. In this sense the cooperatives are faced with the dilemma that if they compete successfully they may well lose their very identity.

Strategies for Cooperatives

The proposed implications of the new biotechnologies for agricultural cooperatives will likely require the cooperatives to employ a range of strategies to ensure positive influence in these changes. These approaches range from very active involvement with biotechnology to more passive roles. The particular strategies will depend in part on size, agricultural sector, and organizational structure. Small cooperatives may simply be in no position to participate in the new technologies other than as consumers. The strategies for the larger, diversified, and better-financed cooperatives include the following: (1) develop joint ventures with supply-input companies; (2) utilize influence to ensure that public-sector research is maintained and strengthened to address a range of broad public agendas as well as the important needs of the cooperatives; (3) where possible, directly engage in appropriate biotechnology research; (4) establish equity positions with venture capital firms that can serve the interests of the cooperative; and (5) develop the capacity to monitor, analyze, and evaluate the current biotechnology products and processes from a systems perspective.

For large and mid-sized cooperatives, a major strategic approach may be to embark on joint ventures of various types with supply-input companies that have expertise and development ability in the area of biotechnology. A key element to such joint ventures would be the ability of each partner to use their own competitive advantage. Cooperatives could participate in the delivery of biotechnology products that enter crop and livestock production, and food-processing systems which they are now supporting. Through such joint ventures, the companies supplying the biotechnology could make use of both the excellent distribution and implementation ability of the cooperatives and their interface with farmer groups. Such linkage would allow biotechnology-based companies to avoid the costly development of farm gate delivery systems. The advantage could be used to negotiate an equitable profit margin for cooperatives (Lacy and Busch, 1988b).

A second viable strategy would be to work to ensure that the biological research at land-grant universities is adequately funded and that the flow of information generated at the public agricultural research institutes remains available to the cooperatives. They could use their political clout to lobby for public-sector research which: (1) focuses on subjects of interest and import to their members; (2) is adequately funded with public funds; and (3) is accessible to cooperatives and their members. For example, certain cooperative leaders believe that the public sector should be conducting more work on domestic and international markets, distribution models, and research on federal market orders. Efforts to affect the research agenda of the public sector may require direct interaction with legislators, researchers, and administrators. Cooperatives which employ a self-tax on their sales to fund university research could better monitor the destination of the funds, the purposes for which the funds are used, and the means by which cooperative leaders could influence their use.

A third strategy, albeit less feasible, would be to directly engage in research. This would take various forms. First some cooperatives could conceivably develop their own in-house research and development capacity. This is perhaps the most effective way to capture the benefits of the new biotechnologies. However, R&D efforts could be very costly and risky. Second, cooperatives could form research and development cooperatives or join research ventures to develop appropriate biotechnology between regional cooperatives. A few research cooperatives already exist (for example, Cooperative Research Farms, Farmers' Forage Research), but these interregional cooperative research ventures have been highly applied, short-term, and often lacking in success. The nature of this new type of venture would be even more problematic. It would require hiring new scientific personnel and convincing cooperative members of the merits of investing in relatively expensive long-term research. Such efforts would need to focus on products that tie in well with current needs of members. Consequently, conducting research, regardless of the means, is a highly unlikely strategy for nearly all the cooperatives with the possible exception of some large food-processing cooperatives.

A fourth possible strategy could involve taking an equity position with a venture capital company. Where cooperatives have identified specific biotechnology areas which would give the cooperative and its members a strong economic advantage, they could take an equity position. The venture capital biotechnology company would then develop and commercialize the desired technology for the cooperative. Another recommended strategy involves possible joint ventures with major European farm cooperatives. In some areas, European cooperatives have already entered biotechnology and have had some success. One U.S. cooperative has established a joint biotechnology effort with a French cooperative (Lacy and Busch, 1988b).

Finally, cooperatives need to take a systems approach to the development and delivery of biotechnology products. Cooperatives are in the best position to distribute complete systems rather than isolated products. Cooperatives also need to assign responsibility for monitoring and analyzing the current developments from a systems vantage point. They must ultimately be in a position to glean the necessary information, analyze the new biotechnology opportunities from a broad systems perspective, and execute sound decisions based on that analysis.

Of course, none of these strategies is likely to be the best one for all cooperatives in all circumstances. It is clear, however, that the new biotechnologies are changing the context in which cooperatives operate, highlighting the contradictions and dilemmas inherent in the cooperative structure. Careful strategic planning by informed leaders will be necessary for cooperatives to benefit from the opportunities and to meet the challenges of the new agricultural biotechnologies.

Conclusion

Agricultural biotechnology is beginning to have an impact which is likely to grow in significance in the forthcoming years. As Jack Doyle has noted in *Altered Harvest*, "Biotechnology and genetic engineering hold enormous beneficial possibilities for agriculture, the environment and food production worldwide" (1985a: 384). Biotechnology offers new opportunities to tailor crops to specific needs, a reduction in the use of purchased inputs, an emphasis on nutritional quality, and fewer environmental problems in agriculture. Alternatively, biotechnology could induce further concentration in farm structure and further industrialization of agriculture, with the highly monopolized input and output sectors of the agribusiness community capturing the bulk of the benefits. This paper has traced some of the important technological changes that are occurring in agricultural biotechnology, the impact that technology is having on the structure of agricultural research, and the implications for agricultural cooperatives of those changes. Although the changes in the system are proceeding rapidly, they are neither inevitable nor totally shaped. The ultimate direction this technology takes will be determined by actors who participate in its development and the power they possess to implement their agenda. A key question for cooperatives is the extent of their foresight, imagination, and power necessary to participate in the shaping of the new biotechnologies.

6

Plant Biotechnology Networking in Developing Countries

Robert K. Dixon

Countries within the developing world have a keen interest in the application of emerging biotechnologies to solve the problems associated with a sustained supply of food, fuel, and fiber (Swaminatham, 1982). Growing evidence suggests the substantial increases in agriculture and forest production attributed to the Green Revolution are reaching a plateau. The current challenge is development and application of appropriate biotechnology to farming systems in developing countries without exhausting soil, water, and energy resources. Since food, fuel, and fiber produced from plants are central to basic human needs throughout the developing world, this paper will focus on plant biotechnology.

Future significant improvements in agricultural and forest crop yield will be realized through greater cultural intensity rather than an extension of cultivation into unproductive land (Brown et al., 1987). Many developing countries have plans or programs for harnessing emerging biotechnologies to improve crop yields. For example, India, Indonesia, Malaysia, the Philippines, and Thailand have established national institutes or programs in biotechnology. The United Nations Industrial Development Organization (UNIDO) recently proposed the establishment of an International Center for Genetic Engineering and Biotechnology that would perform research and transfer new biological technologies to developing countries (Newmark, 1983). The national priorities of biotechnology programs vary widely with domestic needs and investment opportunities. Examples of plant biotechnology research and development topics within the developing world include biofuel production and processing, biological nitrogen fixation, enhancement of photosynthesis efficiency, food fermentation, production of antibiotics, specialty chemicals and microbial pesticides, genetic transformation, and immunotechnology (National Academy of Sciences, 1979; International Rice Research Institute, 1985).

Current and emerging plant biotechnologies will improve the culture and yield of food, fuel, and fiber crops in zones now favorable to intensive cropping. A significant aspect of molecular biology is the applicability of techniques to a range of crops and organisms. Biotechnology applications may also greatly expand the geographic sphere in which research and development can be used to stimulate forest and agricultural production. Emerging technologies will permit the extension of agriculture and forestry to regions characterized by marginal soil and climatic factors, including areas where subsistence and commodity production by the rural population have persisted unchallenged. However, the substantial benefits associated with plant biotechnology must be measured against potential environmental risks and negative socioeconomic developments.

The application of biotechnology to crop production improvement may be equally profound in developed and underdeveloped countries. Transnational agricultural, chemical, and forest product companies, genetic research firms, and university laboratories are pursuing the development of improved bioprocesses, crop yields, and product portfolios. Although an apparent urgency exists to realize the benefits of these research and development efforts in the developing world, an understanding of the problems and opportunities associated with plant biotechnology should be realized. The objectives of this chapter are to: (1) identify current impediments and possible mechanisms for implementation of emerging plant biotechnologies; (2) review current and near-future applications in plant biotechnology; and (3) outline the relative merits and challenges of plant biotechnology networking.

Implementation of Plant Biotechnology Innovations

Biotechnology has the potential to benefit agricultural and forest production in the developing world. The challenge is to implement appropriate technology to impart a sustained improvement in the production of food, fuel, and fiber without damaging fragile socioeconomic institutions or the environment. Historically, cycles of rapid institutional development, supported by external resources, have been followed by a decline in productivity as external support is withdrawn (Plucknett and Smith, 1982). Concomitantly, domestic economic and political support for technology or institutions often failed to materialize. Biotechnology differs from past innovations in agriculture and forestry as developing countries will be required to embody a knowledge and infrastructure of biological technology which is well suited to their own resource and cultural endowments.

A unique aspect of global biotechnology development and application is the intimate tripartite relationship of government, universities, and private industry

(Buttel et al., 1985). The overall biotechnology investment philosophy of government, universities, and private industry differs significantly from the development of less technically demanding processes or products. In the 1980s, over 25 percent of the biotechnology companies in the United States were founded by members of the academic community (Dibner and Bruce, 1987). A survey of biotechnology companies reveals that nearly half of the firms support more than a quarter of all biotechnology research at American universities (Blumenthal et al., 1986). Monsanto, a leading agricultural products company, has invested over $50 million in agricultural biotechnology research in the academic community. Biotechnology research, development, and production facilities are capital intensive and federal and state support is also an essential component of the investment strategy. The world's leading 50 genetic engineering firms have a capital investment of over $1 billion (Bylinsky, 1985). Sustained investment in biotechnology applications by developing countries will require a major restructuring of national and international research programs and priorities. Cooperative investments by transnational agricultural, chemical, and forest product firms, national governments, and the bilateral development community will be required to meet this need. Although International Agricultural Research Centers (IARCs) are moving to exploit new biological technologies, limited resources discourage them from meeting the enormous challenge and responsibility of biotechnology research and deployment in the developing world.

A significant influence on the direction of plant biotechnology implementation in developing countries is the shift in research funding from the public to private sector (Buttel et al., 1985; Plucknett and Smith, 1982). In the United States and Europe, universities frequently contract with biotechnology firms to conduct research as traditional government support of laboratories continues to decline. Moreover, the ability to patent genetically altered organisms provides a proprietary incentive for industry and academia to cooperate (Adler, 1984). This trend will probably shape the development and application of biotechnology in the developing world. Unlike the Green Revolution, the IARCs of the developing world can no longer rely on public expertise for development of new technology (Plucknett and Smith, 1982). After several decades of sustained growth IARCs are confronted by declining budgets for research and training programs. Although some IARCs are implementing biotechnology research and development programs, it is unlikely they will be able to maintain a sustained competitive effort (Swaminathan, 1982).

The deployment and application of emerging biotechnologies in the developing world will be substantially motivated by returns on investment from the private sector. In recent decades, forest and agricultural product companies have become increasingly international. As domestic markets in Europe and North America become saturated, the developing world is looked upon as a source of future markets. Similarly, the developing world, with vast genetic resources which provide the raw material needed to drive the biotechnology industry, look to industrial nations for technology, scientific talent, and financial resources

(Office of Technology Assessment [OTA], 1987, 1984a). Transnational companies provide a mechanism for testing and deploying biotechnology innovations to the mutual benefit of industrial and developing countries (see Table 6.1). Companies within the Federal Republic of Germany, Japan, and the United States have numerous joint ventures with firms throughout the developing world. A successful example of cooperation is the establishment of the ASEAN Biotechnology Corporation by the International Plant Research Institute (U.S.) and Sime Darby Berhad (Malaysia). This venture will facilitate recombinant DNA research with tropical crops, exchange of germplasm, and introduction of new products to Southeast Asia.

One of the most significant issues created by emerging biotechnologies is the problem of proprietary information and patents (Adler, 1984). This issue will significantly influence technology deployment in the developing world, which has been historically dependent on public agricultural research and extension agencies. Legislation to protect proprietary information, establish patent rights, and enforce collection of royalty fees may slow the multilateral exchange of information and germplasm between scientists (Bylinsky, 1985). The Union for the Protection of Plant Varieties has initiated steps to institute legislation to protect propriety information within some countries of the developing world (Buttel et al., 1985).

Sustained mechanisms to develop and deliver the benefits of biotechnology to the developing world are sorely needed. The shortfall is dramatized by the substantial investment necessary to conduct biotechnology research and development, as well as the private character of biotechnology deployment. Recent investment patterns by development banks and bilateral development agencies are not sufficient to meet the need for biotechnology research (Buttel et al., 1985; Weiss, 1985). Leaving agricultural priorities to the marketplace may constrain the transfer of technology to small farmers and the rural poor. The full exchange of information, raw materials, and products associated with biotechnology should consider the needs of two billion impoverished people of the developing world (Brown et al., 1987).

The development and application of plant biotechnology in developing countries will be increasingly dependent on investment by the tripartite union of government, universities, and private industry. The IARCs and incipient national biotechnology initiatives will require significant capital investment in laboratories, trained scientists, and prototype production facilities. In the Philippines, investment in biotechnology is seen as an initial step toward biological industrialization which may lessen dependence on imported commodities and energy. W. G. Padolina, of the National Institute of Biotechnology and Applied Microbiology at the University of the Philippines at Los Banos, states, "The national strategy is to transform biomass biologically into food, fuel, fertilizers and chemicals" (International Rice Research Institute, 1985). This initiative includes development of human resources, institutional capability, and low-interest loans which stimulate development of biotechnology-based industry.

Table 6.1

Examples of Transnational Agricultural and Forest-Product Firms with Biotechnology Linkages or Subsidiaries in Developing Countries

Firm and country	Primary product(s)	Developing country linkage
AFOCEL, France	germplasm, plantlets	AFOCEL, Africa (several countries)
Biotec, Belgium	pyrethrum	Biotec, Kenya
CIBA-Geigy, Switzerland	chemicals	CIBA-Geigy, Mexico
Cargill, USA	grain	global (several countries)
Hilleshog, Sweden	germplasm, microbes	Wingo seedlings, India
Native Plants, USA	germplasm, microbes	Phytec, Brazil Plantek, Singapore
Plant Science, UK	opium	Plant Science, Thailand
Shell, UK, Netherlands	chemicals	global (several countries)

Such an approach assures that biotechnology applications will not broaden the scientific and technological gap between developing and industrial nations.

Health, safety, and environmental concerns have been and will continue to be a significant factor in the testing and deployment of plant biotechnology in developing countries. The laws and regulations dealing with this topic vary greatly between individual nations. Most regulations governing plant biotechnology are aimed at research efforts and are essentially voluntary. General environmental legislation enacted in developed and developing countries uniformly applies to biotechnological processes, products, and waste products (OTA, 1984a). Plants containing recombinant deoxyribonucleic acid (DNA) are not considered especially hazardous, nor their release relatively risky, since the genetic material subject to recombination is collected from naturally occurring ecosystems (Brill, 1985).

The benefits of plant biotechnological processes and products must be weighed against the costs of a stringent regulatory environment (OTA, 1984a). Unreasonable restrictions and unnecessary caution may impede the employment of plant biotechnology application in regions where it is most useful. Moreover, excessive regulatory costs may reduce the ability of developing countries to be competitive in plant biotechnology research and deployment. Those countries which have a favorable regulatory arena will have a substantial competitive advantage in the commercialization of biotechnology (Brill, 1985). The challenge to the scientific community is education of the general public regarding potentially volatile issues in the field of biotechnology.

The development and deployment of plant biotechnology outside of industrial nations will be significantly influenced by socioeconomic concerns, particularly employment and income opportunities. The implementation of novel technology has traditionally influenced urban and rural employment patterns in the developing world (Brown et al., 1987). For example, biological process technology will probably result in less labor-intensive methods for harvesting specialty chemical crops such as cocoa or rubber. These developments may initially result in local unemployment problems or a depression in commodity prices. However, the vast plant genetic resources, growing markets, and ability to attract investments by transnational agricultural and forest product companies should create an opportunity for sustained economic development (Buttel et al., 1985). The following section outlines technologies which are nearing maturity and offer opportunity for beneficial deployment in the developing world.

Current and Pending Plant Biotechnology Applications

A sustained supply of natural resources and energy, stimulation of economic development, and preservation of genetic biodiversity are challenging problems confronting society in developing countries within tropical latitudes (Brown et al., 1987). Emerging applications in plant biotechnology may offer satisfactory alternatives for resource-efficient, sustainable economic development. Preservation of crop germplasm, gene transfer leading to crop improvement, improved methods of plant propagation, manipulation of soil microbiology, protection of crops from biotic agents, and biological processing are examples of promising plant biotechnology applications. Within many developing countries an urgency exists to weigh the relative costs and benefits associated with implementing this technology.

Preservation of Rapidly Diminishing Germplasm

Most plant-derived food originates from a few widely grown crops (for example, corn, rice, and wheat). While agronomic and forest crop yields have been generally increasing in the developing world, the genetic base of most of the important crops has been rapidly narrowing. The adoption of high-yielding varieties over broad areas has resulted in subsistence farmers abandoning indigenous cropping systems that were rich in genetic diversity. In rural Nigeria, over 150 species of woody plants previously used by local inhabitants for a variety of nutritional purposes have been abandoned in favor of a few high-yield agronomic crops dependent on expensive, energy-intensive inputs (Brown et al., 1987).

Over 3,000 plant species have historically been used for food, and opportunities for crop improvement innovations appear numerous (Plucknett et al., 1983).

Preservation of tropical forest ecosystems, which contain approximately two-thirds of the world's plant and animal genetic diversity, is probably the most effective mechanism of conserving plant germplasm (OTA, 1984b). However, deforestation and degradation of tropical ecosystems by resource-poor farmers, commercial loggers, and livestock ranchers have precluded protection of genetic resources. Approximately 11 million hectares (an area the size of the state of Pennsylvania) of tropical forests are harvested each year (OTA, 1984b). At this rate, tropical forest resources will be exhausted in several decades.

When the genetic base of crops becomes narrow and vast geographic areas are planted to a single crop genotype, fodder, fuel, fiber, and fruit productivity becomes extremely vulnerable to factors that limit yields. The recent corn blight which dramatically reduced grain yields in the United States is an example of this genetic vulnerability (Brown et al., 1987). Recently, a problem has been encountered with the widely planted multipurpose tree leucaena. Infestation of plantations by the jumping plant lice in the Pacific basin and southern Asia has resulted in mass defoliation and decline of fodder yield and fiber growth (Adams and Dixon, 1986). The wide dependency of farmers on leucaena as a source of soil nitrogen, food, fuel, fiber, and fodder has exacerbated economic problems of the rural poor in the Asia-Pacific region.

To counteract the genetic vulnerability of crops, scientists are collecting and preserving species which provide the resources necessary for biotechnology applications (Plucknett et al., 1983). Collecting and storing crop germplasm, coordinated by the International Board for Plant Genetic Resources, is now a major responsibility of most IARCs. A number of multilateral organizations, including the U.S. Agency for International Development (USAID), support this effort. Gene banks currently store germplasm for only a few major agronomic crops, yet the germplasm of other essential plants, such as nontraditional agroforestry crops (banana, coconut) and multipurpose trees, as well as nitrogen-fixing bacteria, actinomycetes, mycorrhizal fungi, and yeasts, should also be safeguarded. The International Rice Research Institute (IRRI) recently created the International Biofertilizer Germplasm Conservation Center where promising microbial sources of plant nutrients can be evaluated, stored, and distributed (Swaminathan, 1982).

Emerging biotechnologies associated with gene mapping, storage, and transfer will improve the utility of gene banks. Scientists are rapidly developing new bioprocesses in which naturally occurring genes serve as raw material and working models (Goodman et al., 1987). Germplasm collections of crop plants in the humid- and arid-tropics need to be extensively evaluated and documented in order to fully cultivate the genetic diversity of the tropical latitudes (Hinman, 1984). An Asian network of gene banks is being established through cooperative efforts of USAID, Canada's International Development and Research Center (IDRC), the United Nations-sponsored Food and Agriculture Organization

(FAO), and the International Union of Forest Research Organizations (IUFRO) to provide germplasm for developing superior tree crops (Adams and Dixon, 1986). The preservation of plant genetic resources will provide the raw material for future advances in agricultural biotechnology.

Gene Transfer Leading to Improved Crop Health and Yield

Crops of the future will be superior to those harvested today as a result of conventional crop improvement techniques coupled with the tools of the new biology. Classical plant-breeding techniques have already been used to improve several plant genera such as tomato, potato, wheat, and alder (Bonga and Durzan, 1987). Although they are effective, standard breeding and selection techniques are expensive, long-term projects in which few institutions in developing countries are able to invest (Goodman et al., 1987). Historically, IARCs and a select group of universities in developing countries have spearheaded these activities.

Selection of highly desirable traits using any technique assumes their existence in the gene pool of a given plant species. Traditional breeding methods have relied on selection of specific traits from the broad natural variability of genotypes within breeding populations or the introduction of mutated genes. New methods in biotechnology include rapid and efficient transfer of genes into the host plant, and several methods have been developed to accomplish this feat (Goodman et al., 1987). These techniques include biological vector transfer of DNA (for example, plasmids or viroids), fusion of genetic material or cells, microinjection of DNA, and introduction of extra-nuclear genes to organelles (for example, chloroplast of mitochondria). An example is that plasmids from a bacteria *(Agrobacterium)* have been used to introduce a gene that codes for a seed protein in bean seed sunflower (Torrey, 1985).

The introduction of beneficial organisms into the environment, whose DNA has been modified by recombinant technology, merits careful consideration by regulatory agencies of the developing world (OTA, 1984a). The power of biotechnology, uncertainty over the behavior of novel organisms, and 40 years of experience with toxic chemicals in the environment suggest it is reasonable to proceed cautiously. Regulatory frameworks based on a thorough understanding of the scientific issues and commensurate with probable risk and rewards of biotechnology implementation can be effective (Goodman et al., 1987). For example, the addition of symbiotic bacteria or fungi to millions of acres of agricultural soil has not produced a significant environmental impact.

Efficient Propagation of Superior Plant Genotypes

Tissue culture is a dependable method by which a range of plant genera with desirable characteristics can be rapidly reproduced in large quantities (Torrey, 1985). Micropropagation and tissue culture will play a significant role in the reproduction of plants that have been genetically engineered. These techniques include development of plantlets from organs and cell culture (for example, anthers, embryos, single cells, callus). Regeneration of whole plants from single cells has been limited to a few botanical genera. Unfortunately, many agricultural crops, including woody plants and grain crops, are somewhat recalcitrant. The future is promising as over 200 woody species have been established in tissue culture, representing over 40 genera in 20 families (Bonga and Durzan, 1987). Differentiation of plantlets from tissue culture and genetic instability of some cell lines may delay the application of this technology to a broad range of crop species.

In addition to vegetative propagation, tissue culture offers the potential for rapid screening of superior genotypes. Identification and removal of undesirable individuals from breeding stock at the cell or tissue level is biologically and economically efficient (Torrey, 1985). Desirable plant traits, such as growth efficiency, photosynthetic efficiency, and resistance to disease, frost, drought, salinity, herbicides, and toxic soil chemicals may be screened using tissue-culture techniques. Further research may elucidate biochemical traits of cultured cells that correlate with growth and yield.

Commercial propagation of genetically superior crop plants has been successfully implemented at several locations in developing countries (Bylinsky, 1985). The Unilever Company of India has propagated oil palm and distributed superior planting stock to rural farmers. Plantek International of Singapore offers rapid production of virus-free strawberry plants to farmers in Southeast Asia. The TATA Energy Research Institute, India, is developing clonal cultivars of teak planting stock for establishment of plantations which will provide feedstock for chemical production. A French consortium, Association Foret-Cellulose (AFOCEL), is developing a similar program with eucalyptus for rural farmers in northern Africa.

Manipulation of Soil Microbiology to Improve Crop Yield

Soils within the developing world are often nutrient-poor (OTA, 1984b). In Southeast Asia there are 87 million hectares of saline, highly infertile, and drought-prone soil unsuitable for traditionally bred crops. Although it is sometimes economical to use selected fertilizers, such as phosphates, the high price of inorganic nitrogen fertilizer has curtailed its use on certain crops and is changing agronomic methods (Plucknett and Smith, 1982).

Biological fixation of atmospheric nitrogen has the potential to offset the need for application of commercial nitrogen fertilizers to soil (Gordon et al., 1979). Heavy applications of commercial nitrogen fertilizer suppress soil biological activity, while in most instances, a moderate amount of fertilizer will stimulate nitrogen fixation. Symbiotic nitrogen fixation is of special interest because it occurs in close proximity to the plant roots. In the African Sahel, fields planted with cereal crops and nitrogen-fixing acacia trees produce more grain (Brown et al., 1987). The yield of wetland crops such as rice may also be improved through manipulation of major nitrogen-fixing organisms. These organisms include free-living and symbiotic algae and bacteria. Farmers in China, the Philippines, and Vietnam have improved the yield of rice through manipulation of symbiotic nitrogen fixation (Swaminathan, 1982).

Improved methods of agroforestry soil management will encourage growth of nitrogen-fixing microorganisms (Gordon et al., 1979). One alternative is to interplant nitrogen-fixing trees, shrubs, or groundcover with other agronomic crops. Intercropping with nitrogen-fixing trees enhances site productivity by recycling organic matter and nutrients and improving soil texture and rainfall infiltration. Correct management of organic matter may help ensure maximum rates of nitrogen fixation by these organisms, thus enriching the soil. Selection and management of dominant nitrogen-fixing microorganisms is an immediate biotechnology application in agriculture or forestry. Virtually all vascular plants grow poorly unless their roots are colonized by symbiotic fungi that form root-fungus structures known as mycorrhizae. The mycorrhizal organ benefits agronomic and tree crops in many ways, the major one being to enhance nutrient uptake, especially phosphorus and micronutrients. This symbiotic association also has been shown to increase plant disease resistance and tolerance to soil drought, salt, toxins, and pH extremes (Ruehle and Marx, 1979).

Even though the benefits of mycorrhizal associations to plant growth have been identified, little consideration has been given to mycorrhizae in soil management in most developing countries. In many parts of the world, natural inoculum of tree or agronomic crops is absent, and attempts to establish row crops, agroforestry systems, or plantations failed until inoculum was provided (Khan, 1972; Dixon and Marx, 1987). Because there are many species of mycorrhizal fungi that have varying benefits for a given plant species on a given site, natural inoculation, where it does occur, may not provide the optimal association.

Growth and yield responses to large-scale inoculation with mycorrhizal symbionts is likely in the highly leached tropical soils of developing countries (Ruehle and Marx, 1979). The yield of barley, corn, and wheat has been significantly improved in field experiments in Pakistan (Khan, 1972). Inoculation experiments with selected strains of the ectomycorrhizal fungus *Pisolithus tinctorius* have increased pine survival and growth fourfold on adverse sites (Dixon and Marx, 1987).

It may soon be possible to develop clones or varieties of the best crop species among those dependent on soil symbionts (Torrey, 1985). Research priorities include collection of organisms for adaptation to soil and climatic stress, development of methods to stimulate and maintain desirable organisms, identification and manipulation of undesirable antagonistic organisms and predators, and genetic transformation of host or symbiont. Creation of superior symbiotic crops may require genetic engineering of both the host and the symbiont and is a long-term prospect. Achievement of superior nitrogen fixation, drought resistance, and pest resistance in crops could reduce environmentally hazardous and expensive chemical inputs and have far-reaching consequences on crop yields.

Protection of Crops from Pests and Pathogens

Socially acceptable alternatives to environmentally hazardous chemical control of plant pests are becoming abundant and are most effective when amalgamated into integrated pest-management programs (Entwistle, 1983). Insect pathogenic microorganisms or insects that feed on other insects offer solutions for control. Many of the microparasites have merit, including viruses, bacteria, fungi, protozoa, and rickettsiae. Considerable crop protection research has been conducted with the bacteria *Bacillus thuringiensis*. Awareness is increasing that viruses may be an extremely powerful tool to control insect pests in agricultural and forest crops.

Since the early 1900s the Asian species of the rhinoceros beetle has been spreading through the Pacific and Melanesian islands and is severely defoliating coconut and oil palm plantations. Beetle control studies with baculovirus reveal infection and release of virus-infected adults in coconut plantations in Malaysia was an effective method of control (Entwistle, 1983). Identification of other biologically active agents which could be utilized as an alternative to chemical control is underway. For example, in 1982, viruses pathogenic to the tussock moth were released in New Guinea through aerial helicopter applications to combat this serious tropical pest. Genetic engineering can also introduce new properties into biological control agents, such as enhanced virulence, broader host specificity, and longer shelf life.

Biological Processing and Economic Development

The recognition of agricultural and forest crops as important gene pools and sources of chemical and energy feedstocks has led to intensive efforts to develop appropriate technologies for cultivation, harvesting, and processing of new plant products. These organic compounds include oils, resins, tannins, natural rubber, gums, waxes, dyes, flavors, fragrances, pesticides, and pharmaceuticals (Balandrin et al., 1985). Many species of plants in developing countries have not been surveyed or described and biologically valuable constituents remain to be discovered (Hinman, 1984). Biotechnology applications, such as genetic transformation and plant microculture, will provide the means for improving commercial production of plantlets and the chemicals they produce. Thus biotechnology will effectively extend the utility of plants as renewable resources of valuable chemicals.

The plant genetic resources necessary to drive the commercial development of new chemical products are predominantly found within developing countries (OTA, 1987). In order to fully exploit chemical utilization of crops, an intensive screening program of fiber, leaves, fruits, and exudates is needed. The feedstock for these programs may be collected from farms, plantations, natural ecosystems, or harvest residues and the methodology is well suited to the pastoral life of many farmers of the developing world. Historically important oil crops such as oil palm and rubber have been fully exploited within many sections of the developing world. Small-scale bioprocessing technology appropriate for the social, cultural, economic, and environmental conditions of developing countries have been developed. There are well over 200 oil-bearing species in the developing world, of which less than a dozen are currently used. Burley and Lockhart (1985) report that of some 300 multipurpose trees surveyed, five produce waxes, 17 produce essential oils, 30 yield gums, 26 yield tannins and dyes, and one produces latex. One tree species, neem, which occurs on arid and semiarid land, yields at least one extractive from the roots, shoots, and leaves, respectively.

Suspension culture of plant cells is a viable alternative for production of high-value chemicals (Balandrin et al., 1985). The mass culture of cells from specific plants can result in substantial accumulation of secondary metabolites (chemicals) or other plant products. This biotechnology has significant immediate applications in developing countries. As plant habitat disappears and environmental and geopolitical constraints limit production of plant-derived chemicals, it may become acutely necessary to develop alternative sources of economically important plant products (Hinman, 1984).

Forest resources and product development offer abundant biotechnology applications in the developing world (OTA, 1984a). Certain microorganisms, such as white-rot fungi, are able to partially delignify wood, suggesting a potential for small-scale biological pulping by farmers. Degradation of wood or mechanical pulp with these fungi dramatically reduces the energy required for mechanical refining. Minimal capital investment, low energy demand, and high efficiency of biological pulping are attractive to forestry programs in developing countries (Kirk et al., 1983).

Plant Biotechnology Networking

Plant biotechnology applications described in the previous section can immediately improve food, fuel, and fiber production in developing countries. Most of the biotechnologies are relatively simple, inexpensive, energy-efficient, and nonhazardous to the environment. Illustrations describing the successful implementation of this technology in developing countries have been cited in this chapter. Additional sophisticated tools and methods of biotechnology are being implemented to overcome the complex constraints that limit agricultural and forest production in the developing world.

Globally, plant biotechnology has the potential to develop differentially due to uneven distribution of capital, human resources, scientific infrastructure, and socioeconomic opportunity. Plant biotechnologies with obvious financial potential have received initial attention and support from private industry. Due to the rich genetic abundance of countries within tropical latitudes, some developing countries have benefited immensely from the application of plant biotechnology. More importantly, coalitions of private industry, national governments, and bilateral donor organizations have implemented and sustained plant biotechnology research and application efforts. Within some regions of the developing world, plant biotechnology application efforts are progressing under adequate support (for example, Ecuador, India, and Thailand).

Many policy analysts have identified concerns regarding the equitable distribution of biotechnologies and associated economic rewards within the developing world (Buttel, 1985). These concerns may become valid if the multilateral development community does not continue to foster a global scientific and business infrastructure which nurtures equitable distribution of the biotechnology industry. Knowledge and infrastructure favorable to commercial biotechnology should be tailored to capitalize on unique resources and cultural endowments of individual developing countries. Fostering innovative methods to identify, implement, and sustain useful and efficient plant biotechnology in a climate of scarce human and financial resources and keen economic competition is the challenge to the multilateral donor community.

Biotechnology networking sponsored by bilateral development organizations offers an efficient method to systematically organize the earth's scarce plant biology research and development resources to attack some of the major renewable resource and human subsistence problems. In contrast to biomedical research, funds for basic plant science research are meager and resources allocated to individual investigators and institutions are inadequate (Weiss, 1985). Most developing countries have limited facilities and resources for conducting plant biotechnology research on the broad array of problems, in the depth required. Moreover, a system is needed to deploy the benefits of biotechnology applications. Uncertainties regarding the relative costs and benefits of plant biotechnology have hampered implementation of beneficial technology. Sharing of resources and risks through a coordinated program involving national governments, the academic community, private industry, and bilateral development organizations can be more effective than a fragmented approach to marshalling resources, and can explore a wide range of solution options in a shorter time (Dixon, 1988). Sharing of technology, germplasm, financial resources, facilities, and human resources is especially critical to successful development activities where the goal is to solve major problems of broad significance (Adams and Dixon, 1986).

A program of coordinated, cooperative research and extension in plant biotechnology conducted through informal or formal networks which link government, universities, and private industry in different countries and different disciplines can achieve numerous goals. These goals can be to: (1) help organize a larger concerted effort with a wider range of skills, methodologies, and facilities than any one country or institution alone could provide; (2) permit countries with limited plant biotechnology development capabilities to exploit a wider range of expertise and facilities through cooperative exchange programs;

(3) stimulate cooperative plant biology research among scientists and institutions that have skills essential to successful biotechnology research and development related to the cultivation and use of crops; (4) provide a large gene pool of plant species and associated organisms for biotechnology development and practical applications; (5) provide a wider database for testing biotechnology and developing more general principles and techniques; (6) allow a more systematic and comprehensive research and development approach to a given problem, offering a greater chance of successfully producing useful technology with a broader application; (7) offer improved mutual training opportunities among collaborators; (8) link science and engineering programs of private industry, government, and universities and improve opportunities for developing and deploying new technology and novel products; and (9) foster opportunity for bilateral development organizations and private industry to invest in plant biotechnology research and extension as a means of enhancing economic development.

The existing infrastructure and capabilities of most developing countries are not adequate to support the sustained growth of plant biotechnology applications in future decades. The major resources needed for organizing effective national research programs require trained scientists and engineers, supplies and equipment, and current information and literature (Swaminathan, 1982). Networking of human, financial, and genetic resources offers an efficient means of augmenting existing personnel and facilities in the immediate future, and would substantially increase the level, productivity, and effectiveness of biotechnology applications in the developing world within the next 10 years. Recently, IUFRO, USAID, and other bilateral development groups have pooled common resources to meet this challenge (Adams and Dixon, 1986). Because these incipient networking activities have been relatively successful, this approach merits further consideration and enrichment.

Several obstacles to efficient widespread plant biotechnology networking require attention in the future. These obstacles include adequate financial support by the donor community, disruption of information and resource sharing by competitive forces, and horizontal development of network structure. The obvious benefits of networking to the global community should encourage international support and cooperation among private industry, academia, national governments, and the bilateral donors (OTA, 1984a). The cultivation of scientific and commercial talent within the developing world is the object of side-scale training programs sponsored by academia and the donor community (Adams and Dixon, 1986). The lateral and horizontal expansion of networks to the socioeconomic benefit of the developing world will require substantial effort.

Current networking efforts primarily focus on development of a science and commercial infrastructure. Once products or methods of biotechnology are established within the developing world, networks should focus on the user, especially the resource-poor farmer (Molnar and Kinnucan, 1989). Some policy analysts and conceptual models predict farmers of the developing world will not benefit from plant biotechnology. However, substantial empirical evidence suggests farmers have considerable capacity for change and self-improvement (Geisler and DuPuis, 1989). Networking offers the technical and institutional structure required for efficient adoption of plant biotechnology by resource-poor farmers.

Summary

Evidence suggests the substantial increases in global agricultural production attributed to the Green Revolution are reaching a plateau. This factor, coupled with a growing world population problem and debt crisis, has focused attention on recent advances in biotechnology. Emerging agricultural biotechnologies may revolutionize use of genetic resources to improve food, fuel, and fiber production and foster bioconversion applications and efficient processing of specialty products. The complexity of these technologies has led some policy analysts to predict plant biotechnology applications are futuristic. Uncertain costs and benefits of biotechnology have made it difficult to assess the potential impact on the developing world. Incipient plant biotechnology applications require substantial capital investment in laboratories, trained scientists and technicians, and prototype production and risk-assessment facilities. However, recent developments such as transnational investment in technology by the private sector, recognition of the broad genetic base of plants within tropical latitudes, and bilateral efforts to network information and germplasm, have stimulated biotechnology-based industries in developed and underdeveloped countries. Networking of human resources and institutional capabilities is an efficient and cost-effective mode in developing countries where capital is in short supply, new markets are emerging, and genetic resources are abundant. Tripartite biotechnology networking efforts by private industry, government, and the academic community will ensure sustainable agricultural-based productivity and reduce substantially the land and water requirements for meeting these needs. Moreover, networking fosters collaborative efforts to monitor and assess the relative costs and benefits of plant biotechnology applications.

Plant biotechnology is a promising tool for improving the resource efficiency and sustainability of food, fuel, and fiber production in developing countries. According to the Office of Technology Assessment (1984a), "most emerging technologies are expected to reduce substantially the land and water requirements for meeting future agricultural needs." Moreover, the energy needs and negative environmental impact of plant biotechnology applications are projected to be substantially less than previous improvements in crop production associated with the Green Revolution (OTA, 1984a; Plucknett and Smith, 1982). An expanded commitment to public and private research, at the national and international levels, is needed to insure developing world priorities are addressed. Networking of government and academic institutions with private industry and the IARCs will improve the efficient and equitable distribution of biotechnology.

Abolition of institutional and academic barriers between science and technology disciplines in agriculture and forestry, at all levels, will lead to beneficial changes in patterns of rural development in the developing world. Investments by bilateral development organizations to stimulate biotechnology development and application should be expanded to ensure sustainable plant-based productivity.

Note

This research was partially supported by the U.S. Agency for International Development and the Winrock International Institute for Agricultural Development under the Forestry/Fuelwood Research and Development Project. Contribution 9891971P of the Alabama Agricultural Experiment Station.

III
Assessing Potential Impacts of Biotechnology

7

Who Will Benefit from Agricultural Biotechnology: An Analysis of Economic and Legal Influences

Beverly Fleisher

Because biotechnology has the potential to foster the next technological revolution in agriculture, policymakers are anxious to predict its effect on agricultural producers and consumers. Economists studying biotechnology have focused primarily on the changes in input/output relationships that can be caused by specific products. Judging from only physical response patterns, biotechnology clearly has potential to evoke major changes in agriculture. But the potential for increased productivity is only part of the picture. The creation and distribution of benefits from agricultural biotechnology among input manufacturers, agricultural producers, and consumers will be determined by the interaction of numerous factors including the products that are developed, the prices at which they are sold, producers' willingness to adopt the new technology, and the ability of agricultural producers to capture any cost savings brought about by the new technology.

The structure of the agricultural biotechnology industry will play a key role in determining the distribution of benefits from the new technology. The existing financial and market position of agricultural input manufacturers will be a major factor determining the structure of the agricultural biotechnology industry over the next 20 years. The ability of firms to recoup their investment in research and development of new products through patent and trade secret protection will affect both the industry's structure and the products available to agricultural producers, as well as the prices that are charged for both traditional and biotechnologically derived agricultural inputs.

Social decisions about how the possible risks from biotechnologically derived products for agriculture are to be managed will affect both producers and users. Efforts to reduce risk through regulation will impose costs on input manufacturers. Product liability and the cost and availability of liability insurance will affect the financial position of input manufacturing firms, the risks that agricultural producers must bear, and the recourse available to those who may be harmed by biotechnologically derived products.

Anticipated costly patent litigation, the cost of meeting testing requirements for regulatory approval, and the dearth of financing and unavailability of liability insurance for small biotechnology firms will act in concert to shape an input industry characterized by a fairly small number of large firms, each with significant market power. The actual amount of market power exercised through pricing decisions will depend on the substitutability of biotechnologically derived inputs for traditional inputs and the degree of competitive price-cutting used by traditional input manufacturers to maintain their market share.

Adoption of the new technology and its effect on production agriculture will depend in part on the input prices and changes that the technology makes in the physical production process. But producers' decision calculus also will be shaped by forces affecting the agricultural sector as a whole, including excess capacity, financial stress, a decrease in the value of land and other durable assets, and concerns over conservation and long-run productivity of agricultural resources (Harl, 1984), and by concerns over their financial liability for the unintended side effects of biotechnologically derived products. Because agricultural producers are price takers rather than price setters, consumer benefits from biotechnologically derived inputs for agriculture are directly dependent on the cost-saving or output-enhancing effect of the technologies in production agriculture.

To answer the question "Who will benefit from agricultural biotechnology?" we must examine in more detail the forces shaping the structure of the agricultural biotechnology industry, the effect of the structure of the input industry on production agriculture, and agricultural producers' adoption decisions.

The Agricultural Biotechnology Industry Today

Since the 1970s, some 600 companies dedicated to biotechnology have been founded. It has been reported that almost all of the firms focusing on biotechnology have reported financial losses since their formation (*The Economist*, 1988: 1). So far, according to Pollack (1987: D6), no biotechnology company is profitable strictly from selling products derived from recombinant DNA technology. Industry analysts now predict a major reduction in the number of agricultural biotechnology firms as products near the testing and commercialization stage (Klausner, 1988: 14; *New York Times*, 1987: D5).

The financial and market positions of firms whose primary line of business is agricultural biotechnology can be contrasted with those of firms who are expanding into biotechnology from established positions in the agrichemical market. The aggressiveness of larger agricultural input firms in biotechnology demonstrates the market potential for the products of biotechnology in agriculture. For example, Monsanto, a major agrichemical firm, has already invested over $1 billion in research on agricultural biotechnology products (*The Economist*, 1988: 12).

The financial position of agricultural biotechnology firms is reflected in the ratio of their market valuation from public offerings, including stocks, to their liquidation value. For all firms whose primary or sole line of business is biotechnology, total offerings are valued at approximately seven times the firms' liquidation value, while for agricultural biotechnology firms, the average value of public offerings is less than the firms' liquidation value (Klausner and Fox, 1988: 243). The high level of competition from large agrichemical firms is often blamed for the poor financial position of agricultural biotechnology companies (Klausner and Fox, 1988: 244). Many biotechnology firms have licensed their first products to large pharmaceutical or agrichemical firms who have regulatory and marketing expertise and established sales networks (*Business Week*, 1984: 87). Firms engaged solely in biotechnology have concentrated their efforts on research and development and are only now moving into product marketing and sales.

Proprietary Rights and Research and Development

Currently, two-thirds of all agricultural research and development expenditures are accounted for by the private sector (Pray et al., 1988: 1; Ruttan, 1982b: 23). Private investment depends on the establishment of exclusive private rights in the products of research and development in order to recover research investment. Thus, patent and trade secret law are particularly relevant to the agricultural biotechnology industry. Three areas of proprietary rights are especially important for agricultural biotechnology: the breadth of protection offered by patents and trade secrets, defensibility of proprietary rights against challenges from other firms, and proprietary rights infringement by agricultural producers.

In theory, a patent confers exclusive rights to its holder by granting a legal monopoly on an invention for 17 years. A patent may be viewed as a social contract. Society grants an inventor the right to exclude others from making, using, or selling the invention or its products. In return, the patent application must provide enough information about the invention so that someone skilled in the area could duplicate it. In this way, society can immediately begin to build upon the new knowledge embodied in the patent. If, by law, only one firm is allowed to use or produce the patented technology, the firm will be able to charge a higher price for that product than if many firms could produce the same product (Henderson and Quandt, 1958: 164-66).

Patents are now obtainable for plants, microorganisms, and animals through a variety of statutes and agency and court decisions, including the Plant Patent

Act (35 U.S. Code, Sections 161-162) and the Plant Variety Protection Act (7 U.S. Code, Sections 2321-2583). The Supreme Court's 1980 decision in *Diamond v. Chakrabarty* (100 S. Ct. 2204) extended the scope of patent law to include organisms by holding that patentable subject matter includes "anything under the sun made by man" as long as it meets the standards of invention set forth in the original Patent Act (35 U.S. Code, Sections 101-112), namely, that the invention is novel, useful, and nonobvious (Hoffman and Karney, 1988: B3). In April 1988 the Patent and Trademark Office issued a patent for a genetically engineered mouse (Raines, 1988: 64). The issue of patentability of animals is still contentious.

The issue of proprietary rights is particularly fractious in the biotechnology industry. Because of the influence of close substitutes on what a firm can charge for its product, how broadly or narrowly property rights for biotechnology processes and end-products are defined will affect their profitability and incentives for product development. Due to uncertainty about patent breadth and defensibility, firms are faced with a dilemma about when to apply for patent protection. By disclosing information in the patent process, firms lose rights conferred through trade secret protection. Legally, a trade secret consists of any information that has potential or actual economic value by virtue of not being generally known to one's competitors, as long as reasonable efforts are made to keep the information secret (Payne, 1988: 131). This problem is common in industries developing at a rapid pace and is particularly acute in biotechnology, where many companies are working on a limited number of products using the same scientific methods (*New York Times*, 1987: D5). The process of determining proprietary rights is further complicated by the fact that often 4–10 companies are involved in bringing any one new biotechnology product to the testing or marketing stage (*New York Times*, 1987: D1).

Firms are often forced to take out patents of uncertain validity and fight off challenges to them in the courts because their competitors are doing the same. In fact, patents do not guarantee exclusive rights to a technology or process; they convey only the rebuttable presumption of validity (Adler, 1984: 358). However, patent battles are usually won by the company with the greatest financial resources for legal costs. The necessity of litigation and the uncertainty about biotechnology firms' ability to enforce proprietary rights has added to the uncertainty faced by investors, making the biotechnology industry less attractive, at least in the short run. Industry analysts expect the patent scramble to contribute to a trend over the next few years of great consolidation in the biotechnology industry (Klausner, 1988: 114; *Economist*, 1988: 17).

Firms are also concerned about their ability to enforce proprietary rights once products are released into the marketplace. The applicability of royalties to offspring of patented animals has yet to be tested in the courts. Even if these rights are granted, policing costs could prohibit their actual implementation. Although producers could charge royalties on succeeding generations of patented plants under the Plant Patent Act or the Plant Variety Protection Act, they rarely do so because of the high policing costs relative to the royalties actually obtained (Stallmann and Schmid, 1987: 434).

The high cost of policing for proprietary rights infringement may lead to larger investments in organisms that are not reproductively stable, eliminating the farmer as a source of competition. The ability to exclude agricultural producers from infringing on proprietary rights will be an important consideration in how new biotechnologies are packaged. For example, much of the work on improving plant agriculture is being devoted to the development of artificial seed embryos that contain several packages of genetic material. In combination, they will create plants with more desirable attributes. But their seeds will not transmit these characteristics to the next generation, requiring that producers repurchase seed embryos for each planting, as is currently the case with hybrid seeds.

Product Testing for Regulatory Approval

Despite the major effort being made to insure the safety of products through testing prior to regulatory approval, the current regulatory mandate does not allow federal agencies to work towards insuring that biotechnologically derived products will actually reduce the total risk to society. At the same time, the resources involved in conducting tests required for regulatory approval places further strains on the finances of smaller biotechnology firms. Extensive field testing increases the amount of investment required and the time between when the investment is made and returns are seen.

The U.S. Department of Agriculture (USDA), Environmental Protection Agency (EPA), and Food and Drug Administration (FDA) have published policy statements announcing their intentions to regulate the products of biotechnology (51 *Federal Register* at 23302-23393). All three agencies require submission of extensive data and test results as one condition for approval of certain types of testing and use of biotechnologically derived products. The scope of safety that must be shown by these tests varies according to the statute under which a product is regulated (Mellon, 1987: 18.26-18.36).

The developing regulatory framework will require firms to shoulder the expense of compliance and may delay large-scale testing and commercialization of products. The cost of meeting these requirements has a proportionately larger claim on the resources of smaller firms. Therefore, smaller agricultural biotechnology firms may need to form alliances with larger or better-capitalized firms once products reach the development phase requiring regulatory approval.

Firms approaching initial field tests of biotechnologically derived products are faced not only with product testing costs, but the cost of obtaining regulatory and public approval for the test. Consider the testing of an insect-resistant crop variety. If the variety was produced using conventional techniques, testing would require only some plants and the traditional complement of inputs such as land, labor, and fertilizer. The test could be conducted alongside many other tests on a research station field. However, if the new variety is biotechnologically derived, concern about safety makes the process more cumbersome and can boost actual field testing costs.

Before reaching the stage where field testing can be conducted, companies must incur costs beyond those required for product development or field testing of non-biotechnologically derived products. First, there is the assembly of the paperwork and laboratory results necessary for submission to the appropriate regulatory agency for approval of the initial field test (Schneider, 1987: C1). Second, time and other resources are required to gain approval from local government bodies and citizens' groups to conduct the test at the selected site (Melloan, 1988: 39).

To an adequately financed firm, these costs may not prove to be unduly burdensome. But any decision to test a product must weigh both the costs and possible benefits of the undertaking. At the initial field testing stage, the benefits are unknown; the test is experimental, both with regard to the product's safety and its efficacy. Prior to proving the efficacy of a new technology, the decision to proceed with field testing is strongly influenced by the relationship between costs and expected benefits. The decision calculus can be easily influenced by regulatory requirements or delays that increase costs relative to anticipated benefits, particularly in a scarce-resource environment.

Existing regulatory legislation does not attempt to ensure socially beneficial uses of technology. Most legislation attempts only to ensure that products offered are safe; it does not assure that they are the best possible (Mellon, 1987: 18.9). Regulation of biotechnology is in keeping with this pattern. Nevertheless, policies not directly related to technology can and do affect the technologies brought onto the market, which will also be the case for biotechnology for agriculture.

The types of biotechnologies developed for agriculture will be affected by regulation of existing agricultural inputs. The withdrawal of key pesticides may encourage development of specific types of pest-resistant crops. Similarly, regulation of nitrogen runoff and groundwater contamination may encourage more rapid development of nitrogen-fixing soil microbes. Within the current regulatory framework, such events will be unplanned. Under current procedures, it is possible that one agency, acting within its mandate, may take actions that precipitate changes in agronomic practices that would exacerbate the problems of another agency. For example, at the same time that USDA exercises its responsibility by evaluating and approving testing of genetically engineered herbicide-resistant plants, which could lead to increased herbicide use, EPA struggles with regulating groundwater contamination by some of these same herbicides.

The potential of biotechnology to provide substitutes for existing products with undesirable effects provides an opportunity to use existing regulations to shape the types of technology that will be used in agriculture. For example, Virginia has considered the imposition of a tax on fertilizer to reduce its use and subsequent runoff into the Chesapeake Bay. Biotechnologically engineered plants that fix nitrogen, and thus require less fertilizer, would be more economically attractive to agricultural producers facing fertilizer prices that have increased substantially through the use of a tax. Using this opportunity, however, requires a vision of what types of production systems might be most desirable. This vision must be combined with the willingness to develop regulatory initiatives and make regulatory decisions based not only on minimum safety requirements but on the relative risks presented by existing, new, and potential technologies.

Product Liability and Liability Insurance

Although liability insurance is not required for testing, manufacturing, or commercializing of biotechnologically derived products, operating without insurance exposes manufacturers and users of the technology to potential financial devastation. Regulations require that a new product meets some minimum safety standard, not that the new product is safer than others that are already on the market. Biotechnology products are so new that many of the small companies that pioneered them cannot get product liability insurance (Tort Policy Working Group, 1987: 15). According to Bruce Mackler, of the Association of Biotechnology Companies, many firms will be forced to abandon promising new technology as a result (Day, 1985: IV.14). Others will have to test products without coverage and run the risk of suits for amounts larger than their total assets should a product have unintended effects. The lack of insurance for many small firms raises questions about their ability or obligation to offer compensation for unintended side effects of their operations. Larger companies involved in agricultural biotechnology have not been affected as much as smaller companies because they have the size and safety record to give them clout with insurers, offer a diversified set of products across which premiums and potential claim risks can be spread, and can often afford to self-insure. The dearth of product liability insurance for biotechnology firms arises from three related phenomena: how the insurance industry sets rates, uncertainty about the risks associated with biotechnology, and changes in liability concepts in the courts. In addition, insurers' willingness to invest money in a particular line of insurance such as biotechnology products is determined in comparison to the profits that can be made in other lines.

First, the lack of experience with biotechnology means that the insurance industry, which is fundamentally driven by statistics, has no historical information upon which to base premiums. Companies are forced to make decisions regarding biotechnology insurance versus other investments where the actuarial base is better known and potential for profit is less uncertain.

Second, the lack of consensus among experts on the likely risks or adverse effects of biotechnology compounds the problems raised by lack of historical data (Regal, 1987; Sharples, 1987; Davis, 1987a). The most likely risk profile that does emerge gives little comfort to those who might be interested in providing

insurance. Biotechnology can be characterized as a "low probability/high consequence" risk, which means that adverse events are very unlikely, but if and when
they do occur, they are likely to have grave effects. (*Economist,* 1988: 15). In addition, the events are unlikely to be isolated or independent. Instead, they will
probably affect many individuals, such as all users of a particular microorganism, resulting in large indemnity payments in a very short period of time. In
other industries with this risk profile, such as the nuclear power, space, and mari-
time industries, the government has augmented the coverage offered by the private insurance market by providing caps on liability, or assuming the risk of
indemnities above a certain level. The government's willingness to provide this
protection has been motivated by the decision that development of these industries is vital to the national interest (Princeton Synergetics, 1985: 84).

Third, changes in liability concepts in the courts have affected the insurance
industry's willingness to offer product liability insurance to biotechnology firms.
Insurers are concerned about the proliferation of punitive damages awarded, the
trend towards shared liability, and cases where damages are awarded even though
the product causing the injury met state-of-the-art standards at the time it was
made (Lewin, 1986: 37). In addition to the actuarial risk that an adverse event
will occur, insurers are concerned with predicting the likelihood of suit and the
amount that will be awarded by jury or out-of-court settlements. What insurance executives say concerns them the most is the lack of predictability: the loss
of ability to project with reasonable certainty the relations between losses and
premiums paid (Nash, 1986: D1).

Although biotechnology firms are not required to have product liability insurance, its unavailability to small firms is likely to affect their role in the evolving
biotechnology industry. Alliance with major agrichemical firms through licensing agreements may, in the short run, be the only feasible route towards protection from suit for many small agricultural biotechnology firms. However, this
alliance will not come without cost. In return for providing protection from possible liability claims, major agrichemical firms are likely to require lower licensing fees or other concessions.

The Biotechnology Industry's Structure and Production
Agriculture

The structure of the biotechnology industry will play a key role in determining
the distribution of benefits from the new technology. But the influence of the
structure of the biotechnology industry will be conditioned by other factors. One
is the breadth of proprietary rights associated with each new product or process.
Another is the size of the market for the product. Biotechnologically derived
products' complementarity with or substitutability for inputs manufactured by
traditional means and factors of production will also shape adoption decisions
and the ability of firms to capture the benefits of the new technology. For those
biotechnologically derived inputs that are substitutes for existing inputs, the de-

gree of reactive price competition that occurs may be substantial. Although this discussion focuses on the biotechnology industry and treats agricultural producers as a fairly homogeneous group, it is important to note that any one biotechnology product will not have a uniform impact on all producers of any one agricultural commodity.

Financing is the weak link that may bring about a rapid decline in the number of commercially viable, small agricultural biotechnology firms. The current weak financial position of these small firms is unlikely to improve in the near term because of investor concern about the ability of small firms to overcome the hurdles between research and development of new products and their commercial release. Of particular concern is the ability of small firms to gain and enforce exclusive proprietary rights over their products, the unavailability of liability insurance, and the considerable cost involved in testing new products prior to regulatory approval. For instance, uncertainty about the defensibility of patents leads to concern about the ability to recoup investment in small firms. The possibility of liability suits in the absence of adequate insurance leads to the specter of damage awards greater than the firm's total assets and leaving investors without any return. And the time and cost involved in meeting product testing requirements for regulatory approval increases the amount of investment required and the time between when the investment is made and returns are seen.

Because of the difficulty in generating external financing and concerns about liability, many small biotechnology firms will need to move towards joint ventures with, or absorption by, larger agricultural input firms. These larger firms can generate financing internally through profits from sales of existing product lines and often are in the position to provide their own insurance. Although joint venture agreements may allow smaller firms to continue to engage in research and development, the larger agricultural input manufacturers will likely bring the finished product to market. Through these agreements, a few large firms will be the gatekeepers to the final marketplace for biotechnologically derived products for agriculture. Thus, from the farmers perspective as the purchaser of biotechnologically derived inputs, the market will be dominated by a few large firms.

In a perfectly competitive market, producers of agricultural inputs would price inputs at the marginal cost of production. Agricultural producers would purchase enough of the inputs so that the additional benefits gained from using the last unit purchased would exactly equal its additional cost. However, in an input market dominated by a few firms, each of which holds monopoly rights to its products, input firms are not constrained to pricing their output at its cost of production. The upper limit on the price they can charge is determined by the production possibilities offered by their input and the existence and pricing of products that are, if not identical, at least close substitutes. The existence of close substitutes for the products of biotechnology will prevent firms from capturing all of the returns from the increased productivity that their products may offer farmers.

The price that agricultural biotechnology firms will be able to charge for their products will depend on the existence of substitutes for those products. Patent rights insure that competing firms cannot sell identical products. However, similar, although not identical products can be made. Biotechnologically derived products must also compete with existing inputs used in production activities. The true market power of the biotechnology firms will depend upon the extent to which these similar products may be used in farm production activities. In the short run, the development of multiple similar biotechnologically derived agricultural products will be determined by the breadth of patent protection granted, research and development costs, the size of the market, and the pricing strategies followed by producers of existing inputs for which biotechnologically derived products can substitute.

The breadth of patent production granted by current law differs among biotechnologically derived products for agriculture. For example, the Plant Patent Act allows only a very narrow product space because the patented plant need only be "distinct" from other plants. This means that very close substitutes are legal. The Plant Variety Protection Act, on the other hand, under whose purview feedgrains and other major crops fall, grants broader protection, requiring that the plant be a new or novel variety (Schmid, 1985: 133). The question of breadth of patent protection is made more complicated by the fact that biotechnology firms can also patent the processes that are instrumental in developing biotechnology products for agriculture. Firms holding process patents are often willing to license or sell these patent rights. Although this enables other firms to use patented processes, the purchase of patent rights or licenses substantially increases product development costs.

Before firms invest in the development of new products for agriculture, they want some assurance that they will be able to recoup their investment in research, development, testing, and marketing. Thus, agriculture biotechnology firms must consider both the cost of product development and patentability and the market size for the product. Because of the larger size of the market, we are likely to see more competition among firms for a share of the market for major crops than minor ones. However, this competition will be limited by the broader scope of property rights granted under the Plant Variety Protection Act and the nature of the products themselves. With the trend toward development of seed embryos which "bundle" a set of inputs or attributes, markets for products will be limited by the physical characteristics of the environment in which they will be used. In contrast to existing seed varieties, where farmers can vary complementary input use, such as fertilizer or pesticides, to meet the requirements of their own physical production system, a seed embryo with fixed proportions of various characteristics, such as nitrogen-fixation or pest resistance, will be applicable to a smaller set of physical environments and hence salable to a smaller market segment. Thus, while several companies may engage in development of seed embryos for a major crop such as corn, each company is likely to develop a product for which they have monopoly rights for one segment of the market.

When viewed from an aggregate perspective there may appear to be a competitive market for biotechnologically derived seed embryos for corn, but from an individual producers' perspective there may only be one supplier of a biotechnologically derived product that meets their needs. Biotechnology firms' monopolistic position in any one market segment may be limited by the rapid pace of development of the new technology, where product life is limited by introduction of new processes and products.

Although biotechnology firms may have monopoly rights over biotechnologically derived products for a particular market segment, two additional forces will act to reduce the profits that they can make: the cost advantage that must be offered to induce farmers to change existing production practices and reactive price competition from conventional input manufacturers. To induce farmers to change current practices with which they are familiar and in which they often have significant investment, biotechnologically derived products must be priced to offer nontrivial economic advantages. A few farmers may adopt for only a small economic advantage, but others will be slower to adopt, offering the possibility that biotechnology firms can increase total profits by lowering their prices and expanding the volume of sales. The prices charged by biotechnology firms may be driven lower by reaction from the manufacturers of conventional agricultural inputs. In an effort to maintain their market share, input firms producing chemicals and fertilizers, and related service industries, may respond to the threat of a new technology by dropping prices. Biotechnology firms would then face a lower price for substitute products that they must compete with in order to capture a share of the market.

Biotechnology firms' pricing strategies in individual markets may also be indirectly affected by competition among commodities in the total market for agricultural products. Lowering production costs, and thus the cost of agricultural commodities, increases demand. This increases the demand for inputs into agricultural production, including the new technology. Even though the individual biotechnology firms may focus on products for a specific commodity, all agricultural producers compete in the market for agricultural products. The success of the biotechnology firm is thus indirectly tied to the success of the farm market niche it has established. Lowering the cost of production for farmers in a firm's market niche will expand these farmers' share of the market for agricultural commodities at the expense of other farmers and increase the biotechnology firm's market in the process.

Biotechnology is likely to change the proportion of farmers' input expenditures going to individual purchased inputs. The major shift in crop production budgets is expected to be from chemical inputs to seed, where the seed embryos contain biopesticides or nitrogen-fixing microorganisms. The major agrichemical firms have foreseen this trend and it is reported that they have invested over $10 billion to purchase seed companies over the past decade (*Economist*, 1988: 12). This shift toward a group of inputs "bundled" into seed embryos will give producers less flexibility to change the proportions of inputs they use in response to attributes of their own physical production system or changes in the relative prices of different inputs.

Consider a pest-resistant alfalfa seed embryo. The manufacturer of the seed can charge farmers what they would have paid for the traditional input "bundle" of alfalfa seed, pesticides, and the labor and machinery complement needed to apply the pesticides. Such a seed already is being developed. The developer estimates that it can sell its alfalfa seed to the farmer at $12.30 per pound, a premium of $10 per pound over the cost of ordinary alfalfa seed. According to the input firm, the farmer will still realize some cost savings. The seed manufacturer will make an 88 percent gross margin on the sale of the genetically engineered alfalfa seed, nearly double the 46 percent gross margins on the sale of ordinary alfalfa seed (*Economist*, 1988: 13).

Although there are many guidelines for determining the distribution of benefits between the manufacturers of agricultural inputs as a group and agricultural producers as a group, it is not clear how biotechnology will affect the distribution of returns among agricultural producers. For example, the economic impact of bovine growth hormone (bGH) has been extensively examined, but predictions about its effect on the structure of the dairy industry are highly dependent on assumptions made about the technology's effect on the input/output relationships in dairying. These effects remain uncertain. In 1986, an Office of Technology Assessment (OTA) evaluation assumed that the introduction of bGH would lead to a 25.6 percent increase in milk production and dramatically increase the rate of change in the trend towards fewer, larger dairy farms. In contrast, another study assumed that the introduction of bGH would result in an increase in milk production of 1,800 pounds per cow per year (Fallert et al., 1987). The study concluded that although the concentration trend in the dairy industry would continue, its rate would not dramatically increase. Thus, the assumption of a percentage versus an absolute amount of increase in production due to the introduction of bGH masked the differential usage rate according to the size of farms. This approach to analysis led to different conclusions about the technology's effect on the dairy industry. Estimating potential effects of other types of biotechnology products on production agriculture will also be hampered by uncertainty about their exact effects on the input/output relationships in agriculture.

Agricultural Producers' Adoption Decisions

Farmers' demand for biotechnological products and the benefits they garner from the adoption of new technology are conditioned not only by the prices of the products, but also the individual farmer's current production practices and financial position. Possible liability for unintended adverse effects of biotechnologically derived products will also enter into the farmer's decision calculus.

Excess capacity affects the prices producers receive for their products. Although many major commodities have a price floor set by government programs, these price floors have dropped since the passage of the 1985 Food Security Act. For major grain commodities, the producers' eligibility for deficiency payments is conditional on farmers' historical yield records and bases. Therefore, products must offer significant cost savings in order to be adopted. Simply being yield-enhancing may not provide adequate incentive as farmers may not be able to receive returns equal to previous levels for increases in production beyond historical levels.

Biotechnologically derived products may also extend the geographic range in which particular commodities can be produced. But producers in the new areas may be slow to adopt these crops because for the first few years they will not be eligible for government programs, since program eligibility is based on an established record of growing that particular crop through the use of historical "base" and production yield records for the crop of concern.

Producer decisions to adopt will also be strongly influenced by their current financial position and production practices. Biotechnology advances that require significant investments in new machinery or equipment or significant changes in production practices will be adopted at a slower rate. They will be adopted first by producers who are not highly leveraged or experiencing financial stress. Biotechnologically derived products that will reduce costs or increase income without requiring large long-term capital investments will be more rapidly adopted and will be more evenly adopted throughout a specific commodity subsector (Boehlje and Cole, 1985: 3). For example, Larson and Kuchler (1989: 1) have shown that the costs in production are more important than production limits in determining the effect of bovine growth hormone. They note that the costs of bGH adoption, which include hormone costs, increased feed requirements for treated animals, and additional management time and skills, are just as fundamental to the adoption decision as the effects of bGH on per-cow milk supply (Larson and Kuchler, 1989: 3). The diffusion of any one technology through the sector will also depend on the appropriateness of the product to a broad range of operating environments.

The value of inputs currently used in production will also affect producers' adoption decisions. During the middle and late 1980s, the value of land and other durable assets used in production declined precipitously (Boehlje and Cole, 1985: 3). As a result, producers are likely to use increasing amounts of those fixed inputs and try to minimize the use of purchased inputs with higher costs relative to their returns. Therefore, producers will favor the use of products that serve as complements to the resources that they already have in their inventory, rather than products which serve as substitutes for those inputs. In addition, when evaluating the use of any input, farmers equate the marginal returns from that input to the marginal cost of its use. Futhermore, farmers equate the marginal returns from all inputs used in the production process. Therefore, farmers with different mixes of inputs in their current production practice will make different decisions regarding the adoption of a new input. And, even if the cost of the input is small, the farmer may not have an adequate incentive to adopt it if the marginal cost of the complementary inputs increase rapidly as output increases.

One often overlooked parameter in the farmer's decision calculus is the risks they assume in the adoption of new technologies. The risk that the product will not perform as expected is only one risk of concern to the producer. New technologies often change the distribution of production outcomes. While average output per unit of input may increase, the new technology may have a wider dispersion in possible yields. Adoption will depend on producers' attitudes towards risk and willingness to accept the possibility of lower yields in return for the possibility of higher ones.

Farmers are also concerned with the health risk and financial risk through liability for externalities created by use of biotechnologically derived products. Although this will be of little concern for many biotechnologically derived products, such as vaccines or animal growth hormones, it is a very real concern for products designed for free release into the environment such as genetically engineered microbial agents (hereafter referred to as GEMs) and plants designed for pest resistance through the incorporation of toxin-producing genes from other organisms (Fleisher, 1989). There are concerns about the ability of microorganisms to multiply and spread into other environments and exchange genetic information with other related microorganisms. Subtle changes in host range or virulence could have deleterious ecological, property, and human health effects (Betz et al., 1983: 137).

The financial risk presented by the probability of suit from unexpected adverse effects of genetically engineered products will depend in part on how courts treat the damages that may be caused. The appropriate theory for examination of biotechnology in tort actions is the subject of heated debate in the legal profession (Fleisher, 1989). The legal uncertainty surrounding suit over biotechnology products arises in part from the conscious substitution of a pioneering technology of production for a well-understood conventional alternative technology. If recombinant DNA is the only possible means of manufacture of a product, then the producer or user is less likely to be held liable if damages occur (consider, for example, the development of a new vaccine). But if it is simply more economical, the producer or user is likely to be held liable. The type of suit brought and individual state court decisions will determine whether the end user, the agricultural producer, can shift liability back to the manufacturer of the product (Fleisher, 1989).

Although regulatory approval of a product is not a defense in tort actions for pesticides, the level of safety required before a product is approved for commercial release will affect the likelihood of tort actions. The stricter the regulatory standard imposed, the less likely it is that producers will be faced with suits. However, even a strict regime for regulatory approval does not completely protect producers from suits and state courts may set different standards for what is an appropriate level of due care in negligence actions or what they deem to be abnormally dangerous products under strict liability. Neither a "utility greater than risk" or de minimus standard provides consequent insurance against suit for the agricultural producer because, at this point, biotechnologically derived products will serve, in large part, as substitutes for existing products rather than a new function. A regulatory standard that would promulgate less risk for the farmer is one based on relative risk—approval of the products of biotechnology only if they are deemed to be less risky than the products for which they may serve as substitutes. However, at this point EPA procedures emphasize a product by product standard of acceptable risk, rather than a comparison among products. Furthermore, there is little evidence that regulators and the courts view expected outcomes and unexpected adverse effects in the same way (Fleisher, 1989).

In summary, uneven adoption of new technologies among farmers producing any one commodity is likely. Characteristics and pricing of products, combined with firms' current production practices, inventory of fixed assets, financial position, and decisionmakers' attitude towards risk, are likely to lead to varying degrees of adoption.

Consumer Benefits from Biotechnology

The benefits accruing to consumers from the introduction of biotechnologically derived products in agriculture will follow directly from the structure of the agricultural biotechnology input industry, the products developed, the prices charged for those products, and agricultural producers' adoption of the new technology. Because agricultural producers are price takers rather than price setters, any increase in production or reduction in the cost of production from the adoption of biotechnologically derived products is likely to result in lower commodity prices rather than increased profits for farmers over the long run.

The degree to which consumers will see reduced food costs depends, in large part, on the extent that agricultural biotechnology input firms are able to capture the economic gains of product adoption and use. If the input industry is able to price biotechnologically derived products at or near the price of inputs for which they substitute (and the prices of these products do not drop), agricultural production would not likely increase dramatically, and the prices of agricultural products would remain stable. But although biotechnology firms may have monopoly rights over biotechnologically derived products for a particular market segment, several forces will act to reduce the proportion of productivity increases that they can capture, including the cost advantage that must be offered to induce farmers to change their existing production practices, reactive price competition from conventional input manufacturers, and the rapid pace of development of the new technology where product life is limited by introduction of new processes and products. Therefore, like most technological advances in agriculture in the past, the introduction of biotechnologically derived products into agriculture is likely to result in lower costs to the consumer.

Conclusion

The pricing of biotechnologically derived products for agriculture will be a key determinant of the distribution of benefits among input manufacturers, agricultural producers, and consumers. The price of products from the biotechnology industry will be determined by the structure of the industry, the breadth of patent protection offered, and pricing of substitute inputs for agricultural production. Monopoly pricing opportunities garnered through patent protection will slow diffusion of biotechnologically derived products and limit the output response that accompanies the introduction of new technologies in agriculture. The output response to new biotechnologically derived products will increase as patent protection expires, first-generation biotechnology products are made obsolete by new and better products, or traditional input manufacturers engage in protective price cutting to maintain their markets. Although more rapid diffusion would benefit farmers and consumers, without the promise of profits from patent protection the private sector would have little incentive to invest in research and development and incur the costs of regulatory approval that are necessary to commercialize biotechnologically derived products.

Many of the factors that will affect the development of agricultural biotechnology and the distribution of benefits from the new technology have themselves been the subject of debate over the past decade. Patentability, environmental, health, and safety regulation, and liability and insurability have grown in importance in many sectors of the economy, including agriculture. Their emergence and confluence in the discussion of biotechnology reflects increasing awareness of the influence of law on technology and technology on society, and increasing pressure for anticipatory rather than reactive management of effects.

8

Regulating Genetically Engineered Organisms: The Case of the Dairy Industry

*Richard Sherlock and
Amal Kawar*

In the second decade of developments in biotechnology, policy regarding human consumption of genetically engineered organisms (GEOs) is just emerging. Questions of safety and standards for biotechnology policy have been extensively addressed in the earlier debates of the 1970s and 1980s over what hazards the new organisms might pose to researchers, neighboring communities, or the environment if they were accidentally released. The laboratory safety questions were debated in the Recombinant DNA Advisory Committee of the National Institutes of Health (NIH) and in Congress, and culminated in the 1976 NIH guidelines. The NIH policy established a hierarchy of risks for recombinant DNA and set standards for biological and physical containment for the different categories of experiments, presupposing that skilled laboratory personnel voluntarily chose to assume whatever risks remained (Krimsky, 1982). In the ensuing decade and a half, the guidelines have been continually revised as more evidence has surfaced. More recently, the safety of deliberate release into the environment engendered substantial concerns on the part of environmental activists, lengthy review by the Environmental Protection Agency (EPA), and the resulting acrimonious public debate and numerous court cases (Kawar and Sherlock, 1989).

In anticipation of the use of recombinant DNA techniques by the food-processing industry, concern is being voiced that the Food and Drug Administration (FDA) has not made clear how it will regulate such products. Among recombinant DNA researchers, there is a fear that the FDA may deviate from science-based policy and succumb to social and economic concerns raised by critics of genetic engineering (Sandine, 1987; Chassey, 1987).

In this chapter we examine the concerns of the research community and begin the serious discussion of the policy issues raised by the use of genetically engineered organisms in food processing and production. We review two distinct approaches in which the policymaking debate can be framed: the market model and the social regulation model. We review the assumptions and methods underlying these models and discuss the policies that would follow from each. Finally, we examine what we believe is the most likely policy outcome. But first, a very brief review of the state of the scientific research and the potential applications of genetic engineering in the food industry that would have initial impact on dairy and fermentation processes is provided. This review is centered on the likely early applications, mainly in the dairy industry, that will pose the first regulatory issues and establish precedents which will almost surely be applied to more distant cases.

In general, we intend to show that the use of genetically engineered organisms, especially in the dairy industry, presents a sliding scale of issues and cases, not all of which ought to be of regulatory concern. At the most innocuous end of the scale are those cases where compounds already being employed are produced more efficiently through recombinant DNA technology. Since human exposure does not change at all, issues of regulatory concern may be minimal. At the other extreme will be cases where human consumers will be exposed to entirely new bacterial organisms developed from recombinant DNA technology. These cases will pose serious issues for regulatory agencies: just as new food additives have always done.

Current State of Genetic Engineering Research and Development in the Dairy Industry

The most immediately promising use of genetic engineering in the food industry is in those processes that require bacterial action such as fermentation to make the end product. Because of the potential market, the dairy industry has been foremost in pushing research in the potential use of "designer bacteria" to produce cheese and yogurt. If specific organisms can be created that perform the required processes more efficiently, cost savings could be substantial and product quality and taste could be improved.

Lactic acid bacteria represent a group of microorganisms which have been used for centuries for the production of fermented foods such as cheese, yogurt, buttermilk, fermented sausage, olives, pickles, and sauerkraut. In the dairy industry, it is common to add high numbers of specific species of lactic acid bacteria to initiate and carry out the fermentation process rather than relying on the indigenous microflora of the raw substrate. The added bacteria are thus called "starter cultures." During the fermentation process, the starter cultures must perform efficiently and predictably. However, since the 1930s, important functions of these bacteria which allow their growth in milk have been observed to be unstable, causing variability in product quality and safety. Starter strains are also sensitive to bacterial viruses or bacteriophages. Bacteriophages may attack sensitive starter strains and essentially stop their growth. This has been a major problem to the dairy industry resulting in severe economic losses (Huggins, 1984). With the appearance of large, mechanized manufacturing plants with increased production schedules, there is enormous stress on the starter cultures to perform efficiently. Therefore, there has been a need to isolate new and improved strains which are stable and can grow rapidly in milk. The development of improved strains will make fermentation processes more economically efficient for the producer. This can be passed on to the consumer in the form of cost-savings and products which are higher in quality.

Basically, there are two strategies to provide new and improved strains for the dairy industry. The first is the isolation of strains from their natural habitat, which is green plant material or milk. This strategy has been largely unsuccessful since the new isolates grow slowly in milk or they produce undesirable effects in the final product. The second is the genetic manipulation of preexisting strains. This includes isolation of mutants, the transfer of desirable genes among starter strains, and the use of recombinant DNA technology (Kondo and McKay, 1985). Isolation of improved strains through mutagenesis has been used extensively in classical strain improvement programs. This strategy has been applied successfully in developing mutants which are insensitive to bacteriophages.

The use of recombinant DNA technology to develop improved starter cultures for use in milk fermentations has not yet been successful, but several research groups are nearing this goal. Recombinant DNA technology will allow the specific modification of genes and gene products to improve the performance of starter cultures. Of primary importance is the development of resistance to bacteriophages—viruses which attack bacteria. Since starter cultures have various mechanisms to resist bacteriophage infection, use of genetic techniques (gene transfer and splicing) to specifically increase the number of mechanisms each starter strain possesses would be significant (Klaenhammer, 1987).

Much research has been centered on developing strains which will accelerate flavor development and cheese ripening. Another major area is to develop strains which produce inhibitory compounds against spoilage and pathogenic organisms. Of importance is the production of nisin, a compound produced by *Streptococcus lactis*, a common cheese starter culture. Nisin has recently been approved for food use as a preservative in processed cheese (FDA, 1988). Therefore, genetically engineered strains which will produce large quantities of nisin will be needed (Sandine, 1987).

The application of new genetic technology, combined with classical strain improvement programs, provides a vast potential to improve microorganisms that are beneficial to society (Chassey, 1987; de Vos, 1986). However, the federal regulations for approval and use of these organisms are not clear and will depend on the various levels of genetic manipulation and on the sources and types of genes involved. It is very important that proper precautions are taken to ensure the safety of the food supply, but equally important is that federal regulations do not deter innovation and improvement.

Policy Models of Biotechnology Regulation

There are two approaches to the regulatory review of biotechnological developments as they impact food processing and consumption. The first is a market approach that enhances consumer freedom and minimizes government regulation by permitting the use of additives without substantial regulatory review except to require that consumers know what they are purchasing through adequate labeling. The second is a regulatory approach that enhances safety at the expense of consumer freedom by requiring evidence of the safety of products as a prior condition to marketing. Each of these approaches has a substantial body of theoretical work advanced in its behalf and recent examples of its operation.

Market Model

Market approaches to questions of food additives in general presuppose the superiority of individual choice to decisions made for individuals by regulatory agencies, bureaucrats, or courts. Market mechanisms provide a context in which demands can be satisfied by agents who make their own estimates of what they are willing to spend on various goods and services. There is no "right" set of choices; each agent will make his or her own estimate of whether to purchase cheaper food items made with and possibly containing genetically engineered organisms (Lee, 1983). This would presumably be similar to the manner in which some consumers are currently willing to spend more for organically grown vegetables, food packaged without preservatives, or coffee ground in the store. Some consumers believe that preservatives and possible residues of agricultural chemicals are not worth the risk. Other consumers find that cheaper, mass-produced food is sufficient for their needs and would rather spend the savings in other ways. Thus, market models place a premium on that minimum of legal regulation necessary to insure that the individual possesses the necessary information on the basis of which to make rational choices. Freedom and full disclosure are the fundamental values to be furthered by legal and regulatory actions in a market model (Mill, 1912; Lee, 1983; Wildavsky, 1987).

However, the requirement for disclosure need not be enforced by the federal government. If the experience with health food is a guide, it will very likely be the case that market forces themselves will generate substantial incentives for companies to label products that do not contain genetically engineered organisms. Products that contain no added salt or none of the commonly used preservatives are typically clearly marked as such because producers have found that many health-conscious consumers will purchase only such products. Thus, market incentives, in some cases, may exist for proper labeling (Posner, 1979). Market demands for safety testing of products may also generate alternatives to government regulation, such as private testing and certification by organizations like Consumers Union and Underwriters Laboratories. However, available evidence suggests that market incentives may not insure adequate labeling that enhances the freedom of consumers to know the nature of products. It may be necessary, at a minimum, to require proper labeling of food additives, including genetically engineered organisms. This would not mean warning labels unless liability concerns would generate an incentive for private producers to add such a warning. A simple statement of product content would suffice.

Even in the case of food additives, where the FDA typically tries to insure the safety of all additives, there are recent examples of the market model at work (Hunter, 1975). Of these, the most significant is certainly the case of saccharin, which came to a head in 1977. Saccharin has been used as a synthetic sweetener since the early 1900s in various canned foods and, since the 1920s, by diabetics who must reduce their intake of sugar. More recently it had been used extensively by the soft drink industry. For diabetics and dieters, the situation had been regarded as critical after the 1969 FDA ban on the use of cyclamates, a widely used artificial sweetener. The ban was based on evidence that cyclamate caused cancer when given in large doses to laboratory animals (Merrill and Taylor, 1985).

The FDA action in the case of cyclamates was mandated by the 1958 amendments to the Food, Drug, and Cosmetic Act. Popularly known as the Delaney Amendment, its essential requirement was that the FDA must ban the use of any food additive that is known to cause cancer in animals. The amendment permitted no balancing test among various cost-benefit factors (for example, cancer risk versus treatment for diabetics, especially children, who face strong pressures for consumption of sweet drinks). Nor did it permit any assessment of the particular animal experiment and its potential for extrapolation to human beings (Merrill and Hutt, 1980). During the early to mid-1970s, a modest body of evidence was accumulated in both the United States and Canada that saccharin caused cancer in laboratory rats (National Academy of Sciences, 1970; National Academy of Sciences, 1974; Merrill and Taylor, 1985). Pressure from powerful congressional sources and a rebuke by the General Accounting Office, combined with a desire for a coordinated action with Canada (which was preparing to ban saccharin on its own), led the FDA to feel compelled to act once data from Canadian researchers appeared to confirm the fact that saccharin causes cancer in mice (*Federal Register*, 1977: 19996; *H.E.W. News*, 1977: 1-6).

The FDA immediately caught a firestorm of reaction. Unlike actions banning obscure agricultural or industrial chemicals or drugs used by only a few individuals, the saccharin ban was widely criticized by more than the typical industry groups. Of particular importance were diabetics who saw their last sweetener threatened and the millions of Americans who believed, rightly or wrongly, that consumption of diet soda was an effective means of weight loss or control (Burros, 1977; Shales, 1977). These interests, along with a well-financed industry campaign, effectively petitioned Congress to change the rule just for saccharin. Instead of banning the substance, Congress opted for simply a warning on products containing saccharin. For harassed legislators, the warning label approach appeared as a very useful compromise between industry and some consumers who wanted unrestricted access and the FDA, health, and environmental groups who wanted to ban saccharin completely (*Federal Register*, 1977: 19996).

The resolution of the saccharin issue is a classic market model solution. As long as consumers are given adequate information about the products they purchase or consume, they are free to assume whatever increased risks might be present in light of other goals, for example weight loss or diabetic control, which may be more significant to them. Market models are widely employed in regulating access to potentially risky products, services, and activities. In the case of foods, food additives, and drugs, however, the market model is not reflected in existing law and policy except in unusual circumstances such as those that generated the saccharin policy. Broadly, two types of arguments are alleged to provide a rationale for nonmarket regulatory activities by the FDA (Kelman, 1983; Johnson, 1986; Halloran, 1986).

The first and possibly most plausible argument is the claim of consumer ignorance. It is one thing to say that adults in our society are well aware of the risks of alcohol consumption. Even those who do not consume alcohol almost surely have friends that do, have been at social affairs involving alcohol use, or have read about the effects of consumption. It is quite another matter to ask consumers to evaluate the potential risks of particular food additives or complicated pharmaceuticals. Even a minimum assessment of the risks of food additives will require sophisticated physiological and biochemical knowledge that is beyond the reach of all but a very few consumers. Without such knowledge, consumers cannot be in the position of the rational agent contemplated by market economics. If one cannot properly assess risk, one cannot then make individual trade-offs of price, risk, comfort, convenience, and other factors that the liberty provided by the market fosters (Johnson, 1986).

This line of argument in support of FDA regulatory activity is most easily made in the context of those products used by consumers who are without doubt wholly constrained in their use of the product. Children and the illiterate are classes of individuals that come readily to mind.

It is urged that all consumers, however, bear other significant constraints in their purchase of food. To begin with, poor consumers or those with tight family budgets may find themselves constrained to purchase the cheapest available food simply in order to obtain sufficient bulk to avoid hunger for themselves or their families. Even those who are not financially constrained to purchase lowest-cost foods may have psychological and opportunity costs of checking for the safety certification or reading the label on the product. It may simply be too time-consuming and stressful for consumers to insure the safety of their own food. Rational consumers may very well conclude that a program of strict safety regulation imposed by government works best.

Social Regulation Model

A regulatory approach that is deeply embedded in current law and FDA policy is based on an entirely different set of assumptions than those that guide the market model. The strict regulatory activities of the FDA, with respect to the safety of food, presuppose that: (1) consumers do not possess the required knowledge to make safety and health risk judgments for themselves; (2) consumers face significant constraints, both financial and psychological, in food purchasing decisions; and (3) there are no countervailing claims or special cases in which risk substances should be allowed, unlike the case of drugs, and no gate-keepers such as doctors and pharmacists to control access to those few special cases (Kelman, 1983). What these assumptions mean is that current policy is consciously biased in favor of insuring the maximum safety of food and food additives. In assessing the safety of food additives, the FDA does not typically use either cost-benefit analysis or the *de minimus* risk test. In other regulatory matters it does use these tests. In cases such as chemotherapy, cost-benefit analysis permits the use of a known toxic substance, and in cases involving animal drugs, a *de minimus* risk test is used. In the case of food, however, the prevailing standard is that safety must be assured even if a typically untrained consumer consumed large quantities in a relatively short period of time (Hunter, 1975; Kelman, 1983).

One useful example of the stringency of the FDA's typical response to drug and food additive regulation is the decade and a half of discussion about permitting the injectable contraceptive DEPO-PROVERA to be marketed in the United States (U.S. Congress. House, 1978; Green, 1986). Used as an intramuscular injection, it provides up to 90 days of contraceptive protection between injections. For this reason it has been widely used, especially in countries where limitations on the availability of health services make its long-acting feature a decided advantage. Data from studies in over 100 countries show little adverse health effects except for some irregularities in menstrual bleeding. There is no evidence from studies of human use of an increased risk of cancer or other lethal diseases (Gold and Wilson, 1981; Rosenfeld, 1983). However, the FDA continues to prohibit the marketing of DEPO-PROVERA in the United States. The rationale is that some data exist showing that consumption of high levels of DEPO-PROVERA might cause cancer in laboratory animals. Thus, on the basis of its obligation under the Delaney Amendment, the FDA prohibits its use. Though repeatedly petitioned to change its mind, the FDA has shown no indication that it is prepared to do so. And it steadfastly refuses to consider cost-benefit factors in evaluating whether or not DEPO-PROVERA should be available as a contraceptive for women to use in this country (*Federal Register*, 1979, 1983).

It should be noted here that even the well-established exception to pre-use testing for food additives classified as "generally recognized as safe" (GRAS) is still a regulatory, not a market, policy. Substances classified as GRAS are not free from scrutiny. It is simply the case that, like many traditional herbs, spices, and colorings, they have been used for decades or even centuries with no evidence of harm. The GRAS classification permits their continued use, but only if there continues to be no evidence of any harm. They are not exempted from such requirements as the Delaney Amendment (as saccharin was); they are simply judged to have already passed typical pre-use testing requirements by virtue of their long period of safe use.

These two very different arguments are offered in support of the regulatory stringency of FDA policy regarding food additives and most drugs. The first argument trades on the existence of supposed special classes of consumers, for example children and illiterates, for whom supposedly any labeling strategy consistent with the market model would be inadequate (Halloran, 1986; Shue, 1986). These classes of consumers cannot make use of market mechanisms to protect themselves in ways consistent with their own desires. Therefore, it is argued that another mechanism will be necessary to protect such persons from the unreasonable risk of food additives.

Though this argument has a certain plausibility, it is relevant only to a minority of consumers. A second argument with much broader reach is based on the psychological and opportunity costs incurred by consumers trying to employ labeling or certification policies. It is argued that these costs will be so high that rational consumers will prefer to cede the responsibility for food safety to a government agency that will simply insure that all food additives are safe without question. Given unavoidable limitations in time and knowledge, the consumer might very well prefer to have the government insure that all food is safe. It is further argued that this approach may very well improve the overall efficiency of the economic system since productive consumers can spend their energies doing whatever it is they do best and not having to spend time studying food labels, consumer literature, and scientific articles (Kelman, 1983).

Discussion

We have identified two broad policy approaches that might be utilized in the case of genetically engineered organisms in food: a market model that supposedly enhances freedom and a regulatory model that supposedly enhances consumer safety. Which of these policy approaches is finally utilized in the case of genetically engineered organisms in the human food chain will be answered by a combination of scientific and political considerations, including the state and nature of scientific data, the nature of the interest groups involved, the strength of their concerns, and the public visibility and concern surrounding the issue. We believe that a market approach to this issue is both preferable on scientific grounds and likely to result from the current state of policy discussion.

The use of genetically engineered organisms in food processing presents a sliding scale of regulatory issues, from the most innocuous to the most complex. Policy formulation will vary depending on the case being addressed. Based on current scientific advances, we can envision the following sorts of cases for regulatory review in the near future. At one end of the spectrum is the use of engineered organisms to produce other, already employed compounds, such as nisin, more efficiently. The second case may be the use of a variety of techniques to produce, more efficiently, bacteria that are already produced in other ways. The bacteria themselves are already in use and being consumed by end users of food products; only a method of producing the organisms is being proposed. The third category will be cases where existing bacteria will be altered by gene transfer or deletion methods to perform processing or flavoring functions more efficiently. The fourth category of cases will be those where recombinant techniques will be employed to produce new organisms for use in the food industry. Typically the rationale will be enhanced efficiency of production or altered sweetness or flavor of the product.

Of these cases, those in categories one and two are easily disposed of. In the first category, no issues of human consumption are involved and we need not treat them here, except to note that issues of worker health and safety may still be relevant. In the second category, it seems clear to us that if the organisms to which consumers will be exposed are exactly the same as those to which they have been exposed for decades and even centuries, without any adverse effects, then the GRAS exception is clearly appropriate. In fact, this is precisely the case for which the GRAS exception was created and we can see no reason to be concerned with the method of production if the end product meets the GRAS test.

This conclusion is true only if the level of exposure remains the same in genetically engineered cheese and yogurt. For example, in the case of deliberate release of non-ice nucleating pseudomonous syringae into the agricultural environment, a serious concern was the potential to upset the ecological balance by introducing more non-ice nucleating organisms than usual. If these sorts of concerns were relevant to human exposure, a different regulatory problem might be posed. This is consistent with the position taken in the "Coordinated Framework" to classify hazards by product but not by the technique by which the product is produced (*Federal Register*, 1985, 1986).

Cases three and four do pose important issues of regulatory policy. In our view, a market policy is the preferable means of enhancing desirable policy objectives and is most consistent with the available scientific data. We note that this strategy maximizes consumer freedom and enhances technological development by ensuring a faster process of bringing to market the results of technological development. Moreover, the arguments which might be brought in favor of strict regulation do not apply nearly as well in the case of genetically engineered organisms in the human food chain as these same concerns might apply in other biotechnology policy areas.

Chiefly, two concerns seem to be relevant and prominent in the literature (see, for example, Fiskel and Covello, 1986). The first is contamination of the environment. The second is specific harm to uninvolved third parties. Neither of these concerns is relevant at this point, provided adequate information is made available to the consumers. Three points may be made in this regard. First, no consumer needs to be an innocent victim. Those who wish to consume may do so; those who do not, need not do so. Second, we note that genetic engineering will only affect a small spectrum of the food industry. Even if every product in that spectrum came to be produced with and contain genetically engineered material, any consumer could still obtain a perfectly adequate and even lush diet. Third, we note that compromised consumers (for example, children) will have their choices made or heavily controlled by other consumers who are presumably capable of making the necessary safety and health choices for them, just as they currently do in hundreds of individual instances. We see no reason to treat this issue any differently.

Although earlier (Kawar and Sherlock, 1989) we argued for strict regulation in the case of deliberate release of genetically engineered organisms into the environment, we do not believe that regulation beyond the long-standing requirement that anything which is added to food should be properly identified on the label is necessary. Each set of policy issues must be treated on its own merits. In the instant set of cases we believe that a market approach to food additives best serves the twin goals of personal liberty and technological growth and that no countervailing concerns can outweigh this modest form of technological growth in the food industry.

Our view of labeling is also based on the belief that there is simply no way for the dairy industry to avoid labeling of products with GEOs, especially in case four. This is so for two reasons. First, the industry is unlikely to find any incentives to develop new organisms unless the organism can be patented and owned by the developing company. To patent, however, it must be shown that the organism does not occur in nature. If so, then it clearly could not escape classification as a new, nonnatural substance added product. Thus, in the case of GEOs we see no way that the industry could avoid the legal requirement of labeling food additives.

Products under case three might escape the legal requirement of labeling if the resulting bacteria have not been altered enough to be classified as a new artificial (and therefore owned) organism. If not, then these might be seen generally in the same light as cases one and two. However, we note that in this case the same result as labeling may be generated by the market itself. If the example of pesticides is any indication, a number of consumers are willing to pay more for fruits and vegetables grown without pesticides or chemicals. Given the uneasiness of a segment of the public with genetic engineering, there will very likely be a strong incentive to market dairy products touted as "free from GEOs." This surely would produce much the same result as labeling regulation that is currently utilized. In whatever fashion, whether by legal requirement or market incentives, we think that it is almost certain that knowledge of which products contain GEOs, in either case three or four, will be readily available to concerned consumers.

We also believe that the market approach will result from the inactivity of opposition interest groups on this issue. The analysis above, utilizing the research on lactic acid bacteria, suggests that it is unlikely that a controversy will erupt because the use of recombinant DNA techniques is likely to be on familiar organisms that are generally perceived as safe and have been in use in the dairy industry. Since potential products are still in the embryonic stage, the question regarding genetic engineering in processed foods is whether the issue will be created at all. Preliminary interviews by phone with personnel of several interest groups suggests that strong opposition is not in the making. The Consumer Federation of America's only concern is the potential depletion of genetic variety (personal communication, July 24, 1988). The AFL-CIO's attention has mainly turned to worker safety and they have adopted a wait-and-see attitude (Dennis Chamot, personal communication, May 3, 1988). Even the opposition of Jeremy Rifkin's Foundation on Economic Trends (FET) may not be vehement in the area of processed food, since their strategy has been to target issues that have the potential of gathering support around safety, economic, and morality issues (FET 1988; Robyn Rhymes, personal communication, May 2, 1988).

The allocation of resources by the critics is also dependent on what other environmental and biological concerns are placed on the public agenda. Given current activities of such groups as FET and the Committee for Responsible Genetics, by the time the processed-food industry commercializes the first of these products, attention may increasingly be diverted to more pressing national issues such as acid rain, ozone depletion, toxic waste, and biological warfare.

Critics like Rifkin have so far been unable to spark a national movement against genetic engineering, although the public is inclined toward some sort of governmental regulation. The Novo report, an opinion survey sponsored by the Danish Novo Industri A/S, a major manufacturer of insulin, found that nearly 40 percent of the public has never heard of genetic engineering, but that 70 percent of those interviewed said that it should be regulated. The vast majority, however, said that they did not understand the moral and ethical issues to be able to say how it should be regulated (John and Henig, 1988). A recent survey of public perceptions, commissioned by the Office of Technology Assessment (OTA), indicates a heightened awareness of, but an ambiguous stance about, products of genetic engineering. A majority of the nation generally supports the technology, believing that there will be risks incurred, but that the benefits outweigh the costs. Its support, however, varies by product and could change if a major accident happens (OTA, 1987a).

Features of the use of recombinant DNA technology in food additives make the industry less vulnerable to politicization than in such cases as the unavailability of saccharin, genetic engineering of animals, or the testing of germ uses in warfare. Unlike saccharin, the benefits of recombinant DNA technology would primarily be to the manufacturer in the reduction of processing costs. It is also difficult to see how fermentation bacteria, invisible to the eye, could invoke the kind of concern over dignity of life that animal patenting has. However, in the context of environmental release, bacteria has invoked concern over risks.

The OTA survey found that a larger percentage of the public (29 percent) thought that environmental risk is "very likely" from genetically altered bacteria than those (13 percent) who thought so of genetically altered plants and animals. We maintain that the only way the public is likely to develop concern over consumption of genetically altered bacteria is in the remote scenario that it poses risks to health.

The above analysis suggests that it is unlikely that a well-organized constituency, with strong economic or social interests, will develop in support of more stringent regulation in this area. Of course, conflict over technologies may erupt over the non-risk and the value aspects (Winterfeldt and Edwards, 1984). We suggest that, barring the remote possibility of biological catastrophe, processed food using the recombinant DNA techniques falls into the category of risks that invoke little conflict over values, typical of risks incurred in other consumed products (see Johansen and Steinberg, 1986).

Conclusion

Within the next three to five years, scientists in the dairy industry will be ready to begin using specific genetically engineered organisms in the production of cheese and possibly yogurt. Many of these same scientists are now raising questions about the acceptability of doing so and about the sorts of policy decisions that will determine whether they will be allowed to do so. In this chapter, we have argued that a market-based policy concentrating on requiring truthful labeling of products containing genetically engineered organisms is preferable on scientific grounds and will likely result from the way this issue is being addressed by the policy process to date.

The potential uses of genetically engineered microorganisms are so varied and the issues so complex that each issue must be evaluated as a distinct policy question. One important and emerging application is the use of new genetic technologies in the dairy industry (though applications to other areas of food processing are likely to follow). This chapter has reviewed two very different policy approaches to the issues presented by these scientific developments and their attendant assumptions and implications. We conclude that a policy that maximizes consumer freedom is both a preferred policy choice and the one most likely to result from the current policymaking matrix in Washington. First, once the troubling cases of consumer exposure are carefully sorted out and examined, it seems clear that none of the usual reasons offered for more severe pre-use safety testing apply very well to these cases. Second, it appears that none of the groups that usually fight the introduction of genetic engineering and its products are, at this point, concerned about the use of genetic engineering in food processing. In the absence of compelling reasons or strong political forces opposing such development, we think it likely for industry to be able to proceed with the development and use of new technologies with only minimal regulations, chiefly those having to do with proper labeling of products. Ours is only one first step in trying to analyze the policy issues associated with this new technology. We think further analysis is both necessary and desirable, and we encourage other scholars in a variety of disciplines to join us in this task.

Note

The authors would like to thank Jeffrey Kondo of the Department of Nutrition and Food Sciences at Utah State University for his assistance in writing the scientific and technical aspects of this chapter.

9

Regulatory Experience with Food Safety: Social Choice Implications for Recombinant DNA-Derived Animal Growth Hormones

Fred Kuchler,
John McClelland, and
Susan E. Offutt

The potential introduction of recombinant DNA-derived growth hormones for use in milk and meat production raises an important question about food safety: will the material adulterate otherwise safe and nutritious products? If government regulators, the scientific community, or consumers consider the technology to be unsafe, either commercial sale will not be allowed or, once introduced, the product will not survive in the marketplace. Predicting how each of these groups will assess the risks and benefits of the new technology is difficult because the definition of food safety has varied with time and product; the standards applied in making a judgment about product safety depend on opinion as much as scientific fact.

This chapter outlines possible consequences of attempts to commercialize developments in recombinant DNA (rDNA)-derived livestock growth hormones. We argue that interest groups and the unique regulatory treatment of animal drugs will influence whether the drugs are ultimately judged safe. After reviewing the use of hormones in livestock production, and the impact of biotechnology, we examine three historical cases in which livestock and dairy production practices raised questions about food safety. These cases are the early 1900s controversy over the use of pasteurization in milk processing; the 1970s debate over the use of DES in beef production; and the 1982 discovery of the pesticide heptachlor in Hawaiian milk, requiring intervention by public health officials. The discussion of historical regulatory problems highlights the ways interest groups have behaved, reveals the importance of public opinion towards food safety issues, and shows that the definition of safety can change over time, thereby affecting livestock and dairy production and marketing. The debate over the desirability of pasteurization pitted consumers against the scientific community. Illegal treatment of beef cattle with diethylstilbestrol (DES) to promote growth illustrates the difficulties in changing established production practices. Problems with heptachlor-contaminated milk on Oahu during 1982 points out the fragility of public trust in regulatory authorities. These experiences demonstrate the enduring and political nature of food safety and technological development controversies. The latter cases have shaped the current legal and regulatory environment and show the extent to which perceptions and the changing definition of product safety can influence product acceptance and ultimately the form of technological change. We conclude by arguing that safety is as much a matter of preferences and choices as it is science. Regulations and liability laws are two visible ways consumers have expressed preferences for particular guarantees of safety. Consumer unwillingness to purchase some products is a third method.

Biotechnology and Hormone Use in Livestock Production

Developments in the application of rDNA techniques promise change in products and production practices throughout agriculture (Office of Technology Assessment [OTA], 1986). The likely first commercial applications of rDNA technology will be in the manufacture of rDNA-derived animal growth hormones that are known to promote greater milk production in dairy cows and to allow meat animals to grow faster on less feed (Kalter et al., 1984: 3; Meltzer, 1987: 15-26). Production of these hormones can now be carried out on a large scale. For dairy production, bovine growth hormone (denoted bGH or bST) is currently under Food and Drug Administration (FDA) regulatory review. At least four corporations intend to manufacture bGH (Animal Health Institute, 1987: 1). For hogs, porcine growth hormone (pGH or pST) has demonstrated the most potential among the applications for increased meat production.

Hormones are organic compounds produced in the endocrine glands and carried through the vascular system to regulate several metabolic functions. Hormones regulate the rates of synthesis of proteins and fats, among other activities. For many years, farmers have administered manufactured substances to beef cattle that have effects on muscle accretion that are similar to the effects of natural hormones. With these substances, farmers control the flow of hormones through the vascular systems of their animals and improve the efficiency of feed conversion and growth rates. The manufactured hormones are so cost-effective that farmers administer them to nearly all beef cattle. Hormone use is considered a standard farm management practice. The hormone industry claims that gains in feed conversion and growth rates are so large relative to hormone costs that no farmer can afford to forego such treatments (Schell, 1984: 256). These practices are unlikely to change unless federal regulators find evidence that the manufactured substances are hazardous to consumers or unless many consumers decide that federal regulations are insufficient and refuse to purchase meat produced in this manner.

The rDNA-derived growth hormone differs from currently used hormones in several characteristics. Developed through genetic engineering, a nearly exact copy of the animals' own growth hormone is produced. Hence, the biological action of the growth hormone is thought to be identical to the natural hormone. Currently used hormones are less perfect copies of the hormones they are intended to mimic. Most of these compounds are steroids or sex hormones. They differ in the extent to which their biological action duplicates that of hormones naturally produced within animals' endocrine systems. Steroids are fat soluble, implying that residues could be carried through edible products into human tissues. Also, recent advances open up the possibility of hormone use in many types of livestock production that have not yet benefited from this production practice.

For these new products to be commercial successes, they must be putatively safe. Like any product of a new technology, consensus that a biotechnology-derived product is safe requires interested parties to agree that an acceptable level of knowledge (and ignorance) about the product has been developed and that acceptable hazard levels have been established. Human health problems associated with some hormones once used to promote animal growth are the setting for the debate on these new hormones. These antecedent problems could lead to unprecedented health and safety information demands on growth hormone manufacturers. The biotechnology basis for their manufacture could exacerbate those demands.

Argument over food safety predates the introduction of biotechnology. The terms of the debate change with time and product, and its substance may have more or less scientific content. Because technological change often makes some ways of doing things obsolete, financial gains accrue to adopters while losses are imposed on nonadopters. Sometimes safety issues are used to inflame debates, reducing their scientific content. Consensus may become impossible to attain, postponing losses for nonadopters. Varying assessments of risks and hazards also may make consensus difficult to reach. On such shifting foundations, consensus on food safety standards may be difficult to establish.

The initial applications of rDNA technology to agricultural production will set precedents for the amount of product information and time required by federal agencies to decide on safety before allowing commercial sale. Regulatory decisions will reveal whether the process by which the hormone is made is important or whether the hormone will be treated like other animal drugs and be judged on conventional human and animal health grounds: Is the hormone carcinogenic, acutely toxic, or disease-causing? If the process by which growth hormone is manufactured becomes important to regulatory decisions, then the additional demands placed on firms attempting to develop new input products for agriculture could reduce the incentive to do that research.

The livestock and dairy industry has received unique regulatory treatment, relative to all other components of the food industry. The Federal Food, Drug, and Cosmetic Act (FFDCA) contains several reasons for not allowing a new animal drug or food additive to be commercialized. The Food Additive Amendments of 1958 contained the first Delaney Clause, banning the use of carcinogenic substances that enter the food supply. The Delaney Clause pertaining to new animal drugs contains an exception, known as the DES exception (Council for Agricultural Science and Technology, 1977: 34-35; OTA, 1979: 2). This single exception was granted to allow the continued use of DES in animal feed, even though the substance had been shown to cause cancer in laboratory animals. The DES exception established a "no residue" criteria for use of animal drugs. Animal drugs, while regulated under some of the same legislation as food additives, are different in use and effect than food additives. Drugs are not added directly to consumable food products, but are an input in animal production. The question regulators have asked about animal drugs is whether residues remain in the meat and dairy products that consumers purchase. The DES exception can be interpreted to mean that regulations should preclude the use of a carcinogenic substance only if consumer exposure could be shown. That a substance was known to be hazardous under some circumstances was not, by itself, sufficient reason to preclude use.

There are three ways food products have been regulated (Marraro, 1982). Most food products fall under the Delaney Clause, which prohibits marketing products when there is any demonstrated risk of cancer. There is no balancing of risks and benefits when products fall under the jurisdiction of the Delaney Clause. Only cancer risks matter. Decisions to allow marketing food products with contaminants (for example, fungi on peanuts) have been made using cost-benefit comparisons, which consider trade-offs between consumer health risks (costs) and the sum of consumer benefits from having the product (even with its contaminants) and benefits to producers from product sales. *De minimus* risk standards are an intermediate method of regulation, allowing agencies limited flexibility in trading off costs and benefits of their decisions.

Animal drug regulation has employed *de minimus* risk standards. Any substance subject to Delaney Clause regulation faces inflexible risk standards. Any evidence, no matter how small, that a substance is carcinogenic is sufficient to preclude use. In contrast, animal drug regulations do not require regulatory agencies to make decisions on drug safety based on results from the most sensitive scientific methods capable of detecting drug residues in food. Instead, regulations require that drug residues produce no significant increase in human risk of cancer. This requirement is interpreted as no more than one cancer in one million lifetimes (Marraro, 1982: 224). The *de minimus* risk standards do not permit cost-benefit comparisons (as the Environmental Protection Agency may do with pesticides under the Federal Insecticide, Fungicide, and Rodenticide Act), but the standards do permit the decision calculus to be more flexible than does the all-or-nothing Delaney Clause criterion.

The unique regulatory treatment animal drugs receive affects the regulatory issues raised by growth hormones. The inability to distinguish natural hormone from the injected growth hormone in an animal carcass or meat product makes deciding which substances are residues a daunting regulatory problem. However, abnormally high levels of hormones resulting from a specific treatment could be considered a biological residue, requiring control measures (condemning the carcasses and edible tissues prepared from them) under current meat inspection laws (Jones, 1983: 282). Unlike DES and the currently used hormones, the growth hormone is a water-soluble protein and therefore should not last long in animals. Growth hormone should be especially fragile in the human digestive system if it were carried through meat or dairy products. Even if elevated growth hormone levels are defined to be residues to which consumers might be exposed, regulators must decide whether such exposure is hazardous.

How any hormone promotes growth and feed efficiency is not completely understood, but it is widely recognized that nutrients are diverted from the development of fat to milk or muscle tissue: nutrients are repartitioned. Re-partitioning agents may speed up the rate at which fat is degraded back to fatty acids and slow the rate at which nutrients flow to the adipose tissues, thereby slowing fat accretion. Thus, more muscle can be built from the same nutrient intake. Growth hormone, unlike other repartitioning agents, regulates many metabolic functions that regulate growth, including the rate of bone formation.

Growth hormone use in red meat production could be contentious because product quality could change. The reduction in meat lipid content (intra-muscular fat) could be of value to consumers concerned about reducing serum cholesterol levels. The medical science community could support the technology on this basis. Available evidence suggests that this benefit is not especially important to consumers. If consumers really value lean meat then meat from growth hormone-treated animals could command a premium in the marketplace. Currently, however, lean meat is graded lower and sells for less than more heavily marbled meat. Consumer reactions to hormone use for the production of meat products are likely to be negative, especially if consumers can easily recognize and differentiate meat products based on growth hormone treatments. A large reduction in fat could change the appearance and flavor of meat and could signal to consumers that the hormone was used. This change would be most noticeable for pork because hormones are not now part of pork production and potential productivity gains are considered larger than beef productivity gains. Labora-tory experiments indicate that growth hormone technology could extend use to sectors of the livestock industry that have not yet employed hormone therapy (for example, dairy, swine, and lamb production). Whether growth hormone could replace or complement sex hormones in beef production is not known.

Growth hormone experiments in pork production indicate up to 28 percent greater feed efficiency, 19 percent greater growth rates, 33 percent reductions in backfat, and a 20 percent larger loin eye. These changes reveal that growth hor-mone could reverse patterns in meat consumption. Poultry feed efficiency gains have led to poultry prices falling relative to red meat prices. Increased feed efficiency in poultry is due to conventional husbandry practices rather than growth hormone therapy. During the 1970s and 1980s, per capita consumption of red meats declined while poultry and fish increased, but total meat consumption changed less than one percent. Red meat consumption declined 7-8 percent, while poultry increased 39 percent. Greater red meat production and the concomitant lower prices could lead to larger red meat diet shares.

The growth hormone-induced productivity changes indicated by laboratory experiments are quite variable, but the largest observed changes imply that widespread adoption could significantly change agricultural commodity markets. The largest annual milk yield increases shown in experiments are 25-26 percent (Bauman et al., 1985). The first economic studies of the implications of widespread growth hormone adoption began appearing in the mid 1980s (Kalter et al., 1984).[1] At that time, government price supports had created Commodity Credit Corporation stocks (government ownership) that peaked at more than three billion pounds of dairy products (butter, cheese, and nonfat dry milk). Additional production represented additional government expenditures in a time in which government deficits were soaring.

Historical Cases

The regulatory environment in which livestock growth hormones are now being examined has characteristics that can be revealed by examining historical cases in which health and safety questions were raised over dairy and livestock production practices. The pasteurization debate shows that health and safety questions are an enduring part of technological development controversies. Health and safety issues are sometimes raised by those whose personal wealth would be reduced by technological developments, hoping to swell the ranks of technology opponents. The more recent controversies over DES and heptachlor show that scientific advance will continually raise health and safety questions.

The current controversy regarding bovine somatotropin (bST), or bovine growth hormone (bGH), is reminiscent of the debate among scientists, consumers, and milk producers over pasteurization at the turn of the century. By the end of the last century, the scientific community had recognized the importance of reducing disease-causing bacteria in milk to improve public health, particularly in the areas of infant mortality and tuberculosis. The scientific community was nearly unanimous in its advocacy of pasteurization. Pasteurization is now an accepted practice in milk processing and has been a legal requirement in most states for many years.

In the early 1900s, large-scale pasteurization spread rapidly through the industrialized areas in the eastern U.S., but the technology was resisted in the West by debate that pitted consumer groups, favoring raw milk, against large milk producers and public health professionals, advocating pasteurization (Fusonie, n.d.: 4). Consumer interests argued that pasteurization would adulterate an already safe, wholesome product and would allow milk producers to abandon existing sanitary practices. Smaller-scale milk producers supported this position partly because the economics of volume of the pasteurizing equipment would increase their average costs relative to the larger dairies. Larger dairy owners favored pasteurization because the technology gave milk greater shelf life and opened geographic markets (Fusonie, n.d.: 5-6).

Parallels between the bGH and the pasteurization controversy exist. Both conflicts contain arguments over scale economies and firm size likely to receive greatest advantage from the new technology (OTA, 1986: 190-202). Dairy farm organizations from areas where small-scale operations predominate have argued against bGH use, demanding information on changes in their number and size distribution (Annexstad, 1986: 22). Pasteurization also raised distributional issues. The smallest dairies could not adopt the new technology and many recognized that the new technology would provide a cost advantage to their largest competitors. Distributional questions were addressed in the pasteurization debates, but opponents refocused the discussion, leading to a long debate over product safety, even while raw milk continued to cause health problems. Similarly, in the case of bGH, legal actions by the Foundation on Economic Trends against the FDA have focused on the lack of information on health of bGH-treated dairy cows and environmental problems caused by the associated increased crop production (U.S. Department of Health and Human Services [USHHS], 1986: 3-5). But the FDA is legally bound to grant approval for limited use in the initial stages of the regulatory process based on product efficacy and safety, not on balancing benefits and costs. These legal actions are attempts to alter the decision rules under which regulatory approval can be granted and to expand the scope of issues to be debated over a new animal drug.

Both pasteurization and growth hormone use have the desirable characteristics of making milk production more efficient (bGH implies more milk per cow while pasteurization implies less spoilage). Both technologies have raised distributional issues through their potential for uneven allocation of benefits. In both cases, groups believing themselves disadvantaged have used their resources attempting to delay or prevent use of the new technology.

The more recent controversies over DES and heptachlor have shaped the regulatory environment by making dairy and meat product consumers sensitive to the health and safety consequences of changing farm production practices. Consumer sensitivity to health and safety questions is the result of scientific advance occurring in two directions. Scientific advance may make agricultural production more efficient, but it also may refine scientists' ability to causally link human health problems to agricultural production techniques. When new linkages are alleged, that sensitivity may be expressed through the demand for new regulatory actions. Scientific debate and recognition of uncertainty can reduce consumer belief that their interests are being protected. Heightened health and safety concerns also can be expressed through changes in the legal system. The

DES controversy was instrumental in initiating changes that made mass toxic tort litigation possible.

Scientific information may show growth hormone use to have no deleterious human health consequences. That does not mean human health issues are trivial. The history of DES use set the stage for discussing potential use of any new animal growth promotant. DES, a synthetic estrogen, was used as a growth promotant in beef cattle beginning in the 1950s. The substance was known to cause cancer in laboratory animals almost from its first production in 1938 (USHSS, 1984: 1). DES was also used by women to prevent miscarriage. Over the period 1947 to 1971, between 500,000 and 3,000,000 women are estimated to have taken DES (Epstein, 1980: 159).

Evidence first appearing in the 1970s indicated a causal link between DES use and a rare form of vaginal cancer in the daughters of women who used DES, demonstrating that DES is a human carcinogen. The Council for Agricultural Science and Technology argued that evidence of human cancers from medical treatments aroused the fear of cancer hazards from residues in meat derived from DES-treated animals.[2] The Delaney Clause would have eliminated DES use in animal production, but a "no residue" exception (the DES exception) inserted in the Animal Drug Amendments of 1968 allowed continued use in food animals. The FDA banned DES in feeds and animal implants on evidence of residues in beef livers, but the withdrawal was vacated in 1974 over disputes over testing methods (OTA, 1979: 21-22). The FDA had used a detection method that was more sensitive than those used previously. The implant ban was finally mandated by the FDA and sales of the animal drug were ordered to cease in July 1979. Use became illegal on November 1, 1979. DES manufacturers were unable to prove cancer risks were less than one in one million lifetimes. During 1980, widespread illegal use occurred among ranchers who felt that the ban was unreasonable meddling by the government in their affairs (Schell, 1984: 222-25). Over 500,000 cattle in more than 300 feedlots were illegally implanted with DES.

In the case of DES, regulation failed to prevent its unauthorized use. When enforcement of public health regulations is not thorough, consumers may be skeptical of information received from public health officials. The heptachlor contamination case shows that consumers initially trust and quickly react to particular types of information provided by public health officials. Statements that a potential health problem exists elicit rapid abandonment of some food products. Statements to the contrary do not cause the opposite reaction. The importance for livestock growth hormones of this type of behavior is that any scientific evidence linking human health problems with growth hormone use would quickly impede development.

Van Ravenswaay et al. (1986) explain both the positive and negative effects of publicity on milk consumption in Oahu following the discovery of heptachlor contamination. Heptachlor is an insecticide that was once widely used in the United States. A chlorinated hydrocarbon, it is in the same chemical family as chlordane and DDT. The Environmental Protection Agency cancelled registration for most agricultural uses of heptachlor in the 1970s because of its carcinogenicity, persistence, and ubiquity. In March 1982, 80 percent of the milk produced on Oahu was found to be contaminated with heptachlor. Heptachlor-treated pineapple plants had been sold for feed, and the heptachlor was passed through to milk. Immediately following discovery of the contamination, approximately 36 million pounds of milk were removed from the market. Public health officials assured the public that all remaining milk was uncontaminated, but milk sales were depressed for 16 months following the discovery, indicating that consumers did not completely accept the assurances of safety (Van Ravenswaay et al., 1986: 328). Media coverage, both positive and negative, had a negative impact on sales. The Federal Dairy Indemnification Program bought the contaminated milk for $8.5 million. Lost sales, after the contaminated milk was destroyed, were estimated to cost an additional $30,000 per producer.

FDA statements indicate that the agency believes milk produced in current bGH trials is safe for human consumption (Borcherding, 1987: 30). However, there are reasons why human health concerns might be raised when new pharmaceutical products to promote animal growth are introduced. Problems beyond the link between DES and cancer have been recognized. Poultry production involving hormone use (in other countries) has been linked to abnormal sexual development in children consuming poultry products (Schell, 1984: 279-94). The long-term human health consequences of consuming beef from animals treated with existing hormones are not yet fully understood. But the conventional technology is relatively well-documented compared to the new. So the human health issues of substituting growth hormone for the sex hormones in beef production are far from resolved.

Are Growth Hormones Safe?

At least two human health and safety issues are raised by the proposed use of growth hormones in livestock and dairy cows. The obvious question raised is whether meat and dairy products produced from animals treated with growth hormones will be safe for human consumption. This question can only be answered in part by scientific studies. No innovation has been adopted with all the possible ramifications for human health and well-being understood in advance. The expense of carrying out studies to answer safety questions, the inability of liability laws to offer complete consumer protection, and product developers' demands to end regulatory delay all lead to the introduction of new technologies prior to fully understanding all possible consequences.

To answer whether hormone use is safe, a more general issue must be resolved. A definition of safety is necessary before a judgment about safety can be made. The history of technological change in the dairy and livestock industries shows that safety has been a variable concept, changing over time and among various interest groups. One of the Delaney clauses in the Federal Food, Drug, and Cosmetic Act specifies that no residues of animal drugs or feed additives can be allowed in food products if the drugs or feed additives are carcinogens. Approved methods of analysis determining whether chemical and drug residues exist are mandated. Determining which methods are approved was problematic for DES regulation. The Council for Agricultural Science and Technology (CAST) argued that that provision codified into law the idea that the most sensitive testing methods available would be required. Consequently, as testing methods become more sensitive, some products once considered safe would no longer receive such approval. The ability to detect residues is claimed to have increased many orders of magnitude in recent years (Marraro, 1982: 225). Further, products could be deemed unsafe even if residues were below the threshold at which a substance might cause cancer. The more recent *de minimus* interpretation of risk means that the concerns CAST expressed are not now an issue for animal drugs. Regulatory agencies may use the most sophisticated residue measurement techniques available, but have some flexibility in setting standards. This flexibility in decisions for animal drugs, which does not exist for food additives (they have no exception to the Delaney Clause requirements), means that health and safety standards can vary over time because administrative preferences matter. Predicting whether the growth hormones will be judged safe is therefore equivalent to predicting the way scientific information will be strategically used and interpreted, possible misperceptions, how health and safety standards might change, and how scientific knowledge might advance. Safety is not an objectively definable and timeless concept.

There are obvious necessary, but not sufficient, conditions that growth hormone technology must fulfill before human health issues are resolved. At least three identifiable groups must agree that milk and meat from growth hormone treated animals are acceptably safe for growth hormones to be fully adopted. These groups include consumers, government regulators (FDA and USDA), and the scientific community.[3] Each group can unilaterally prevent a product from successful commercialization. If government regulators consider the technology to be unsafe, adoption will not be allowed. If consumers judge the technology unsafe, it will not survive in the marketplace. The scientific community can influence both consumers and regulators, but it should be noted that scientific studies demonstrating deleterious health consequences from consumption of a product gain more attention than the converse. Consensus requires that all the groups agree that the scientific evidence on the question of safety is reliable and unambiguous.

Optimal Social Choices

There are several ways health and safety decisions can be made. Empowering a government agency to make decisions for the entire population reduces the costs of decisionmaking for each individual and society as a whole (Buchanan and Tullock, 1962: 97-116). When government agencies make decisions, individuals do not have to become expert in animal physiology or biochemistry. However, government-mandated decisions imply some costs. In practice, such decisions usually either prohibit everyone from using a product or allow anyone to use a product, perhaps subject to a small number of restrictions. Individual and idiosyncratic needs may not be well met when all are treated alike.[4]

Regulations that prohibit the sale of products that might be hazardous to some portion of the population raise distributional questions by creating net benefits for some (reductions in decision costs along with protection from hazardous products) and costs to others (impossibility of acquiring desirable products). Regulations also raise efficiency questions through their potential to delay commercialization of all products, including those eventually judged safe. Any regulatory process will require time, thereby implying consumers will forego some benefits of innovations, possibly including enhanced safety or reduced production costs. The latter benefit could lead to reduced consumer prices and greater product availability.

Balancing the cost reductions promised by social rather than individual decisionmaking against costs imposed by regulations is not easy in a politically active environment. Individual economic incentives can compound the problem. Turning health and safety management over to a government agency and setting the standards of health and safety is a collective decision. High standards may offer protection to even the most risk-sensitive individuals, but those benefits come at a cost of reducing opportunities to those less sensitive. When the distribution of benefits from a new technology are not uniform and relatively large groups believe their interests are not served, additional collective action attempting to change decision procedures could be expected.

The major positive contribution health and safety regulations can offer is to protect some portion of the population from exposure to substances that might cause harm. The use of DES shows that advances in scientific knowledge and the discovery of new information imply that decisions made at one time may not be reasonable at a later time. Several types of information changed during the period in which DES was used in animal production. Findings that suggested animal health might be impaired with DES use became available. Human health concerns and development of more sensitive testing methods provoked scientific debate.

What Is and What Ought to Be

The rules by which society makes health and safety decisions can affect research and development. When regulatory agencies impose regulations on firms attempting to develop products, demanding additional information, agencies raise the cost of bringing products to market. When costs rise and benefits from commercialization remain unchanged, fewer new products ought to be expected and some benefits from enhanced production forgone. Regulations, setting minimum standards, are an attempt to define what levels of health and safety ought to be.

Other arms of government deal with what actually occurs. When the courts more liberally assess harm from products, product developers see the benefit stream expected from commercialization falling, while development costs remain unchanged. Again, government action changes the expected cost-benefit ratio from research and development.

Several changes in the legal system have the potential to influence commercialization of growth hormone. Mass toxic tort litigation has become almost common (Schuck, 1986: 26-34). These disputes first involved DES and asbestos, but now include Agent Orange, toxic shock syndrome, Dalkon Shield, and Love Canal, among others. The changing nature of product liability and the associated awards hold out the possibility of bankrupting product manufacturers. Product liability laws are likely to grow stronger so long as products are sold in national or international markets and regulated by tort law generated at the state level (Epstein, 1988: 311-12). Often, out-of-state product manufacturers may benefit from legislation limiting product liability. Local interests (both potential defendants and their lawyers) may prove to be stronger coalitions for expressing interests to state legislatures.

Schuck (1986) argues that this type of class action suit has become common because the legal system has made several fundamental changes. A manufacturer's duty to design and produce safe products has been expanded as product liability standards have moved from negligence to strict liability (some products are unreasonably dangerous) standards and from manufacturing defect to design defect (some products ought to have had a different design) standards. The categories of persons entitled to sue to enforce that duty have multiplied because the attempt to award only traditional compensable damages (for example, medical expenses, lost earnings) has given way to awards for emotional distress (for example, fear of cancer after exposure to toxic chemicals). Requirements of proof of causation of injury have eased as statistics and epidemiological information have substituted for proof of exposure, causation of injury, and demonstrable injury. Unprecedented damage awards have been upheld both because compensatory damages have grown and punitive damages have been extended to product liability cases.

Traditionally, tort cases were used to resolve isolated disputes, allocating losses between well-defined wrongdoers and victims. When victims and wrongdoers are not so easily identified, as with toxic substances, a new source of uncertainty must enter the product manufacturer's profit calculations. When the court and jury function as social problem solvers and risk regulators, demands for safety are being expressed. Changes in tort and product liability law are well known to drug manufacturers. Many have direct experience. Litigation undertaken by women whose mothers had taken DES established a new solution to identifying defendants when defendant identity is in question (Abrahams and Musgrave, 1982: 682-85). The drug had been used many years before problems appeared. Additionally, the pills were manufactured by firms estimated to number in the hundreds (Sheiner, 1978: 964). Identifying the specific firm that manufactured the pills that a woman may have taken a generation earlier has been nearly impossible. However, manufacturers' liability has been established on the basis of market share. Market shares have been developed for use in litigation.

The willingness of firms to undertake product testing and commercialization in the presence of legal risks capable of bankrupting any corporation must be interpreted as a belief in the safety of growth hormones. Whether consumers will ultimately share that belief is unknown. If government regulators believe growth hormone is safe, the most positive statement regulators will make is that growth hormones have no impact on human health. A much more positive statement can be made about pasteurization. Nevertheless, consumer fears delayed its use.

Conclusion

Consumer response to scientific studies of the growth regulator daminozide show a more extreme example of the behavior demonstrated over heptachlor contamination. Agricultural inputs can lose their economic viability when safety is questionable. Regulations can set minimum standards for society, but that does not prevent consumers from demanding higher standards at times. Daminozide, sold under the name Alar, was widely used in apple production to increase storage life, enhance color, and to prevent fruit from falling. The sensory qualities of treated fruit were improved and a larger supply of fresh fruit was possible with treatments because smaller quantities rotted in storage and less fruit fell from trees prior to harvest. Alar was also used on peanuts, grapes, cherries, peaches, nectarines, and pears.

In July 1984, the Environmental Protection Agency (EPA) announced it had initiated a Special Review (cost-benefit analysis) of Alar, based on studies showing that the chemical and one of its metabolites were carcinogenic, oncogenic, and mutagenic in laboratory animals (*Federal Register*, 1984). The EPA has demanded additional information from the manufacturer, but has not imposed any new restrictions on use of Alar. Consumers responded to the information to the extent that most major food processors and grocery chains claim they refuse fruit that has been treated. Alar use was claimed to have ended (*Consumer Reports*, 1987: 594). Although that is less likely than initially indicated, new and more sensitive testing procedures are available to enforce consumer demands for its end (*Consumer Reports*, 1989: 289).

The initial regulatory decisions and the decisionmaking process will be important to research and development incentives throughout the biotechnology industry. Demands for information from the industry could be considered onerous, depressing further research and development. The pasteurization example shows that there are real costs to slowing technological change. Those costs can include incurring otherwise preventable death and disease as well as sacrificing greater product availability and reduced consumer prices. Alternatively, if regulators demand too little information, fearing that regulations would otherwise be onerous, the likelihood of a regulatory mistake could rise. Two types of wrong decisions are possible. If growth hormones are deemed unsafe when in fact they are harmless, the products probably will never be marketed. Recanting, and allowing commercial use of a product it once banned, would be an unusual act for any regulatory agency. If growth hormones are deemed safe, but are later shown to be harmful (like DES), skepticism of public health officials' statements (as in the heptachlor case) should continue (OTA, 1987a). Further developments in rDNA and application to agriculture would not be well-received by consumers, resulting in depressed commodity demand and adverse effects on the agricultural sector.

Notes

The views expressed are the authors' and do not necessarily represent policies or views of the U.S. Department of Agriculture or of the Office of Management and Budget. We would like to acknowledge Tanya Roberts who directed us to literature on several of the examples discussed here.

1. Economic studies have not all treated the scientific literature alike. The OTA (1986) assumed that all dairy farms would produce 25.6 percent more milk once adopting bGH and that all eventually would adopt bGH. The USDA (1987a) assumed a yield increase approximately half that of OTA and assumed adoption would never exceed 75 percent of all dairy farms.

2. The Council for Agricultural Science and Technology (CAST) disputed the findings that DES use in animal production could cause health problems. They claimed that the human epidemiological evidence linking DES use to cancer is weak. They also argued that agricultural use of DES is not likely a source of problems with estrogen levels. CAST argued that all animals produce some levels of estrogen, implying it is not a foreign substance.

3. The USDA and FDA have concurrent jurisdiction over certain meat and poultry products through the Federal Meat Inspection Act and the Poultry Products Inspection Act. The FDA has authority over feed additives and animal drugs through the Federal Food, Drug, and Cosmetic Act.

4. Regulation of artificial sweeteners shows that regulations may affect individuals differently. Diabetics and weight-conscious consumers of artificially sweetened products have viewed potential bans on saccharin (after cyclamates were banned) with dismay, arguing that low-calorie products were more important than a perceived cancer risk. Cummings (1986) argues that low-calorie product demanders have made action against saccharin impossible since the cyclamate ban.

IV
Public Policy Responses to Biotechnology

10
Biotechnology: Issue Development and Evolution

L. Christopher Plein

As we begin the 1990s, the controversy over the social, environmental, and economic impact of biotechnology has reached a point where debate turns not on whether the processes and products of this new technology *will* be adopted, but on how and to what extent they will be used and regulated. The controversy surrounding biotechnology involves lack of agreement and understanding regarding the potential impacts of this new technology. Over the years, issues of government jurisdiction, regulatory procedure, safety, ethics, and social and environmental impacts have come to characterize biotechnology as a policy issue. Emphasis on certain issues associated with biotechnology over others at distinct times has contributed to identifiable phases in the evolution of this complex policy issue. The emphasis on human ethics in the late 1960s and early 1970s marks the first phase of issue development. Health and environmental safety concerns in the middle and late 1970s characterize the second phase of biotechnology's evolution in the policy arena. And during the 1980s the economic dimensions of biotechnology provided a third distinctive phase in issue development. Taken together, these phases reveal the evolution of biotechnology as a complex policy issue. In short, biotechnology has been transformed from an issue primarily associated with ethics, to an issue associated with safety, to one associated with economic impacts. This chapter uses these phases of policy issue development to examine and explore the evolution of the issue of biotechnology. After exploring these three phases of evolution, prospects for the future are considered.

For the past two decades the issue of biotechnology has been a subject of policy consideration. Certain events, in the form of scientific advances, shifts in public opinion, and actions and decisions in the policy arena have served as catalysts in moving biotechnology from one phase to another in policy evolution. The earliest high-level policy discussions of biotechnology can be traced to 1968, when hearings were held by the Senate Committee on Government Operations to consider the potential ethical consequences of genetic engineering (see U.S. Congress. Senate, 1968), setting the stage for the first phase of issue evolution. These ethical concerns reflected a larger social trend which centered on whether scientific advances were far outstripping our ability to reason and assess their moral and ethical consequences (see Dickson, 1988). A second phase of issue evolution was initiated with advances in recombinant DNA techniques. No longer the domain of theory, the recombination of genetic structure had become reality. Public attention turned to the potential health and environmental dangers of biotechnology. The publication of a letter by leading scientists calling for a moratorium on rDNA experimentation in 1974 brought these concerns to center stage in the policy arena. Through the middle and late 1970s, Congress and federal agencies dealt with matters regarding laboratory safety and environmental protection. The third phase of issue development came in the wake of rapid scientific advances making commercial applications of biotechnology feasible. From an economic and legal standpoint, the commercialization of biotechnology was highly influenced by the 1980 Supreme Court decision in *Diamond v. Chakrabarty* (U.S. Reports, 477: 303-22) allowing for the patenting of simple-celled organisms. The decision encouraged investment in research and product development (Wehr, 1984: 3094) and throughout the 1980s much of the policy consideration associated with biotechnology turned on issues relating to the commercialization of this new science. Recent events suggest that the emphasis on the economic dimensions of biotechnology will continue and that current actions in the policy process will have significant bearing on the future course of this policy issue.

In the sections that follow each of these three developmental phases will be discussed in greater detail and possibilities for the future offered. In order to understand the dynamic history of biotechnology as a policy issue, the forces that helped to shape and define each phase will be examined. Among the most influential forces in the development of biotechnology as a policy issue have been: (1) the role of public opinion, (2) the dynamic scientific nature of biotechnology, and (3) the participation of interest-groups and governmental actors in the policy process. By understanding how these events and forces have influenced the past, we are better able to understand what future policy issues associated with biotechnology might entail.

Biotechnology and Genetic Engineering: 1968-1974

With genetic engineering—who are the beneficiaries, who makes the decision as to who participates in genetic engineering? Is it widespread? Is it to everyone? Do we use it just to breed a master race? (Senator Abraham Ribicoff [D-CT], March 1968)

Twice before in the history of Western civilization, the scientist-philosophers, the humanists, and the politicians found common ground for broad intellectual discussions. There was the Golden Age of Pericles and there was the Renaissance Period. I see a prospect of a new period of enlightenment in which we can begin to understand the molecular foundations of human nature. The American people and the Congress that represent them have a trust to make this prospect a reality. (Arthur Kornberg, Nobel Laureate, March 1968)

On February 8, 1968, Senator Walter Mondale (D-MN), acting on behalf of himself and such noted senators as Birch Bayh (D-IN), Robert Byrd (D-WV), Edward Kennedy (D-MA), and Robert Kennedy (D-NY) introduced a joint resolution to establish a Commission on Health Science and Society to examine the implications of such issues as genetic engineering and the property rights of human tissues (U.S. Congress. Senate, 1968: 415, 417). Hearings that followed in March and April of 1968 to review the need for such a commission revealed the emerging controversy surrounding genetic engineering. In conducting the hearings, both Senator Walter Mondale (D-MN) and Senator Abraham Ribicoff (D-CT) expressed their concern for the ethical and social consequences that genetic engineering might create and emphasized the need for social, legal, and ethical evaluation and oversight. Prominent scientists, such as Nobel Laureate Arthur Kornberg, testified at these hearings. The hearings constitute the first time Congress deliberated on the potential consequences of genetic engineering and biotechnology. The proceedings of the hearings, from which the quotes at the beginning of this section have been drawn, reflect the mood of public opinion and the social context in which biotechnology emerged on the political scene. The debate over biotechnology as it related to the role of science in society came to define the first phase of this policy issue's evolution. A debate, which when compared to events to come, was low-key, and confined to the concerns of relatively few actors.

The new science of biotechnology emerged in a society which had begun to sour towards the prospects of scientific and technological achievement. Public opinion was shaped in large part by mounting concerns over the role that science was playing in the political process and the effects that technological advancements were having in the environment. In post–World War II society, the link between scientific knowledge and public policy had become very strong (see Price, 1965). The interdependence between science and politics was based on the need for policy expertise in government, the nationalistic goals of scientific and technological superiority, and the need for federal support for increasingly expensive methods of research. This close relationship dates back to World War II when the scientific community was called upon to develop military technologies. Leading scientists of the time, such as Vannevar Bush, then director of the President's Office of Scientific Research and Development, stressed the need for continued government support for medical, military, and especially basic research in the postwar years (Bush, 1945: 14-15). Bush identified scientific progress as a force in protecting "liberties against tyranny" and advocated a partnership between government and science in which the former played an active role in providing research support and resources while maintaining a *minimal* role in oversight (Bush, 1945: 6, 14-15). These views were adopted as the blueprint for postwar relations between science and government (Price, 1965: 2). This was made possible, in large part, by the public's faith in the legitimacy of scientific autonomy and self-regulation.

As science became more intertwined with political life, it became more politicized and subject to scrutiny. By the time that biotechnology emerged as a policy issue, the public's faith in the sanctity of science had been shaken. In 1961, a series of lectures published by C. P. Snow called into question the neutrality of science advice in the government. In 1962, Rachel Carson published *Silent Spring*, which questioned the ability of the scientific community to assess impacts and risks of technological developments and helped launch the environmental movement. In *The Scientific Estate*, published in 1965, Don K. Price observed the growing influence of scientific knowledge and expertise in policy decisions and the technological complexity of new policy issues requiring consideration of political problems thought to have been "disposed forever by simple Constitutional principles" (1965: 18). Concerns over the political, social, and environmental impacts of science and technology meant that technological change was no longer held in positive light (Dickson, 1988: 266). These factors worked against science in general, and the development of biotechnology in particular.

The fear of potential ethical dilemmas unleashed by unbridled scientific enterprise led to legislative activity in which controls on research were sought. Throughout the late 1960s and early 1970s bills were considered in Congress to initiate oversight arrangements for scientific research. In 1968 and again in 1971 and 1972, unsuccessful efforts were made to establish commissions designed to evaluate and assess the potential social, ethical, and legal dimensions of advances in the research and application of genetic engineering techniques (see U.S. Congress. House, 1972: 39). In large part, the primary reason why Congress did not act to pass legislation designed for oversight rests on the fact that the issue failed to galvanize substantial public support—the issues being debated were, after all, the subject of conjecture, not pressing realities.

The 1968 hearings on genetic engineering provide a microcosm of the emergent debate over biotechnology. For its proponents, genetic engineering had become an issue of scientific freedom. For its opponents, it represented another example of science's lack of regard for social responsibility. During the hearings, these positions were encapsulated in exchanges between Senator Ribicoff and Nobel Laureate Arthur Kornberg. Ribicoff referred to the dangers of creating a master race and alluded that scientists might fail, as they did in the case of the development of the atomic bomb, to consider the consequences of their work (U.S. Congress. Senate, 1968: 47-48). Kornberg tried to defuse the charge by stating that biochemistry was an enterprise whose fundamentals should be familiar to any high school student (U.S. Congress. Senate, 1968: 53). He blamed the press for sensationalizing scientific research and giving the public a false image of genetic science (U.S. Congress. Senate, 1968: 41). In accentuating the positive he stressed the need for scientists, policymakers, and the public to work together in making the most of the opportunities offered by advances in genetic science (U.S. Congress. Senate, 1968: 47).

Concern at the federal level over the dangers of human avarice in genetic engineering continued through the early 1970s. A Congressional Research Service report prepared for the House Committee on Science and Astronautics in 1972 mentioned that "each time a new advancement in genetics or cell biology seems to bring some type of genetic engineering closer to reality, there is a reaction from the public which appears almost to border on real fear" (U.S. Congress. House, 1972: 34). Much of the concern during this period appears to have focused on eugenics and how genetic engineering might promote nefarious enterprises in selective breeding. This fear figured in popular accounts that warned of selective breeding reminiscent of the quest for a "master race" in Nazi Germany (U.S. Congress. House, 1972: 35).

In retrospect, in the late 1960s and the early 1970s biotechnology was primarily associated with the potential human applications of genetic engineering. Such sensational rhetoric as the development of a master race and the selective breeding of various social classes recalled more the fiction of Huxley's *Brave New World* than the realities of a limited state of knowledge about genetics. Biotechnology came to be associated with potential fears rather than the potential benefits of application in the fields of agriculture, industry, and medicine. Prevailing currents of public opinion revealed a transformation from unbridled support for scientific achievement to skepticism over the consequences of scientific "advances." Set against this backdrop of public concern over the marriage of science and politics and the detrimental impacts that technology could render in society, biotechnology received a less than hospitable greeting in the policy arena. The tenor of debate focused squarely on what might be done with the newfound skills and knowledge of genetics. This dimension, more than any other, distinguishes this period in the evolution of biotechnology as a policy issue.

The Debate Over Health and Environmental Risk: 1974-1980

Recent advances in techniques for the isolation and rejoining of segments of DNA now permit constructions of biologically active recombinant DNA molecules *in vitro*. . . . Several groups of scientists are now planning to use this technology to create recombinant DNAs from a variety of other viral, animal, and bacterial sources. . . . There is serious concern that some of these artificial recombinant DNA molecules could prove biologically hazardous. ("Berg Letter" [Berg et al., 1974])

We don't seek to suppress science. We do seek to protect the public health and safety, reconciling the two sensibly is difficult, but not by any means impossible. (Senator Adlai Stevenson, III [D-IL], November, 1977)

In the summer of 1973, DNA from one organism was successfully combined with that of another. This singular event served to move biotechnology from theory to the laboratory. The implication of this, in turn, served to politicize the issue of genetic research. Biotechnology became associated with the issues of environmental safety and health risk. Attention turned away from the potential consequences of deliberate scientific manipulation and focused instead on the specter of accidental release and ecological disaster. While the debate over this topic originated in the scientific community, the controversy quickly moved to the public and policymaking arenas, resulting in an expanding group of participants and a flurry of legislative activity. Scientific advances made biotechnology an immediate and pressing topic. The second phase of biotechnology's policy evolution marked an intensive, often speculative, debate over the health and environmental risks of this new science. The widening scope of participants involved in the policy process revealed a distinct change in the nature of this policy issue.

It was the science community itself that set into motion the wheels of policy debate over research safety. Published concerns by leading scientists in the field of genetic engineering created the spark that ignited debate over the issue of DNA research (*Congressional Quarterly Almanac*, 1978: 492). In a letter to *Science* published on July 26, 1974, a group of scientists representing the Committee on Recombinant DNA of the National Academy of Sciences outlined concerns over the potential dangers of rDNA microorganisms and the ability of existing research guidelines to ensure safety (Berg et al., 1974: 303). Known as the "Berg Letter," for the senior biochemist who organized it, the letter called for a moratorium on genetic research. Many in the science community opposed such a ban, and a highly visible, internecine conflict ensued which became the central focus of meetings held in Asilomar, California, in February of 1975. The Asilomar meetings, which garnered much media attention, gave the issue of genetic research even greater visibility and resulted in a call by the scientific community for a restriction on research until self-governing guidelines could be developed by the National Institutes of Health (Curry, 1986: 28). As a result of the highly visible debate within the scientific community the issue spread to the public arena and the policymaking process. In both cases there was resistance against genetic engineering in particular and a sense of skepticism towards science in general (see Krimsky, 1982).

In the 1970s, preexisting public conceptions of biotechnology fueled resistance to genetic research. While applications of genetic engineering were not developed until the 1970s, the theoretical dimensions of biotechnology had been around long enough for terms like "cloning," "selective breeding," and "genetic engineering" to have attained negative symbolic weight. As a scientific development, biotechnology had to suffer from the burden of its own verbal baggage before it in fact was a reality. The mass media used these images of risk and uncertainty to frame the issue of biotechnology both through news reporting and fictional depictions. Warnings of potential hazards and dangers of biotechnology dominated news stories associated with biotechnology (Nelkin, 1987: 38). In the wake of the Berg Letter, such headlines as "A New Fear: Building Vicious Genes" and "Genetic Scientists Seek Ban—World Health Peril Feared" appeared (Hutton, 1978: 53). The specific science of biotechnology, in which the first issues of debate would focus on topics of experimental procedures and protocols, was simplified and made socially relevant by its portrayal in the mass media. These portrayals helped to generate public awareness and fueled activity in the policy process.

In June 1976, public opposition to genetic research crystallized in Cambridge, Massachusetts, when controversy emerged over the DNA research plans at Harvard University. Plans to build a DNA research laboratory raised the ire of local citizens groups and gained nationwide attention through such sources as the *New York Times* (Hall, 1987: 41-43). Prompted by the Cambridge controversy, Senator Edward Kennedy (D-MA) initiated hearings before the Senate Subcommittee on Health and the Senate Subcommittee on Administrative Practices and Procedures to consider the adequacy of existing regulatory frameworks for biotechnological research (see U.S. Congress. Senate, 1976). Kennedy's high stature gave the issue even greater visibility on the policy agenda and in the public arena.

The question of research safety, not only in the laboratory setting but for society as a whole, sparked legislative activity in 1977. In the House, no less than seven bills were introduced aimed at revising or replacing existing research guidelines with more stringent policies (see U.S. Congress. House, 1977). In the summer of 1977, disclosures of alleged violations of National Institutes of Health (NIH) regulations at a leading genetics laboratory at the University of California-San Francisco (see Hall, 1987: 149) led to investigative hearings into the research conduct of leading scientists. Paradoxically, the controversy focused on one of the original signers of the Berg Letter, Herbert Boyer. Hearings held before the Senate Subcommittee on Science, Technology, and Space in November of 1977 by Senators Adlai Stevenson, III (D-IL) and Harrison Schmitt (R-NM) reveal the heightened controversy and debate surrounding the ability of the scientific community to regulate itself and assure environmental and health safety in the wake of advances in genetic research (see U.S. Congress. Senate, 1977).

In many ways the hearings were similar to the Ribicoff-Mondale hearings of spring 1968 in which the key issues turned on the topic of scientific responsibility, except this time the focus was not on deliberate genetic manipulation but on accidental genetic mutation. A review of the hearing reveals that the senators were not sympathetic to the concerns of many in the science community that more stringent government regulation would restrict scientific freedom and hinder technological advance. When the president of the National Academy of Sciences emphasized that scientific research was a constitutional right, Senator

Stevenson reminded the witness "not to spend much time on questions of law at which we may be more expert than the witnesses" (U.S. Congress. Senate, 1977: 17). Both senators expressed doubt over the ability of the biotechnology science community to regulate itself in the face of increasing private commercialization (U.S. Congress. Senate, 1977: 19-20). In Senator Stevenson's view this entrepreneurial climate had led to a situation in which protocols designed for basic, cooperative research were being circumvented (U.S. Congress. Senate, 1977: 210). Herbert Boyer, a principal witness, would later protest in a letter to Senator Stevenson against the biases of the senators and the "inquisitional manner in which [the] hearing was carried out" (U.S. Congress. Senate, 1977: 224).

The November hearings also revealed the entrance of environmental groups into the research safety debate. Emphasizing themes of uncertainty and risk, representatives from such groups as the Friends of the Earth and the Natural Resources Defense Council sought to expand the scope of conflict through analogies to nuclear energy safety and government competency (U.S. Congress. Senate, 1977: 300-301). Beyond the hearings themselves, other groups such as the Environmental Defense Fund and the Sierra Club took public stands in favor of more stringent research guidelines to ensure health and environmental safety (McAuliffe and McAuliffe, 1981: 174).

The scientific community, divided as it was over the specific issues of biotechnology, realized the precedent-setting dangers of new regulatory legislation. Many commercial and academic researchers, universities, and professional organizations balked at calls for reform and additional regulation. The proposed actions were a threat to the autonomy that science had enjoyed since World War II. The specter of close nonscientific scrutiny, including devolution of oversight to citizens groups, presented potential precedents so broad that the debate mobilized opposition from policy actors not immediately in the fray of biotechnology debate (*CQ Almanac*, 1978: 633).

The outcome of the research safety controversy was, in large part, the result of negotiation between scientists and environmentalists (McAuliffe and McAuliffe, 1981: 179). Efforts to reform and implement new research regulations achieved some success while the scientific community retained considerable autonomy. New research guidelines did not, however, come in the form of new legislation. Instead, a compromise was reached with the establishment of the Recombinant DNA Advisory Committee under the auspices of the National Institutes of Health in 1976. Empowered to implement guidelines and review research procedures, the advisory committee was composed of members primarily from the scientific community. For example, in 1977 only four of the committee's 20 members were not scientists (Curry, 1986: 29). Environmentalists continued to press for greater public participation in research regulation. In 1978, the advisory process was opened up through the establishment of local regulatory arms called Institutional Biosafety Committees to oversee research at universities and laboratories. In addition, the number of nonscientists on the

Recombinant DNA Advisory Committee was increased (McAuliffe and McAuliffe, 1981: 179).

In retrospect, many in the science community felt that they had made a great mistake in precipitating the debate on the research safety of genetic experimentation. Nobel Laureate James Watson commented, "As one of the signers of the original moratorium I apologize to society. The dangers of this thing [rDNA research] are so slight—you might as well worry about being licked by a dog" (McAuliffe and McAuliffe, 1981: 176). An issue of scientific protocol, the research debate served to exacerbate divisions within the science community already simmering over the issue of applied and entrepreneurial work. Once the debate moved into the public arena, the issue rode "piggy-back" on the larger environmental movement of the 1970s. However, the science community retained enough organization and mobilization to thwart efforts to adopt more stringent regulatory legislation, and compromised by developing revised regulations through the National Institutes of Health. As the 1980s dawned, larger social trends would act to benefit research and entrepreneurial interests while eroding support for the policy agenda of the environmental movement.

Taken together, the events of the 1960s and 1970s provide evidence of the impact that public opinion has on the development of a policy issue. Uncertainty and trepidation replaced expectation in matters relating to scientific and technological developments. In this climate of opinion, biotechnology received an inhospitable greeting in the public arena. The review of congressional activity in 1968 and again in 1977 shows how sustained this reluctance and opposition towards this new technology was. The Ribicoff-Mondale and the Stevenson-Schmitt hearings serve as snapshots of legislative action which encapsulate the lasting anxiety over biotechnology while capturing the nuances of change which marked the evolution of biotechnology as a policy issue. It is this nuance of change which makes for two identifiable phases in the evolution of this complex policy issue in the 1960s and 1970s. For there was a marked transformation of this issue from one of foreboding towards humanity's dominion over nature to our clumsiness in experimenting with the design of nature. This climate of fear and lack of faith in biotechnology would have a lasting impact on the evolution of this policy issue. In one aspect, it would shape the commercialization of biotechnology in the 1980s by delaying investment by large-scale firms (Sylvester and Klotz, 1987: 67). In another aspect, it planted seeds of doubt which would color much of the controversy and debate over biotechnology in the 1980s.

The Commercialization of Biotechnology: The 1980s

Imagine farm animals that produce leaner meat and more milk at less cost. Biotechnology offers new ways to improve the health and efficiency of farm animals. . . . New ways to improve the competitiveness and profitability of farmers. . . . And, new ways to make food healthier for consumers. Monsanto scientists are working with nature to develop innovative products for people of today and the future. (Monsanto Corporation Advertisement, Fall 1988)

The new [patent] policy transforms the status of the biotic community from the common heritage of us all to the sole possession of major corporations. (Representative Charlie Rose [D-NC] in Spitler, 1987)

The debate over the advantages versus the disadvantages of commercial applications of biotechnology defines the third phase in the evolution of this policy issue. The emphasis on commercial aspects was influenced by advances in research and product development, supportive public opinion, new participants in the policy process, and important policy decisions. As new possibilities for the application of biotechnology in the fields of agriculture, medicine, and industry expanded, so increased the number of associated issues and the scope of interested participants in the policy process. No longer an abstract cause of concern, nor an issue centered on the prevention of ecological disaster, the economic impact of pending applications stood to affect the lives of many. Within this context, proponents extolled the virtues of biotechnology, emphasizing its promise of cheaper and better goods in the marketplace and the role that the new industry would play in achieving economic recovery and development in the United States. Opponents challenged the new industry from two points of view. Citing ethical concerns, one set of opponents favored the absolute termination of genetic research and product development. Another set of opponents, afraid of what biotechnology might do to the structure of agriculture and research, sought assurances and policies protecting their interests. Within this arena of debate, such issues as patent rights, federal research support, and the regulatory process moved to center stage. In particular, debate crystallized around the subject of animal patents, which originated with the Supreme Court's 1980 decision in *Diamond v. Chakrabarty* (U.S. Reports, 477: 303-22) ruling genetically engineered organisms patentable. In the wake of the events of the 1980s, two trends stand clear. First, a well-organized, cohesive pro-biotechnology coalition emerged in the policy arena. Second, those opposing biotechnology were divided by differing concerns, priorities, and tactics to influence the course of policymaking.

The dawn of the 1980s marked important changes in public attitudes towards science and technology, providing a supportive social context against which biotechnology was judged and considered in the policy arena. Public concerns turned away from such issues as environmental safety and government oversight of research. A troubled economy and growing conservatism in the United States reoriented the policy agenda away from issues which dominated in the 1960s and 1970s. Even the Carter administration, having relied on the support of environmental groups in the 1976 election, shifted emphasis away from related regulatory issues in the face of stiff opposition from corporations (Dickson, 1988: 276). As the tide of social and political opinion turned against environmental and public-interest groups, the scientific community experienced rehabilitation in the public arena. By the early 1980s, calls for American reindustrialization renewed the need for scientific and technological innovation (Dickson, 1988: 267). Both Congress and the Reagan administration placed scientific research support high on the policy agenda. At the popular level, the mass media abandoned negative attacks on science and turned to promotion of new scientific discoveries as a cure for economic and social malaise (Nelkin, 1987: 51). In the case of biotechnology, it was transformed from a "runaway science of genetic engineering" to a new "technological frontier" (Nelkin, 1987: 40).

The development of new research techniques and the development of biotechnological products and processes attracted both private investment and public research dollars. Advances in theory and technique provided opportunities for commercial applications of biotechnology. These advances contributed to the growth of a biotechnology industry which allied entrepreneurial scientists with large pharmaceutical and agribusiness firms. At first, pharmaceutical firms with an interest in developing synthetic insulin, interferons, and human growth hormones provided the impetus for the commercialization of biotechnology (see Hall, 1987). But by the early 1980s potential agricultural applications of biotechnology had been realized, swelling the ranks of the pro-biotechnology coalition. Agribusiness firms, the United States Department of Agriculture, and the American Farm Bureau Federation perceived the advantages of agricultural biotechnology and supported its development. In order to participate effectively in the policy process, well-funded trade associations were formed and alliances with established public and private actors were forged (see Plein, 1989). Acknowledging the power of public opinion, these interests sought to cultivate public support through publicity campaigns launched by trade organizations (see Scott and Plein, 1988) and the United States Department of Agriculture (see, for example, USDA, 1987b).

In the 1980s, public opinion and advances in research and product development served to strengthen the pro-biotechnology coalition. These same forces altered the composition of the opposition coalition, weakening their influence by dividing their goals and priorities. Opponents who had established themselves as the voices of challenge in the 1970s moved to the sidelines of debate. A clean track record in research eased the fears of concerned scientists who had earlier helped to elevate laboratory research as a predominate issue of debate. In the face of a changing policy arena, which embraced economic competition and scientific development, environmental interest groups disengaged from the fray of debate.[1] In their place a fragmented coalition of groups ascended as the cacophonous voice of opposition. This coalition was made up of *conditional* and *absolute* opponents, who were divided over priorities and strategies.

Groups troubled by the ecological, social, and economic consequences of biotechnology emerged as *conditional* opponents of biotechnology. Specific developments in biotechnology, say the introduction of a growth promotant into the dairy industry, mobilized those interests most affected by the issue. The science of biotechnology was not their concern, what it could do was. As a result, groups with conditional concerns moved in and out of the fray of debate as specific issues mobilized their concern and then subsided. Through the years, conditional opponents grew to include agricultural groups, concerned scientists, environmental groups, and public-interest groups. These interests were frequent participants in the policy process, providing hearings testimony (see Plein and Webber, 1989) and agreeing to compromises with proponents of biotechnology. The enactment of National Institutes of Health guidelines for rDNA research and the establishment of Institutional Biosafety Committees in the late 1970s are examples of the accommodations worked out between participants in the biotechnology debate. As we will see later, the recent controversy over animal patent policies reveals how these groups participate in the policy process and rely on compromise and negotiation to resolve conflicts.

Whereas conditional opponents are concerned with the implications of biotechnology as a tool which enables a host of applications, *absolute* opponents challenge the new science out of a deep-seated belief that the manipulation of life is inherently wrong. Their position is essentially nonnegotiable. Where the cast of conditional opponents has changed with the issues under consideration, this small but highly visible set of opponents has been a near permanent fixture in the biotechnology debates of the 1980s. Winning concessions from the biotechnology industry may satisfy conditional opponents, but for absolute opponents they are only steps towards the total rollback of biotechnology. While frequent participants in legislative hearings (see, for example, U.S. Congress. Senate, 1984; U.S. Congress. House, 1986), absolutist opponents have utilized the more confrontational tactics of litigation (see, for example, *Federal Supplement*, 1986), publicity campaigns, and public demonstrations in an effort to focus public opinion on a subject which has lost visibility as it has been broken up into specific economic-related issues in the policy process (see Von Oehsen, 1988; Wheeler, 1989). These activities have garnered substantial media attention and press accounts frequently portray absolutists as leaders in biotechnology opposition (Plein, 1989). Reflecting on the state of public debate on biotechnology, Representative John Dingell (D-MI) commented in 1985 that "the mainstream environmental organizations have left center stage to Jeremy Rifkin, a clever advocate with an apocalyptic view of scientific progress" (Dingell, 1985: 30). Rifkin, the leader of the Foundation on Economic Trends, is well known for his commitment to the termination of biotechnological research and applications. The differences in tactics and priorities between the absolutists and the conditionalists were revealed in the debate over the patenting of genetically engineered organisms in the 1980s.

A number of observers (see Wehr, 1984; Raines, 1988) point to the Supreme Court's September 1980 decision in *Diamond v. Chakrabarty* providing patent eligibility for genetically engineered organisms as the driving force behind the commercial development of biotechnology. In the words of one author, the decision "opened the floodgates" of investment into biotechnological research and product development (Wehr, 1984: 3094). The Supreme Court decision had an immediate impact on the scope of debate surrounding biotechnology, both within and around government. First, it opened up a new set of issues to be entertained which suggested the following questions: How far could patenting now go—could human genes be next? What impacts would there be on the structure of the biotechnology industry in terms of product development and application? What role would Congress and the bureaucracy take in regulating the patent and proprietary process? By bringing to the forefront of debate issues of ownership and control of genetic products, resources, and technologies, policy debate moved away from issues of safety and environmental impact. This reorientation served the advantage of biotechnology's proponents while undercutting the position of those opposing biotechnology on environmental and safety grounds.

The patent issue involved questions of ethics, animal welfare, corporate domination of knowledge, and the structure of American agriculture. The history of this issue after the *Chakrabarty* decision illustrates how questions of economics had come to the forefront in policy deliberations. The decision set into motion further policy actions that expanded the range of genetically altered life forms qualifying for patent review. In 1987, the patent office ruled that genetically engineered animals qualified for patent review. An early response to the patent office's policy took the form of a moratorium effort in Congress which sought to pass legislation banning animal patents for a period of two years while the implications of the patent office's actions were evaluated. Congressional interest in the subject peaked in the wake of the patent office's 1988 decision to award a patent to a mouse developed by a group of Harvard University researchers that expressed a cancer-causing gene. The media quickly dubbed this transgenic animal the "Harvard Mouse."

Backed by a broad coalition of animal rights organizations, religious groups, ethical opponents, scientists concerned over the control of research, and groups representing small-scale farmers, legislators sought to enact the animal patent moratorium. Ethical and religious opponents favored the moratorium in order to derail the biotechnology industry, arguing that it was morally wrong to alter life forms and then award them proprietary status. Concerned scientists and small farmers favored the moratorium as a means of achieving assurances against corporate domination and control of biotechnologies (Taylor, 1988: CRS6).

While absolutist opponents garnered substantial media attention, the tenor of discussion in Congress turned increasingly towards economic issues in the course of policy debate over the issue of animal patents. Interests with an economic stake in animal patents, such as independent researchers and small-scale farmers, became major participants in the debate. The moratorium bill, sponsored by Representative Charlie Rose (D-NC) enjoyed widespread support in Congress until a compromise was worked out securing royalty exemptions for farmers and researchers (*CQ Weekly Report*, 1988: 2623). By the end of the 100th Congress, the moratorium effort had been defeated, but no clear-cut course of policy action had been adopted because the exemption bill was not acted on (Office of Technology Assessment [OTA], 1989). In the 101st Congress, patent exemptions were taken up again. A recent bill introduced by Representative Robert Kastenmeier (D-WI), HR 1556, would amend the patent code to provide exemptions to farmers from paying royalty fees. For years a similar provision has been provided for most plant patents (OTA, 1989).

In the history of biotechnology as a policy issue, the 1980s may well be remembered as the decade of the animal patent. The Supreme Court's *Diamond v. Chakrabarty* (1980) decision helped to reorient policy debate towards economic issues and a series of administrative policies by the patent office sustained this debate. More than any other issue associated with biotechnology in the 1980s, the patent issue illustrated how policy debate over biotechnology had moved from an emphasis on environmental impact and safety to an emphasis on economic concerns. The debate also revealed the dynamics of interest group participation in this phase of policy issue evolution. While absolutist opponents generated substantial media coverage over their opposition to the granting of animal patents, in the halls of Congress it was conditional opponents, such as small-scale farmers' organizations, who emerged as important participants in the policy process.

In reviewing the development of biotechnology as a policy issue in the 1980s, the role of interest groups and public officials in influencing the character of policy debate stands out. The nature of interest group participation in the biotechnology debate was as crucial as the climate of opinion and the impact of policy decisions in making the consideration of economic issues a distinguishing trait in this phase of policy issue evolution. Mancur Olson (1982: 25) has noted that organized groups with homogeneous interests are advantaged in terms of participation in the policy process, for heterogeneous groups tend to split and fracture. In the 1980s, the pro-biotechnology coalition represented a cohesive coalition of research interests, industry firms, and trade associations, while biotechnology's opponents consisted of a fractured alliance of interests. Together, these allied interests engaged in activities to advance their concerns and agendas in the policy process through publicity campaigns, alliance building, and lobbying (Plein, 1989). Public opinion, advances in research and development, and policy decisions greatly aided the pro-biotechnology coalition while diminishing the position of opposition groups. Thompson (1988) has commented on the fragile alliance among opponents to biotechnology because they have differing views on the role of the state in mediating conflicts which arise out of scientific and technological change. Rapid advances, heralding widespread applications of biotechnology, exacerbated these tensions. On the other hand, the pro-biotechnology coalition, standing on the common ground of commercial enterprise and research support, profited from a debate structured along economic lines. In large part, the future of biotechnology as a policy issue will be influenced by whether this coalition remains cohesive or starts to fracture as differences emerge among its members and opposition from detractors becomes less challenging.

Prospects for the Future: Biotechnology in the 1990s

I believe that biotechnology has more potential to reshape the world as we know it than any other technology besides nuclear power. This time, public policy implications should be handled a little bit better than the implications of technology have been handled in the past. (Representative Albert Gore, Jr. [D-TN] 1985)

Right now, the United States is the world's leader in biotechnological innovation. A fierce international competition is underway, with our greatest trade rivals devoting enormous resources to obtaining equality—if not eventual superiority—in this area. (Senator Patrick Leahy [D-VT], 1988)

By reviewing the history of biotechnology as a policy issue, some idea of its future evolution can be offered. Barring the equivalent of a "Three Mile Island" crisis where public attention is riveted on safety or environmental dangers, it is likely that the economic issues that have come to be associated with biotechnology in the 1980s will continue to characterize the nature of policy considerations in the coming years. However, changes within the coalition of interests making up the pro-biotechnology community will give future considerations of biotechnology a different character than that of the 1980s. In particular, it is likely that cleavages will emerge among supporters of biotechnology as economic issues regarding commercial ventures and the control of resources turn the axis of debate away from issues of safety and ethics. Among the chief concerns voiced by the pro-biotechnology coalition is the lack of regulatory policy coordination and growing international competition which threatens the future well-being of the biotechnology industry (see Fox, 1987; *Bio/Technology*, 1988; *IBA Reports*, 1989). As the quotes from Senator Gore and Senator Leahy illustrate, policymakers also believe the nature of policy responses to these concerns will determine, in large part, the future course of biotechnology.

Tensions are emerging within the pro-biotechnology community as a result of a "shake-up" within the industry which has seen a number of firms fail. While a similar falling out of firms occurred in the early 1980s, and some analysts have predicted that failures will be offset by the merger of small firms into corporate giants (see *Financial Times*, 1989: 22), the recent performance of the industry has shown signs of instability. In 1988 over 24 biotechnology firms failed. Studies suggest that approximately half of the nation's 500 companies will go under in the next ten years (Naj, 1989: B1). The industry-wide shake-up has not cut evenly; large firms have fared better than small firms (Fleisher, 1988).

The poor performance of the biotechnology industry is linked to the delay in introducing new products on the market, which in turn is linked to a regulatory process which the industry has labeled ineffective and uncoordinated (see Fox, 1987). Delays in product introduction due to regulatory hurdles have been blamed for raising undue public concern over product safety and in dissuading potential investors (see, for example, Fox, 1987; *IBA Reports* 1989). In the case of bovine somatotropin, which many in the agricultural biotechnology industry have heralded as the vanguard in livestock applications of the new technology, approval by the Food and Drug Administration has been delayed because of recent congressional calls for additional testing. This action in turn has been linked to dairy industry pressure on Senate Agriculture Committee Chairman Patrick Leahy (D-VT) to delay the regulatory decision (Larrabee, 1989: 3A). Small-scale dairy farmers, such as those found in Vermont, fear the potential economic impact of bovine somatotropin on the structure of the industry. Members of the biotechnology industry favor a more streamlined regulatory process which would avoid the hurdles of the highly political legislative process.

In recent years there has been substantial congressional support for biotechnology research and commercial development (see, for example, Gore, 1985; Harkin, 1988; Leahy, 1988). Efforts have been made in Congress to revise and reorganize the process by which biotechnology is regulated in order to streamline the process. However, these efforts have been thwarted by disagreement over how to best regulate the new technology and reluctance among both administrative and legislative interests to sacrifice any jurisdiction and thus influence over research and regulation. The ill-fated attempt to pass regulatory reform in 1987 and 1988 bears this out. During the 100th Congress, the Biotechnology Competitiveness Act was introduced into both houses of Congress. The purpose of the proposed act was to implement a comprehensive regulatory framework to provide biotechnology firms and research concerns a stable investment climate to facilitate industry growth. But the three committees that the bill was referred to in the House were not willing to place parochial interests aside in favor of a bill which would reform existing research funding and regulatory arrangements. As a result the bill died (*CQ Weekly Report*, 1988: 2553; Plein and Webber, 1988).

Currently, at least 16 congressional committees have a stake in biotechnology policy (Plein and Webber, 1988, 1989). At least 20 federal rules, policies, and statutes have been identified as applying to biotechnological research and products. At least 11 federal agencies have some stake in biotechnology regulation and policy (Plein, 1989). A recent General Accounting Office report (1986) found that when it came to defining what "biotechnology" and "biotechnological research" meant, various definitions had been adopted by federal departments and definitions even differed among agencies within the same department. In an effort to coordinate regulatory policies and actions between federal agencies, the Office of Science and Technology Policy issued the Coordinated Framework for Regulation of Biotechnology in 1986. Since its inception, the Framework has been faulted for ineffectiveness by private and public actors (see, for example, Fox 1987).

Perhaps in an effort to spur the streamlining of federal regulatory procedures, the effect of international competition on the biotechnology industry has been highly publicized by the industry and supporters (see Industrial Biotechnology Association, 1989). The issue of international competition, and America's role in the world economy, has been a salient topic throughout the 1980s (see Dickson, 1988). Supporters of biotechnology have allied this issue to their cause in order to secure support and beneficial policy actions (see Plein, 1989). Their efforts have met with some success, as evidenced by the recent Omnibus Trade Bill which provided for long-sought protections of process patents (Wehr, 1988: 2215). The domestic biotechnology industry has cause for concern with regard to their fortunes in the future. The development of the biotechnology industry in the United States has been paralleled in Europe and Japan. It has been estimated that by the year 2000 upwards of a $100 billion worldwide market will exist for biotechnological processes and products (OTA, 1984a: 4). More recently, attention has turned to foreign investment in the American biotechnology industry. In 1988, Japanese firms initiated partnership arrangements with a number of American firms (Naj, 1989: B1).

The multiplicity of federal actors involved in policy matters is in large part the product of the biotechnology coalition's success. The development of new products and processes in the fields of agriculture, energy, defense, and medicine have expanded consideration of policy issues into those arenas which consider specific topics. The commitment of federal research dollars to biotechnology has also mobilized the interest of actors within the federal arena. It is quite possible that in the future, a once cohesive biotechnology coalition will splinter into alliances with specific policy arenas relevant to their agendas. If this is the case, then the complex and ambiguous evolving policy network that currently characterizes biotechnology as a policy issue may be replaced by more institutionalized relations.

The biotechnology industry's concerns reveal the important role that policy activity and decisions will play in setting the future course of biotechnology as a policy issue. In the past, policy decisions such as the *Chakrabarty* decision and the administrative actions of the patent office reveal the power that public officials have in redefining issues in the public arena. Lack of federal coordination will likely foment divisions among the interests that presently form the basis of the pro-biotechnology coalition, leading to the fracturing of alliances and diminishing the effectiveness of the lobby as a player in the policy process. Since the early 1980s, proponents of biotechnology have been successful in structuring debate in economic terms. The new science has been embraced as a means of achieving economic growth and influence in the world market. Challenges from opponents have been persistent, but no longer do they occupy center stage as they did in the middle and late 1970s. Many proponents believe that the agenda of the pro-biotechnology interests has essentially been set in the policy arena—but remains to be acted upon (see, for example, *IBA Reports*, 1989; Industrial Biotechnology Association, 1989). Without clear-cut regulatory arrangements and federal support for emerging commercial developments and applications in biotechnology, the future is unclear. For these interests, favorable policy decisions are seen as the best insurance against an uncertain future.

Conclusion

The evolution of biotechnology as a policy issue reveals three distinctive phases of development. The first phase, running from 1968 to 1974, focused on the ethical and moral dimensions of what was, essentially, a theoretical science. In 1974, scientific concerns over genetic research in the laboratory signalled the beginning of a second phase of issue development featuring intense debate over environmental and safety risks. In the 1980s, policy decisions and the development of commercial applications of biotechnology heralded the third phase of issue development, featuring debate over economic opportunities and impacts. As for the future course of biotechnology as a policy issue, it appears that economic issues will continue to characterize policy discussion and debate.

In reviewing the evolution of biotechnology as a policy issue, each phase reveals how the forces of public opinion, policy participants and actions, and technological advances influence the way biotechnology has been dealt with as an issue in the policy arena. In the case of public opinion, its influence both shaped the controversy that surrounded the emergence of biotechnology in the 1960s and 1970s and, as opinion changed, contributed to positive responses to biotechnology in the 1980s. The dynamic and changing cast of participants in the policy process was another influence figuring prominently in the evolution of biotechnology as a policy issue. The agendas and actions of interest groups supporting and challenging biotechnology helped to define specific phases in this policy issue's evolution. For example, the presence of environmental groups in the 1970s helped to emphasize ecological concerns. In the same manner, the emergence of a cohesive pro-biotechnology coalition contributed to the placement of such issues as trade policy on the policy agenda in the 1980s. Public officials have also played a role in issue definition. For example, policy decisions, such as those by the patent office, can spark debate and controversy and set the stage for future events. The legislative process, through its hearings, provides visibility and forums for debate that shape the nature of policy consideration. Scientific developments are another force, outside of the policy process, making biotechnology a dynamic policy issue. Rapid advances moved biotechnology from the blackboard, to the laboratory, to the marketplace. In the wake of these developments, new policy concerns emerged.

As a policy issue embracing a set of issues spanning environmental, safety, and economic concerns, biotechnology has achieved some sense of permanence in the public arena. Yet for a set of issues which has been around for over 20 years, it has yet to be defined as a consistent set of policy alternatives, tools, and decisionmaking arrangements. No committee in the House or the Senate has primary jurisdiction over matters relating to biotechnology. No government agency has primary responsibility to administer policies relating to biotechnology. And while there have been many bills concerning biotechnology, very few laws have been passed and thus there is no legislative framework to guide policymaking. In short, biotechnology is a policy issue without a policy niche. Throughout biotechnology's history as a policy issue, this lack of policy coordination has been a concern of both opponents and proponents of biotechnology. In large part, this is because the policy process plays an important role in shaping perceptions of issues in the public arena. Uncertainty in the present policy arena translates into uncertainty for the future course of this policy issue.

The complex evolution of biotechnology as a policy issue can be summarized by an analogy using the genetically engineered Harvard Mouse. In the 1960s the question of the mouse would have centered on whether in theory such an accomplishment in genetic engineering *could* and *ought* to be done. In the late 1970s the question would have focused on the implications if the mouse escaped from the laboratory. In the 1980s the question of who owns the patent on the mouse takes center stage. In the 1990s it is likely that the focus of debate will be on who will build the better one and where.

Notes

The author's work on this research project has been made possible by a two-year research assistantship provided by the University of Missouri-Columbia's Food for the 21st Century Program.

1. This is not to say that environmental groups have been absent from biotechnology debate, but rather that their prominence has subsided (for recent evidence of lack of environmental group involvement see U.S. Congress. Senate, 1984; U.S. Congress. House, 1986).

11

Policymakers Address Biotechnology: Issues and Responsibilities

Morris Bosin

Public policymakers in many federal agencies are attempting to interact with the private sector and academia in guiding the evolution of biotechnology along a course that they feel will best promote the public interest. The aim of this chapter is to help these officials appreciate the wide range of factors that can enter into the determination of *responsible* action as they undertake this task. First, major issue areas that public officials are grappling with in the biotechnology arena will be briefly outlined. Second, some of these issues will be utilized to illustrate the diverse elements that enter into a definition of responsible action. Finally, some possible trends for the future are identified.

Biotechnology is a rapidly growing industry. The industry shows prospects of growing to leviathan proportions as its potential continues to be unveiled. Total private investment in dedicated biotechnology firms through 1987 is estimated to be $4.5 billion (U.S. Department of Commerce 1988). Federal spending in biotechnology research and development was $2.7 billion in 1987 alone (Office of Technology Assessment [OTA], 1988).

Authors such as Zilinskas (1983) and Grobstein (1983) have characterized biotechnology as Janus-like. On the negative side they see such potential problems as disputes over intellectual property rights, disposal of biowastes, the large-scale environmental release of genetically altered organisms, and even the possibility of illegally using new techniques for biological warfare. On the positive side, the prospective benefits of biotechnology include better disease diagnosis and prevention, fostering of new and improved foods, and environmental cleanup. These benefits can be transferred internationally, provided institutional mechanisms are established which encourage the flow of information across borders.

Because of the need to balance these benefits and risks, and given the fact that over 1,000 firms are currently applying the tools of biotechnology (Young and Burril, 1988), public administrators and other public officials are becoming acutely aware of the daunting responsibility associated with governing this rapidly expanding industry. This chapter is about the responsibilities of policymakers as they deal with biotechnology issues. To act responsibly is to act ethically. Ethical behavior means acting in accordance with certain standards (Sherwin 1983). The question is: whose standards? This chapter is not intended to suggest what is and is not acceptable behavior. Rather, it is intended as a guide to help government officials understand the various standards they need to be attuned to, and balance, as they face a diversity of issues in the process of facilitating the emergence of biotechnology.

Some Key Biotechnology Issue Areas

Policy issues associated with biotechnology have been characterized in many federal documents over the past several years (see, for example, OTA, 1984a, 1988; *Federal Register*, 1986; General Accounting Office, 1986; and U.S. Department of Agriculture, 1986). The many issues covered in the above sources can be consolidated into the following focused issue areas: (1) how federal policies can be directed toward effectively assessing and managing the risk associated with products produced via biotechnology, (2) available alternatives to catalyze the efforts of both the private sector and academia in bringing biotechnology to fruition, (3) the appropriate institutional arrangements/infrastructure between the public and private sectors, *and* among government agencies in this endeavor, (4) how the federal role in biotechnology can effectively be incorporated into achieving broader national goals such as increasing U.S. competitiveness in the global market, and (5) how the federal stewardship of biotechnology can effectively be "marketed" to the American public. To discuss each of these issue areas in depth is obviously beyond the scope of this chapter. However, some observations will be made about each area to set the stage for exploring how responsible action might be interpreted in some of these instances.

Risk Management

The effective management of risk associated with biotechnology-based products means that regulatory agencies such as the United States Department of Agriculture (USDA), the Environmental Protection Agency (EPA), and the Food and Drug Administration (FDA) are faced with the question of what is an appropriate balance of effort between assessing the risk, managing the risk, and communicating the risk to the public. Generally, regulatory strategies applied to biotechnology have been based on increased optimism by federal officials. These federal agencies are essentially regulating the new products through existing legislative mandates such as the Federal Insecticide, Fungicide, and Rodenticide Act (FIFRA), the Toxic Substances Control Act (TSCA), and the Pure Food, Drug, and Cosmetic Act (FD&C) (*Federal Register*, 1986). Congress, thus far, has deemed this preferable to enacting new special-purpose biotechnology laws.

Even with this general strategic agreement, many specific questions of implementation remain. For example, each agency is faced with the question of which mix of approaches to risk management should be adopted—mandatory vs. voluntary or self-regulation; how much risk assessment is sufficient; and what proportion of the regulatory attention should be paid to the product as opposed to the process by which it is produced? To what extent, for example, should regulatory resources be directed toward assuring the safety and efficacy of the process by which enzymes are genetically engineered to aid in the fermentation of beverages—as opposed to assuring the quality and safety of the final product? Although it is apparent that both product and process should be attended to, federal resources cannot be all places at all times.

Federal Incentives to Catalyze Private and Academic Efforts

The public sector can offer a variety of incentives and disincentives to at least partially control the pace of biotechnology research and development. These incentives include positive and negative tax incentives and federal support for biotechnology research through direct federal research expenditures, grants, and technology transfer programs. The issues for public policymakers center on the appropriate blend of incentives that works the best in achieving national goals. The mix question becomes a "nested" one, in that within each of the specific incentive areas there are further questions of appropriate strategy mixes. To illustrate, once the decision has been made to support biotechnology research and development with federal funds, the question of the most appropriate balance between basic and applied research remains.

Institutional Arrangements

Institutional arrangements focus on the appropriate kinds of working relationships that should be established between government, industry, and academia and among regulatory agencies. The advent of biotechnology has prompted questions on the part of government and industry alike. For example, will traditional lines between private and public sector roles be adequate to address the complexity of biotechnology? Or are new institutional arrangements called for? Some of these questions are being answered with action. In Maryland's Montgomery County, for example, the Center for Advanced Research in Biotechnology (CARB) has been established in hopes of attracting new biotechnology firms to that area. The center will be funded by the county, the

University of Maryland, and the National Bureau of Standards. Several other states have followed similar "center" concepts in pursuing creative multisector initiatives to make the biotechnology dream a reality, not to mention an economic boon for the region (OTA, 1988).

Other institutional relationship questions arise in the form of jurisdictional issues among federal agencies. Several biotechnology innovations currently on the drawing board are influencing federal regulators to clarify jurisdictional responsibilities among agencies. For example, a standing committee has been established between the FDA and the Veterinary Biologics Staff at the USDA to determine which veterinary biotechnology products should be regulated under the Virus, Serum, and Toxin Act or under the Pure Food, Drug, and Cosmetic Act. Some genetically altered food-producing animals or plants may also require careful distinctions between USDA and FDA areas of responsibility. For example, tomatoes have been modified to express the *Bacillus thuringiensis* toxin that kills caterpillars (Baum, 1987), bringing into question whether such plants would be regulated under FIFRA, or as a food additive under the Pure Food, Drug, and Cosmetic Act.

National Goals

Biotechnology presents the potential to help the United States achieve several national goals, including offering a potential solution to the nation's and world's hunger problems, increasing the productivity of our private sector, and improving American competitiveness in international markets by helping to overcome the current growing trade deficit. Each of these goals, of course, is surrounded by tough policy decisions facing public administrators. To illustrate with the competitiveness goal, to what extent should we adopt flexible export controls, antitrust laws, patent policies, and tax incentives to raise our international competitiveness? Some of these elements may themselves be in potential conflict. For example, stringent approval regulations for new biotechnology products, but less restrictive export laws may be adopted. Federal policymakers face the unenviable task of coordinating these incentives and restrictions into a strong initiative which utilizes biotechnology as part of a total strategy geared toward enhancing U.S. competitiveness.

Risk Communication

A major issue area for policymakers concerns the communication of risk associated with biotechnology. In short, how do policymakers relate to the general public their current assessment of biotechnology's safety, and steps that they are undertaking to minimize risk? Policymakers are keenly aware that this is a major issue, and that they have the power to influence public perceptions. This is evidenced by the presence of the topic "public perceptions of biotechnology" at virtually every federally sponsored biotechnology conference. Although administrators have a hand in shaping such perception through their approach to risk communication, these perceptions are by no means totally within their control. National surveys were conducted in the early 1980s with the aim of determining how the general public viewed biotechnology (USDA, 1986). The survey data point to several interesting conclusions: (1) despite attempts on the part of agencies like the National Academy of Science to allay public fears, the public still has real concerns about biotechnology research (Vobejda, 1987: A3), (2) few Americans really understand biotechnology, and (3) the more informed the public is, the more likely they will be to have favorable reactions.

Policymakers have some control over public perceptions, such as the terminology that they use in communicating to the public. But there are other factors shaping public opinion which lie largely outside of the policymaker's control. Two such factors are the media's treatment of biotechnology, in which newsworthiness may sometimes override considerations of comprehensiveness, and the personal ethics of individual citizens. For many, even the broad specter of gene research may have foreboding moral consequences because it implies the capability to blur the integrity of the human species. In the case of public perceptions, policymakers find themselves in the situation of changing what they can through more effective communication of risks associated with biotechnology; but at the same time they recognize and accept that to an extent, control over public perception lies beyond the federal realm.

Considerations in Determining Responsible Action on the Issues

With the almost limitless range of biotechnology issues facing policymakers, a reasonable question to ask is: how do they decide what is responsible behavior? That is, what standards do they follow? Two major sources of guidance proposed here are environmental forces which are external to the policymaker and his/her agency and which influence viewpoints on appropriate behavior, and guidance drawn from the policymaker's own agency, functional, and personal frames of reference. Policymakers heed these sources of guidance, and then they *act*. The outcomes of their actions make them responsible in a "causal" sense, because they are in a position to make things happen. In this section, responsibility for biotechnology policy will be examined from each of the above perspectives.

Many environmental forces can help to shape policymakers' views on responsible action in each of the issue areas discussed above. Some prominent forces that appear to be influencing biotechnology regulation include fiscal constraints on federal spending, current administration philosophies regarding appropriate government roles, and the sheer pace and complexity of biotechnology developments.

Fiscal constraints can exert direct influence on risk-management strategies, institutional arrangements with industry, and the degree and type of incentives offered to industry to encourage biotechnology development. First, limited federal dollars could lead to diffusion of the responsibility for managing risk, with the result being an increased reliance on industry to assess the safety of their own products of biotechnology and a diminished role for federal regulators. This might be necessary because of inadequate numbers of federal regulators to review biotechnology-based products before they enter the marketplace and a lack of trained compliance officials to monitor the products once they are on the market. Fewer dollars for the federal payroll could also mean less ability to recruit, train, and retain the kind of quality scientists and regulators who can understand the new products and processes well enough to communicate with industry. Inadequate understanding on the part of federal officials doesn't eliminate accountability for reviewing new products developed through biotechnology. However, it could cause regulatory officials to hesitate before accepting responsibility for ultimate outcomes. Such a reaction might be expected when long-term effects of biotechnology-based products and processes are uncertain.

Second, fiscal constraints can act as a motivator for government and industry to modify existing instrumental arrangements through such resources as dollars, skills, and facilities. The need for pooled capital is at least part of the reason why several states have launched initiatives hoping to attract biotechnology firms as a way to strengthen local economies. Notable among these states are North Carolina, New York, Iowa, Wisconsin, and Maryland (OTA, 1988). At the federal level, fiscal constraints influence the degree and type of federal incentives offered to industry to further biotechnology development. In tight fiscal times, incentives may, for example, be offered more frequently in the form of technology transfer activities and less restrictive legislation and regulation, rather than via direct grants to the private sector, particularly academia.

Consideration of appropriate federal roles, particularly regarding intervention in industry activity, has historically been influenced by the prevailing political and economic orientations of the Congress and administration in power. Classical public economic theory provides us with a broad framework for understanding the rationale underlying federal intervention. Generally, government intervenes to provide goods and services when the market is not able or willing to provide them. Steiner (1977) describes three types of market failures that warrant the provision of public goods: (1) those resulting from externalities that are not effectively marketed, (2) those arising from shortcomings in the market mechanism itself—such as the lack of adequate and/or timely information and lags in directing appropriate labor inputs into industry sectors, and (3) those public goods that result from particular qualities of the changing economic environment.

Biotechnology developments can be associated with the production of any one of these three externalities. In the first instance, undesirable externalities may be associated with a disruption of the ecosystem that occurs as a result of deliberate release of genetically engineered organisms into the environment. There have been extensive dialogues within and outside of government circles, as well as court decisions, regarding the legitimacy of government intervening to prevent such potential adverse effects from occurring (USDA, 1986: 32-37). In the second instance, federal intervention in private-sector biotechnology may be warranted on the basis of such market mechanism failures as inadequately trained personnel. And the success of biotechnology in this country depends on adequately trained scientific and technical personnel. Federal agencies such as the National Institutes for Health, the National Science Foundation, and the Department of Defense have seen fit to sponsor fellowships and trainee grants in those disciplines that undergird biotechnology (OTA, 1988).

In the third category of market failure, general environmental outcomes, the international competitive milieu provides a clear example of justification for federal intervention. Aggressive product initiatives on the part of international economic powers such as Japan and West Germany may result in the United States losing competitive ground in world markets. This kind of shift in the economic climate represents a changing environmental quality that is perceived not to be in the public interest. It might warrant federal intervention in the form of altering strategies for governing biotechnology and more effectively utilizing the industry and academia infrastructure. Coordinated and coherent public-private sector strategies offer a challenge and an opportunity for this country to regain a competitive lead in world markets (OTA, 1984a).

Such coordination has gained legitimacy and is considered responsible behavior by public officials because international competitiveness has become a national goal. In each of the above three kinds of market failures, a theoretical gap exists between public demand and private provision of goods and services. How unacceptable that gap is, how it is filled, and whether indeed it is filled at all, is at least partially determined by the administration in power. In an administration characterized by a strong free market advocacy, some would argue that there are few important distinctions between sector roles. In such an administration, responsible behavior would be that which results in the job being performed in the most cost-effective manner (Moe, 1987). To reap the fruits of biotechnology for the American public, this administration would likely advocate that research and development be carried out by the sector with the money and talent to produce results. Institutional arrangements between government, industry, and academia would be considered appropriate if they got the job done.

Conversely, in an administration where a stronger federal role is presumed desirable, the perspective on what constitutes responsible public sector action might be expected to shift. Public issues such as what is an acceptable risk-management strategy for biotechnology products, may be answered with a much stronger regulatory role for the public sector. Thus, for example, stringent federal standards for environmental release of genetically engineered organisms may be considered necessary, and thus responsible action. This is not because private market alternatives to controlling these organisms is impossible, or even impractical, but simply because federal intervention is deemed appropriate by those in power. That philosophy places government and industry into closer alliances when the foundation of the cooperation is consistent with the competitive spirit. Maryland's Center for Advanced Research in Biotechnology, mentioned earlier, is one example of public and private-sector organizations sharing financial, managerial, and technical resources. At the same time, the two recent administrations have not seen the need to regulate biotechnology as a special category (*Federal Register*, 1986).

The sheer complexity and growth of the biotechnology industry is a third type of environmental influence on policymakers' view of responsible action. From a few dozen "dedicated" biotechnology firms in 1976, the industry has expanded to over 1,000 firms active in biotechnology pursuits (Young and Burril, 1988). In a study conducted by the Food and Drug Administration (1988), experts from the public and private sector cited over 1,200 examples of biotechnology advances in the foods area alone. In addition to the growth in both firms and products, the industry structure has become complicated by extensive networking among firms and between firms and academia. Joint ventures, ownership arrangements, and collaborative agreements characterize much of the industry (FDA, 1986).

Industry size and complexity, from both a technological and structural standpoint, require that public policymakers develop a flexible response in their working relationships with industry. Flexibility is required in two senses. First, multiple roles must be played. At times, the roles call for close integration between government and industry, as in the case of the development of research guidelines by NIH's Recombinant DNA Advisory Committees. At other times the roles require a dynamic tension, as in the case of enforcing the guidelines. Second, government-industry actions become more reciprocal. How government attempts to steer this new industry has a direct bearing on industry's research and development decisions, and these decisions in turn could influence such government policies as product approval approaches. These decisions bear on the direction of government research expenditures, and government resource allocation decisions as they pertain to biotechnology. Reciprocity is also evident in the mutual need among industry, academia, and government for information and understanding about these new developments.

As we have seen, external forces can play a significant role in determining policymaker stances toward the various biotechnology issues. However, the individual policymaker ultimately decides what is and is not appropriate behavior. It then becomes incumbent upon the federal official to be self-conscious about the sense of responsibility that is being employed to decide on the appropriate response to issues. This personal sense of responsibility is manifested in three dimensions: (1) to whom (or what) accountability is felt, (2) internal values and associated frames of reference that serve as guides for behavior, and (3) the particular position that the policymaker occupies which gives him/her power to effect particular outcomes (causal responsibility).

The above three components of responsibility have a long history in public administration theory, and together they compose the classical definition of administrative responsibility (see, for example, Friedrich, 1966; Finer, 1966). Accountability essentially implies rewards and punishments that are forthcoming as a result of obeying or disobeying authoritative sources. To be accountable is to feel an obligation for one's actions to other people within one's own organization. The performance of each function is guided by embedded organizational cultures that have evolved over the years. These subcultures involve a pattern of basic assumptions that each functional group has developed in learning to achieve internal cohesiveness, and to adapt to its external environment (Schlein, 1984).

Separate paradigms have evolved in research, enforcement, administration, education, and rule making. These models serve as strong reinforcements for federal officials to approach the issues in a characteristic manner. Each function imparts differing signals concerning how to share biotechnology's risk with industry, which kinds of positive and negative incentives to offer industry, and the particular kinds of working relationships to engage in with industry. Public policymakers have to consider the likelihood that their responses to biotechnology will be a composite of activities emanating from very different organizational and perhaps functional cultures. On one hand, they may very well be feeling the press of fiscal constraints, biotechnology's complexity, and the general need and ability to share great amounts of information with industry. These forces could be driving the public-private intersect into new dimensions. It is not difficult to see, however, that such pressure at least has the potential to create great conflict within certain governmental functions when the outside forces are redefining roles in a way that goes against the grain of long-standing culture-based assumptions about appropriate and responsible public sector behavior. For example, it would appear that the current administration's philosophy is to aggressively utilize biotechnology as an economic opportunity in order to achieve competitive parity in international markets. At the same time, several laws mandate regulatory agencies to ensure the safety of products such as drugs and foods that are marketed to the American public.

It is not too difficult to envision uncertainty felt by the policymaker as regards the *pace* of product approval. This uncertainty stems in part from accountability to two sources: current administration philosophy, and legal mandates to ensure health and safety. An even broader kind of accountability may be felt to the principles of the democratic process (Lilla, 1981). The whole chain of accountability reaching from immediate rules and regulations all the way back to the sovereign will of the people, may provide a framework for ethical action as regards biotechnology, but not a very tight framework. This chain of accountability may be hindered by several factors, including: (1) the existence of many possible mechanisms to carry out the public will, including decision rules used by regulatory agencies, interest group interpretations of what the public wants, and press interpretations of the public interest, (2) the lack of complete information available to the policymaker or the general public, and (3) conflicting signals—as in the case where the public wants complete assurance that genetically engineered products are safe, but is unwilling to support levels of federal spending to guarantee safety.

In the absence of unequivocal guidance on appropriate behavior from the various sources of accountability, policymakers will resort to their internal value orientations to determine what is or is not acceptable. This determination, sometimes referred to as "inner checks," is based on personal frames of reference and the associated values that prevail within those frames. Individual public officials may rely on embedded views of the working world which surrounds them. How is the biotechnology milieu being incorporated into these views? If they view their world as one of "war" with other factions in the private sector and with other nations, then biotechnology adopts the role of a set of weapons in that war. Decisions on the biotechnology issues mentioned earlier will conform to their metaphorical frame of reference. If they view their world as "puzzle solving" or "truth seeking," then obviously biotechnology plays quite a different role.

Many possible metaphorical interpretations are accessible to increase understanding and to guide action on biotechnology issues. Sources include organizational cultures and subcultures, professional, familial, or religious contexts, or broader societal mandates. While it is difficult to predict the combination of frames of reference and associated values any particular policymaker will bring to bear in shaping his/her concept of responsible action on the issues, ultimately it is the policymaker who does the shaping.

Regardless of the intent of action, and irrespective of the particular frame of reference that the action is grounded within, a policymaker is a cause of, or at least a contributor to, certain outcomes because he/she created conditions that led to the outcomes. To have causal responsibility is to have control of the following four elements, which are usually present in varying degrees: (1) resources to make things happen, (2) knowledge of likely consequences that various courses of action may produce and a choice among alternative courses of action, and (3) a purpose in mind beforehand (Harmon, 1981). By having these elements under rein, policymakers have an ability to shape and direct actions that take place outside their organization.

Skilled policymakers have many tools available to achieve intended purposes. These include the ability to assist in the social construction of meanings which surround the topic of biotechnology as it is addressed by public and private-sector officials. This notion is contrary to a perhaps commonly held image of the public official hamstrung by inflexible policies and procedures. Policymakers can design meetings and other communication mechanisms in desired directions. For example, they can select who will attend such meetings. They can, through agenda design, focus "air time" on particular topics and not on others. They can set the tone of dialogue through the structure of meetings (Forrester, 1982). They can also attempt to control the symbols surrounding communications, in order to achieve certain aims (Smircich and Stubbart, 1985).

Finally, they can at least *attempt* to manage the kinds of media messages that are constructed for public consumption and which paint certain pictures of biotechnology events as they transpire. Public-affairs officials in formal agencies can carefully screen and construct press releases, under close guidance of top policymakers, that will leave the desired impression with the general public. In short, policymakers are causally responsible to the extent that desired outcomes result from the social constructions that they shape.

Future Trends

And what of the future? It is highly likely that policymakers will be faced with more, not less, complexity as they attempt to help steer the course of biotechnology. But they will also hopefully have more effective tools to help them deal with this complexity. Despite some recent evidence of pessimism about technology companies demonstrated on Wall Street (Gladwell, 1989), the long-term prognosis appears bright. Both in terms of numbers of firms and products, the industry will continue to grow. The onslaught of biotechnology products is just beginning. Experts predict that genetically engineered food products will not start to affect the marketplace until the mid-1990s (FDA, 1988). Public policymakers will have to match such a pace of industry development with enhanced scientific understanding and capability, communication ability, and innovative institutional arrangements.

At the level of scientific and technological understanding, federal agencies will have to upgrade their efforts. Effective biotechnology policy will simply not be possible unless federal understanding of both product and process at least matches that of industry. Advances in communications technology will help the public policymaker address the challenge of keeping pace. The emergence of communications technology, particularly telecommunication advances such as computer conferencing and other linked computer networks, will give government and industry the potential to communicate more rapidly, incorporate a greater number of people in the communication, and cover a more diverse range of subjects. The opening of an electronic pipeline between government and industry offers the opportunity for closer interaction, more accurate interpretation of each other's positions, and more rapid adjustment through more rapid feedback. Multimedia techniques may permit simultaneous oral, graphic, analytical, and narrative information exchange.

As communications technology facilitates greater volume and frequency of information exchange, it may well affect participants' conceptualization of the boundary between government and industry, particularly in the case where the government agency has traditionally been the regulator of industry activity. For example, electronic transmission of information between the regulated drug industry and the FDA is changing from a potential benefit to a reality (Abbott, 1988: 55). This places both parties in more of an information inquiry and exchange mode, for the ultimate benefit of all affected stakeholders—including the American consumer. In some, although certainly not all instances, the traditional metaphorical depiction has been one of a military border. Regulatory agencies protect the territory (the territory being the health and safety of our citizens). The metaphor of the military boundary could become less applicable in situations where public and private sector must communicate clearly and frequently about complex new developments in biotechnology. A more appropriate boundary metaphor would be an estuary, where important exchanges of energy, matter, and information occur. This could certainly become more characteristic of the boundary relationships between regulatory agencies and industry. As the need for timely information about biotechnology developments becomes even greater, communications technology has the capacity to create an osmosis-like relationship. In this way, knowledge and understanding will be equalized by government, industry, and academia. The potential of electronic networking may be particularly well-suited for products developed via biotechnology, given the number of different public and private-sector organizations associated with the development of genetically engineered products.

Spurred on both by complex technology developments and the ability to communicate more effectively, government policymakers might well see a blurring of the line between the public and private sector. This will occur *not* in the responsibility for carrying out federal legislative mandates, but in the philosophy and implementation strategies necessary to bring the fruits of biotechnology to the general public.

New and innovative institutional arrangements are likely to evolve and result in shared human, technical, and physical resources. Institutional innovations between the sectors have already made their impact in other endeavors. Regional public-private sector management bodies have been active for 13 years in the area of marine resource management following the adoption of the Resources Conservation and Management Act in 1976. Public corporations, Urban Development Grants, and model cities projects have all demonstrated how multisector efforts can realize success in such areas as housing and economic development. And closer to the biotechnology area, centers of excellence such as the North Carolina Biotechnology Center again show the advantages of multi-sector efforts.

Such arrangements have several benefits. First, they represent the opportunity for efficient and effective resource expenditures in a time of fiscal constraint. Cooperation rather than competition among resource pools may be the byword for the future. Second, several of the arrangements mentioned above are consistent with the philosophy of decentralizing a complex sociotechnological challenge such as biotechnology. This permits greater responsiveness to regional/local concerns, while not relinquishing the ability to manage biotechnology's evolution. Finally, the very nature of such joint undertakings stands a good chance of imbuing government, industry, and academia with a stronger sense of public-mindedness—but in a way that acknowledges the existence of "multiple publics," not just a monolithic national public.

Summary

In this chapter some aspects of responsible action have been outlined for policymakers to consider as they address biotechnology issues. This is offered in the hope that practitioners will do some "reality testing," and in the process discover just how they construct their own personal standards of "responsible action." The concept of responsible behavior as government officials engage biotechnology is a complex one.

Policymakers are being fully responsible when they acknowledge all elements that influence the actions they embark upon. Officials need to explicitly acknowledge to whom, or what, they are being accountable as they break down the traditional formalities between regulator and regulated. Is it a personal standard, an administration standard, or a democratic standard they are living up to when they exchange needed information with industry—for example, about the risks associated with a genetically engineered organism being unintentionally released into the environment? They must also take responsibility for the outcomes that result from their actions. Ultimately, policymakers must be sufficiently comprehensive in their outlook to see the overall linkages between external forces which may be driving their policy decisions regarding responsibility, their own personal and institutional frames of reference, and the outcomes that result. Officials will then see that they and their agencies, and how they play their role with the other biotechnology actors such as industry and academia, have a joint shaping influence over biotechnology in the future—and its impact upon the American public.

Note

The views expressed by the author do not necessarily represent the policies or views of the Food and Drug Administration.

12

Economic Development and Public Policy: What Is the Role for Biotechnology?

Mack C. Shelley, II,
William F. Woodman,
Brian J. Reichel, and Paul Lasley

As a number of state and local governments seek ways to expand their economic base, high technology, including biotechnology, has taken on increased importance in the minds of policymakers and elected officials as a means to produce major and long-lasting improvements in the industrial and service sectors. This chapter will first briefly outline general patterns of thought regarding economic development strategies pursued by state and local governments. The discussion then turns to an in-depth analysis of the state of Iowa's commitment to fund research and development activities in biotechnology. This discussion examines Iowa's Biotechnology and Bioethics Program and Iowa State University's Research Park, international trade dimensions, and several economic development programs at Iowa State University. In the process of policymaking for economic development, different views may be held by key groups of actors as to how best to provide a high-technology infrastructure. In the case study of Iowa, the views of academic, corporate, farm operator, and legislative participants in policymaking about the role of public universities in economic development are examined and the context for considering the role of state support for research in various aspects of high technology is made clear. This analysis presents a portion of an extended case study in the state of Iowa of funding for research in biotechnology. We report on some potential implications drawn from statewide, local, and national surveys addressing that biotechnology emphasis. We present selected results from some of our core items addressed to all target groups, along with an analysis of attitudes toward university-industry cooperation through research parks. A concluding discussion attempts to place our findings in broader perspective.

Issues of State Development of High Technology

Gurwitz (1982) refers to "the new faith in high tech," which, to him, is a "fad" fraught with four major problems: (1) the vagueness of the concept of "high technology," (2) the likelihood that many or even most attempts to develop high-technology industries and services will fail when they become widespread, (3) the absence of large numbers of leading technical universities to provide personnel and research results for such industries and services, and (4) the inability of most governments or civic and business interests to stimulate activities which have a high probability of success.

In contrast to Gurwitz's skepticism about the future of high technology as an engine of economic development, Denny (1982) sees the possibility that competition among the states and municipal governments for high-tech industry will produce social benefits from attempts to lure such industries through adoption of policies which encourage public and private investments in education and research, tax structures that reward research and development (R&D), and taxing consumption and after-profits income. He foresees advances in urban and rural infrastructure, corporate philanthropy, and cooperation among the public, private, and nonprofit sectors on many fronts, particularly in labor relations. Denny also envisions that competition among states and municipalities for high-tech industry is helping to ensure the competitiveness of the United States in international markets by encouraging regional diversification and specialization in different aspects of high technology.

A case study (Dorfman, 1983) of the emergence of Boston's "Route 128" center for high technology, however, found that its development was largely indigenous and spontaneous, and did not result from strenuous governmental efforts to attract industry to the Boston area. Dorfman attributes the Route 128 phenomenon to its proximity to local universities and their research laboratories, a strong existing technological infrastructure, positive externalities from the colocation of related high-tech firms, and the previous success of local minicomputer manufacturers (notably Digital Electronic Corporation). Other researchers (Klausner and Van Brunt, 1987; Trewhitt, 1985) have assessed various regions' or cities' likelihood of joining the front ranks of biotechnology research centers.

In the rush to attract high-technology industries, leaders of the dominant companies have a major role to play in concert with government officials and with those universities that place a heavy emphasis on technology-relevant research. Hagstrom (1982) reports, though, that successfully communicating high-technology industry needs to elected officials is often difficult because political authorities, who are ready and willing to offer assistance, commonly fail to understand the complexities of this emerging sector of the economy, particularly its demands for engineering talent, capital, and entrepreneurial effort.

An assessment by the U.S. Bureau of Labor Statistics (Riche et al., 1983) suggests that the common arguments by elected officials that high technology will generate large numbers of high-quality new jobs may be misleading. The study found that high-technology industries accounted for a relatively small proportion of all new jobs created nationally from 1972 to 1982, with 60 percent of high-technology jobs concentrated in the most populous states, and that high-technology industries can be expected to account for only a small proportion of new jobs created through 1995. Nonetheless, the common perception that high-technology industry is a solution to unemployment generally and manufacturing-sector unemployment in particular is widely shared. This equation of jobs with high technology commonly involves the promotion of economic growth and development by major universities through selectively encouraging research in relevant areas of science and technology, with examples including Stanford University and the Massachusetts Institute of Technology. Some states tend to encourage closer university-industry relationships (commonly abbreviated as UIRs) when economic conditions or expectations dictate the political need for the state to become active in job creation (Abelson, 1983).

David (1983: 28) argues that "the nation's fine research universities are still largely untapped as an element for innovation despite increasing connections between industry and the universities" and that "industry can lend new life to at least some university research by sponsoring work related to corporate objectives but encouraging creativity by avoiding the bureaucratic impediments of government funding." Thus one view, which we take to be widely shared by many in both industry and academia (and perhaps in government, as well), is that universities are indispensable to the success of high-technology endeavors, that research universities can and should do more to promote economic development, and that the universities in turn will benefit in at least some of their research endeavors from both the infusion of industry resources and the lack of bureaucratic red tape. However, Fusfeld (1980: 221) argues that "university-industry relations in science and technology have long been characterized by curious mixtures of respect and condescension, of affection and irritation, of strong mutual interactions and barriers, planned or philosophical." These interactions, he asserts, are essential for continued progress in science and technology.

Abelson (1986) focuses on the expanded role of state governments in promoting UIRs. He points to the leadership role in this area taken by the National Governors' Association, which preceded the federal government in emphasizing the importance of interaction between universities and industries. This conclusion was predicated on studies showing that a majority of all new jobs were created by small firms, and on the supposition that activity by state and local governments to promote science and technology could stimulate the formation of small firms and thereby improve the record of job creation. Abelson notes that common features of state activities in high-technology promotion include research parks located near universities, incubator facilities on or near campuses, start-up support for companies, encouraging faculty entrepreneurship, joint research centers, and providing extension services to larger numbers of companies.

In this respect, it is particularly instructive to realize that colleges and universities, combined with state and local government, account for only about three percent of the more than $100 billion spent nationally on research and development (Lindsey, 1985). However, universities, which conduct about 10 percent of the nation's R&D, receive nearly two-thirds of their R&D funding from the federal government and about five percent from industry. Thus, there is a large role to be filled by both industry and state governments in encouraging university R&D work. Lindsey (1985) proposes various mechanisms, modelled after the experience of the state of North Carolina, by which states can encourage this activity. He concludes that "the common feature of state efforts should be the *identification* and *removal* of public barriers and disincentives to industry/ university cooperation and technological innovation and the *creation* of incentives" (emphasis in the original). State government interest in the R&D capacity of academia is easily understood by considering that roughly two-thirds of the Ph.D.-granting research universities are public institutions supported by state and local governments, and that many of the private research universities also receive some form of state support (Lindsey, 1985).

The State of Iowa's Program in Biotechnology and Bioethics and Iowa State University's Research Park

In 1985, the 71st Iowa General Assembly empowered the Iowa Development Commission to allocate to the state's public Board of Regents' institutions or to the independent colleges and universities the sum of $10 million for the purposes of economic development and research and development. This funding, and subsequent state financing for such efforts, was derived from proceeds from the state's recently enacted lottery. The funded institutions were required to certify that matching support would be received from other sources. Proposals from the Regents' institutions, including Iowa State University, were to be filtered through and submitted by the state Board of Regents to the Iowa Development Commission. Proposals not acceptable to the commission could be rejected if they were judged to be inconsistent with the plan for economic development in the state.

In its 1986 session, the General Assembly amended the relevant legislation to provide more specific instructions for the allocation of funds for biotechnology-related economic development. The sum of $500,000 was allocated to Iowa State University for agricultural biotechnology research and development for the fiscal year beginning July 1, 1985. Further, for the fiscal year beginning July 1, 1986, an additional $3.75 million was allocated to Iowa State for biotechnology

R&D. For the fiscal year beginning July 1, 1987, and for each of the two succeeding fiscal years, $4.35 million was allocated for the same purpose.

The 1986 legislation also provided that $50,000 for each of the fiscal years beginning July 1, 1986, and July 1, 1987, was to be used to develop a program in "bioethics" at Iowa State University. The legislation, authored by legislators Paul Johnson and David Osterberg, stipulated that this program should address socioeconomic and environmental implications of biotechnology research (Iowa, State of, 1986). Subsequently, additional external grant funding was obtained for the bioethics research program from the Joyce Foundation and the Northwest Area Foundation. A Bioethics Committee was established, along with a number of task-oriented subcommittees, and research proposals were solicited. A series of informal discussions on agricultural bioethics issues was inaugurated late in 1987. Also in 1987, an external advisory group was established to help direct the efforts of the committee into critical aspects of agricultural bioethics. The committee was actively involved in three major national conferences from 1987 to 1989. Other developments in related areas were moving at a similar pace.

The initial legislative funding of both economic development and bioethics research could be said to reflect a major reality of the political culture of Iowa, and perhaps of much of rural America. That the state was in need of a stronger, broader, and more modern economic base was generally accepted. At the same time, the views of many members of relevant policy publics held that the traditional family farm should not thereby be threatened and that the virtues of Iowa's quality of life should not be sacrificed to economic developments that might carry threats to the physical environment, cultural norms, and consumer safety.

By early 1986, plans were well underway for the establishment of a university research park near Iowa State University linked to the perceived need to enhance existing resources in biotechnology and to transfer advanced technologies to private industry. A research park working group, established by the Vice-President for Planning and Development, included economic development consultants and experts from Iowa State University, Ames Laboratory (a Department of Energy facility), and the Iowa High Technology Council. Its mission was to implement an economic development plan for the university including the following elements: (1) establish an incubator program on campus to foster entrepreneurial activities, (2) develop research parks near the campus to facilitate technology transfer between the university and corporate researchers, (3) attract high-technology companies to Iowa, and (4) develop industrial parks in the Iowa State-Ames-Ankeny-Des Moines area to create new jobs.

The research park was established as a joint project of the university and the city of Ames, with the goal of creating as many as 6,000 jobs and millions of dollars of investments in the state over roughly a 20-year period. The first phase of construction was supported by the board of the Iowa State University Research Foundation (ISURF), which assisted in acquiring land for the park in the furtherance of the university's role in stimulating the state's economy. A total of

$2.5 million was raised for purchasing the land through the Achievement Foundation of the Alumni Association. Local political leaders were strongly supportive of the project as a mechanism to generate more jobs and reverse the state's population decline.

In July 1986, a director of the research park was selected with the expectation that the companies to be attracted to the research park would come because of the university's established strengths in areas such as microelectronics and biotechnology. Both the state of Iowa and the university expected to gain from the development of this mechanism for technology transfer for both domestic and foreign markets. The park was set up to be managed by the ISU Research Park Corporation, a not-for-profit affiliate of the university accountable to the Board of Regents. The university was to exercise control over which firms located in the park, with the length of the lease to depend on each firm's ability and willingness to meet criteria set by the park's management and to participate in the advantages afforded by proximity to the university.

University officials hoped that the park would become a midwestern "Silicon Valley" through its unique status as the first research park in the state to be linked with a university. A variety of technologies were planned in order to make the park less susceptible to softness in the economy of any given sector. The park was envisioned as the beginning of a high-technology belt to run along an axis created by Interstate 35 between Des Moines and Ames, including several intervening towns. At the same time, the Iowa State Innovation System (ISIS) was established as a high-tech business "incubator" designed to help transform business ideas into fully operational companies. One specific goal of the research park is to nurture the companies that are already growing in the incubator and to enhance relationships with other firms that wish to invest in their research and development.

In June 1987, the Board of Regents gave the university conditional approval to spend $750,000 for land acquisition and operating costs for the first two years, under the university's bonding authorization, provided that other projects were funded first. The Regents also authorized Iowa State University to proceed with planning for a $30.5 million Biochemistry and Molecular Biology Building designed to house about 50 scientists by 1990 and to consolidate campus-wide research on biotechnology.

In September 1987, Iowa State University hosted the Iowa Biotechnology Showcase, designed to highlight the state's university-based biotechnology research program. The event was sponsored by the Iowa Biotechnology Consortium, which included representatives from Iowa State University, the University of Iowa, and the Iowa Department of Economic Development. About 60 agribusiness and research companies were represented at the Ames showcase, including officials of foreign firms and major American corporations, in addition to over 200 members of the public, including faculty and students. A railroad parlor car was loaned by a state senator for transporting the participants between Des Moines and a developing research park near the University of Iowa campus.

The consortium has also made presentations designed to market Iowa biotechnology in San Francisco, New Orleans, and London, and participated in the AgBiotech '88 international conference and exposition for agricultural biotechnology industries held in Washington, D.C.

A major success of the state's effort to attract biotechnology-related industry was the 1987 announcement by Eastman Kodak of its decision to locate a $50 million plant on about 80 acres owned by Iowa Electric Light and Power Company in Cedar Rapids, Iowa. The plant, a project of Kodak's Bio-Products Division, was expected to employ between 75 and 100 workers to manufacture "Snomax," an artificial snow, and to utilize fermentation processes to manufacture other products, using corn and soybeans in the production of food additives, pharmaceuticals, industrial enzymes, and specialty chemicals.

A strategy for accomplishing economic development in Iowa through biotechnology research and applications emerged, with an emphasis on technology transfer from universities to industry and field trials. The ties between corporate and academic interests necessary for this strategy to be successful inevitably gave rise to manifest and latent stresses. Many of the state's political leaders had tied their electoral appeal to the reputed virtues of biotechnology-led economic growth, while corporate needs for short-term payoffs from university-based research potentially conflicted with farmers' interests in the viability of the family farm, and with academics' concerns for the integrity and independence of basic research. Furthermore, divisions within academia—between administrators and students or faculty, between faculty and students, and between faculty in and not in biotechnology research—were widely expected. Some of these sources of possible conflict were evident in the international focus which Iowa biotechnology acquired.

International Trade Dimensions

The international dimension of economic development through biotechnology in Iowa is perhaps best exemplified by the participation of state and university representatives in the October 1986 Bio Fair in Tokyo, Japan. The purpose of the fair was to promote an exchange of knowledge and technical information in order to expedite the industrialization of biotechnology research. Held under the sponsorship of the Bioindustry Development Center and the Japanese Association of Industrial Fermentation, in cooperation with Japanese banks, trade and industrial organizations, scientific societies, and government ministries, the fair attracted 62,000 participants. Several possibilities for research leading to technology transfer in a number of plant and animal science areas were explored. One Japanese company (Ajinomoto) has already invested heavily in biotechnology in Iowa through a $50 million lysine plant, owned jointly with a French firm (Orsan), at Eddyville. The plant exploits genetically engineered modifications in lysine-producing bacteria which may be facilitated by recombinant DNA techniques.

In December 1987, Nittobo American, Inc., a California subsidiary of Nitto Boseki, announced that it would locate a new biotechnology production and distribution facility at Boone, Iowa, under the name of Midland BioProducts Corporation. The company produces immunodiagnostic antisera raw materials for the veterinary and agricultural industries. The Iowa Biotechnology Consortium was instrumental in attracting this start-up facility in the state. The firm's decision was no doubt made easier by the fact that the president and chief operating officer of Midland BioProducts is an Iowa native and an alumnus of Iowa State University. A major factor in the company's decision was its access to research facilities at Iowa State University, as well as the nearby Animal Disease Center and the National Veterinary Services Laboratory.

This example seems to suggest that while the lobbying efforts of economic development organizations are beneficial, the crucial factors may be the same as those in Dorfman's (1983) list of "Route 128" attractions: proximity to local universities and laboratories, existing technological infrastructure, and similar factors. The crux of the matter clearly is that success builds upon success and can encourage subsequent development.

Economic Development Programs and Iowa State University

Under the motto "Iowa State Means Business," Iowa State University has tied its research very closely to business development, jobs growth, and economic diversification. Both Iowa State University and the University of Iowa have come to be regarded by the state's political leadership as the focus for their hope of rebuilding an economy that has long been too closely tied to the vicissitudes of agriculture. However, doubts have been raised about the ability of any university to meet the high expectations thus placed on it, especially in light of concerns of the transferability of high-technology success from other parts of the nation, the projected small role for high technology in job creation, the relative paucity in Iowa of military research and development expenditures, the limited entrepreneurial experience of university faculty, and uncertainty about continued state and private support (Westphal, 1987).

An effort to foster economic development was undertaken in late 1987 with congressional approval of a National Center for Food and Industrial Agricultural Product Development, with an initial 1988 fiscal year appropriation of $6.4 million. Planning began on a $14 million facility to be situated on the Ames campus. The goal of this center was to encourage the development of new markets for agricultural commodities by pulling together researchers active in crop and livestock utilization in three existing centers at Iowa State: the Food Crops Processing Research Center, the Meat Export Research Center, and the Meat Irradiation Technology Center. The university will have the capability to determine the properties and possible uses for new products or processes involving the state's agricultural commodities, solve scale-up problems, obtain licenses and patents, and transfer newly developed technologies to interested industries.

Companies may also engage the center to do contract research or to analyze the properties and potential uses of new grain or meat products that have been developed by an industry.

Meanwhile, Iowa State University's Food and Industrial Crops Process Research Center was charged with examining ways to make industrial products, such as chemicals and biodegradable plastics, from corn and soybeans, the state's chief agricultural crops. One of the goals is to replace nonfuel, petroleum-based products with products developed from Iowa crops. Other scientists are working on biological and genetic controls for major crop pests, with the goal of minimizing production costs and reducing dependence on massive application of fertilizers and petrochemical derivatives which can threaten environmental degradation (Eaton, 1987).

Different Viewpoints and Concerns Regarding Universities' Roles in Economic Development

A number of practical and ethical issues have been identified as arising from the commitment to biotechnology research for economic development at Iowa State University (Rose, 1987). Among these concerns are: the lack of structures within the university to create jobs when the major function of an academic institution is the conduct of research, teaching, and service activities; the possibility of classified weapons-related research; the uncertain risks posed by releasing genetically engineered microbes or plants into the environment; the development of herbicide-resistant crops which will allow greater concentrations of chemical inputs into agriculture, with advantages to the chemical firms sponsoring such research and the risk of possible environmental damage; the differential benefits of biotechnology for larger farm operations at the expense of traditional small family farms; the danger that researchers and university officials may come to prize profit more than scholarship; curtailment of information derived from this research due to commercial constraints; exploitation of students for commercial reasons; the use of public funds to finance private projects; and pecuniary jealousy among faculty colleagues.

Yet another dimension of the concern was brought out in a December 1987 commencement address at Iowa State University delivered by the director of the Ames Laboratory, who emphasized the importance of translating the findings of higher education into practical applications, the role of the university in broadening the state's economic base, concerns by the faculty that involvement with industry is nonacademic, and the fact that researchers must expect to show benefit to the funders of their research (Bullers, 1987). Afterward, the local newspaper editorialized that the trends discussed by the director were beneficial to all involved:

A trend toward university-corporate partnerships is growing across the nation rapidly and we're in on the ground floor ... "In terms of technology transfer and exposure to some of the brightest scientists in the world, you can't beat university research," Edwin Przybylowicz, Eastman Kodak's director of research recently told the *New York Times*.

Universities, which had been stand-offish from corporate ties for fear of taint, are now clasping business hands. Federal research funds are drying up and schools are looking to corporations to fund the work of the best and brightest. Their previous, and many existing, fears have not been borne out. Compromises have been reached with companies that allow professors to publish findings of research involving proprietary information. And, scholars are finding that business contributions supplement, rather than detract from or inhibiting, their traditional pursuits.

Iowa State has had a long association with the agricultural industry that it can cultivate even more as the biotechnology phase takes hold. In this area, we are on the cutting edge of a trend that is helping universities expand on all their traditional functions—teaching, research, and service (*The Daily Tribune*, December 21, 1987).

Although not all observers of this phenomenon tend to be as sanguine about the virtues of closer university/industry research collaboration, it seems virtually certain that the future of university research will be tied closely to connections with the industry. It is a signal event, then, that Iowa State University recently appointed its first biotechnology industrial liaison person, an individual who was formerly group leader for plant biotechnology for Standard Oil.

The Iowa State University Surveys on Biotechnology

As part of Iowa State University's research agenda on bioethics, a series of surveys were mailed to relevant populations, a total of seven groups being targeted. Virtually all the faculty members at Iowa State who were listed in the 1987 biotechnology directory (except for department executive officers [DEOs]) were sent surveys through campus mail, along with a systematic random sample of non-biotechnology faculty also contacted by mail (a total of 450, of which 59 percent responded). A systematic sample of graduate students (250, of which 38 percent responded) was also surveyed, both by mail and by telephone, without regard to their involvement in biotechnology-related work. Virtually all of the university's administrators with the rank of DEO through vice-president were mailed surveys (161, of which 71 percent responded). In the spring of 1988, a survey instrument was sent to all members of the Iowa state legislature (150, of which 55 percent responded). Finally, results from a large parallel survey sample of 1983 Iowa farm operators (conducted by the Iowa Farm and Rural Life Poll) were compared to those obtained from the university, biotechnology corporation, and legislative surveys.

The samples were designed to produce a diversity of views on issues related to university research in biotechnology. Specific areas of interest addressed in the surveys (but not necessarily repeated for all respondent groups) included: the likely impacts of biotechnology on U.S. agriculture; university participation in biotechnology research; the role of research parks in economic development;

university relations with biotechnology companies (regarding contracts, patents, and the like); the use and benefits of state lottery funds to support research in biotechnology; effects of biotechnology funding on the university environment (regarding salaries, teaching, relationships among faculty and between faculty and students, and the like); barriers to cooperative research between industries and universities and ways to reduce them; and general background data about the individual respondent or corporation.

A total of 11 questions were asked of all sets of respondents. Owing to variations in question wording for the Iowa farm operators as compared to the other respondent groups, and because of space limitations, we do not present the results here for the first six of the common-core items, which are focused on possible economic development consequences arising from the research emphasis on biotechnology in Iowa (for those results, see Shelley et al., 1989; Woodman et al., 1989). The latter group of five common-core questions (Table 12.1) pertains to various aspects of university research agendas which might be affected by the push for biotechnology applications. This set of five items addresses the sometimes uneasy research partnership among universities, industry, and government which is at the heart of many proposals for economic development, as noted above. Results of these items have been discussed previously (Shelley et al., 1989; Woodman et al., 1989).[1] (For a detailed investigation of state legislators' reactions to biotechnology as a means of economic development, see Reichel et al., 1989.)

A brief overview of the data in Table 12.1 reveals that some systematic differences in response structures exist between university respondents and nonuniversity groups, and that the university respondents' attitudes are relatively similar to each other. The consensus among academic respondents to the surveys includes agreement that it is all right to work closely with industry, that scientists should determine the direction of university research, that universities should sell patent rights, and that private consulting by faculty should not be curtailed. On the contrary, the selection of research problems by scientists is opposed by farm operators and biotechnology company respondents, both of whom also resist university control of patent rights. In addition, farmers and state legislators tend to be more inclined to favor limits on consulting, and farmers favor increased public funding for the development of new agricultural commodities.

Findings from Other Surveys

Given that about half of the annual federal R&D monies destined for universities and colleges end up in biochemical and biomedical research projects oriented toward disease control or eradication, it should not be surprising that there would be a substantial scramble by both universities and companies for these funds. Given also that these funds are oriented toward applied (and highly profitable) outcomes, it should also not be surprising that companies in these areas have made themselves part of this process through cooperative research agreements,

Table 12.1

Summary Statistics for Five Items on Structural Effects of Biotechnology Research

		Biotech Faculty	Other Faculty	Grad Student	College Admins.	Biotech Company	Farm Oper.	Legislators
Universities should work closely with private businesses and industry, including the agri-business sector.	Mean	2.254	2.611	2.411	2.263	1.686	2.10	2.608
	sd	1.081	1.191	1.160	1.040	0.922	0.91	1.372
	n	134	113	90	114	121	1,911	79
Scientists, rather than the agri-business community, should determine what types of problems need to be investigated.	Mean	2.614	2.726	3.156	2.842	3.642	3.48	3.154
	sd	1.202	1.128	1.235	1.110	1.083	1.13	1.280
	n	132	113	90	114	120	1,917	78
New discoveries by university scientists should be patented by the university and sold to the highest bidder, who would then make these products commercially available.	Mean	2.431	2.598	2.736	2.327	2.958	3.00	2.449
	sd	1.173	1.035	1.163	0.901	1.177	1.42	0.907
	n	132	112	91	113	120	1,913	78
The amount of private consulting by university faculty should be curtailed.	Mean	3.820	3.616	3.473	3.652	3.689	3.07	2.911
	sd	1.065	1.059	0.993	1.052	1.053	0.89	0.909
	n	133	112	91	115	122	1,902	79
More public funds should be used to support the development of new uses for agricultural commodities.	Mean	2.149	2.339	2.411	2.157	2.213	2.07	2.354
	sd	1.037	1.027	0.959	1.065	1.070	0.97	1.050
	n	134	112	90	115	122	1,912	79

direct funding, and university-industry contacts. Surprisingly, there has been a very small number of studies of such a financially significant phenomenon in our society. Among the most frequently cited such studies of recent years have been those of Blumenthal et al. (1986b, 1986c). In a survey of over 1,200 faculty members at 40 major universities in the United States, Blumenthal et al. (1986b) revealed that biotechnology researchers supported by industry publish at higher rates, patent more frequently, participate in more administrative and professional activities, and earn higher incomes than colleagues lacking such support. At the same time, industrially funded faculty were more likely than other biotechnology faculty to report that their research had resulted in trade secrets and that commercial considerations had influenced their choice of research projects. Although the data did not establish a causal connection between industrial support and these faculty behaviors, the findings strongly suggest that university-industry research relationships carry with them both benefits and risks for academic institutions.

In addition, Blumenthal et al. (1986c) found that almost half of all biotechnology companies funded university research. This funding may comprise as much as half of all U.S. university funding for biotechnology research, and is apparently returning a higher rate of patents per dollar invested than any other industrial research. However, it is a commonly voiced concern that traditional university values, such as openness of communications among university researchers, may be jeopardized in these relationships.

When asked to agree with a statement that "universities should work closely with private companies, businesses, and industry," a large majority of all surveyed parties agreed, with biotechnology companies expressing the strongest (89.2 percent) agreement among all groups. Along this line, while Blumenthal et al. (1986c) found that 46 percent of industry respondents were sponsoring university research at the time of their survey (1984), the authors found that 66.1 percent were supporting university research in 1987 and, even more impressive, that fully 78 percent of the companies anticipated funding such research in the future. Thus, the evidence from Blumenthal et al. (1986c) indicated that there was a growing movement toward industrial support of university biotechnology research, and the Reichel et al. (1989) research verified that the trend is gaining momentum. Lasley and Bultena (1987), in a statewide survey of Iowa farmers, also found farmers' faith in science and their orientation toward economic development to be the best predictors of constituency support for university-industry linkages. They concluded that although farmers are generally supportive of university-industry linkages, it is too early to predict accurately whether that support will be sustained into the future. Similarly, Lasley and Bultena (1987) found that for the most part farmers enthusiastically endorsed expected improvements in production efficiencies as a result of biotechnological research in agriculture.

The net effect of the small amount of research on the topic of university-industry relationships to date is that a consensus clearly exists among some seg-

Table 12.2
Summary Statistics for Nine Items on the Development of Research Parks*

From your point of view, to what extent do you see the development of a Research Park in Ames by Iowa State University resulting in:		Biotech Faculty	Other Faculty	Graduate Students	Adminis-trators	Legis-lators
Shifting emphasis to applied research?	Mean	2.150	2.035	2.079	1.895	1.920
	sd	0.812	0.550	0.661	0.615	0.587
	n	133	113	89	114	75
Creating pressures for faculty to spend too much time on commercial activities?	Mean	2.767	2.761	2.899	2.535	3.600
	sd	1.014	0.993	0.966	0.942	0.944
	n	133	113	89	114	75
Undermining intellectual exchange and cooperative activities within and between departments?	Mean	3.338	3.177	3.169	3.447	2.800
	sd	1.022	1.011	0.980	0.951	0.959
	n	133	113	89	114	75
Producing patent royalties to increase university revenue?	Mean	2.373	2.496	2.517	2.451	2.480
	sd	0.722	0.670	0.827	0.756	0.601
	n	134	113	89	113	75
Creating conflict between faculty who support and oppose such activities?	Mean	2.699	2.566	2.562	2.640	3.149
	sd	0.945	0.895	0.878	0.913	0.753
	n	133	113	89	114	74
Providing job opportunities for students?	Mean	2.187	2.310	2.079	2.088	2.120
	sd	0.615	0.745	0.661	0.659	0.657
	n	134	113	89	114	75
Creating unreasonable delays in the publication of new findings?	Mean	3.142	3.239	3.326	3.272	2.947
	sd	0.877	0.672	0.823	0.756	0.787
	n	134	113	89	114	75
Enhancing scholarly productivity?	Mean	2.776	2.699	2.404	2.482	2.554
	sd	0.906	0.865	0.808	0.707	0.705
	n	134	113	89	114	74
Altering standards for promotion and tenure?	Mean	3.105	2.761	2.730	3.140	2.932
	sd	0.971	0.794	0.836	0.958	0.669
	n	133	113	89	114	74

* Some small but inconsequential wording differences existed among questionnaires. The wording used here is from the faculty/graduate student questionnaire.

ments of the scientific community and public as to the prospects and promise of biotechnology. That consensus turns on the assumption that university-industry interactions will be good for both the companies and universities involved. There exists much less consensus as to the goals which should be pursued and the means which should be used to pursue them.

Research Parks, Biotechnology, and Economic Development

One major section of the Iowa State University surveys administered to five of the respondent groups (biotechnology faculty, non-biotechnology faculty, graduate students, university administrators, and state legislators) dealt with the role of research parks in biotechnology and economic development. A summary of these results is given in Table 12.2, where the information is arranged as in Table 12.1. Some small but inconsequential wording differences existed in different surveys. The wording used for Table 12.2 is from the faculty/graduate student questionnaire.

It is notable that biotechnology and non-biotechnology faculty showed only minimal differences, except where the issue of promotion and tenure was concerned. That is, biotechnology faculty were notably less inclined than faculty not doing biotechnology research to agree that the establishment of a research park would alter standards for promotion and tenure. Table 12.2 also shows that attitudes of graduate students were quite similar to those of faculty, although they are more likely than the faculty to agree that a research park would enhance scholarly productivity. The university administrators were more likely than the other groups to agree that the research park would shift the emphasis to applied research and result in pressures for faculty to spend more time on commercial activities. Administrators were less likely to agree that intellectual exchange and cooperative activities would be undermined by the research park. Legislators tended to feel that faculty would not spend too much time on commercial activities and that intrafaculty conflict would not be engendered. The legislators were more likely than other respondents to agree that academic cooperation and intellectual exchange might suffer and that publications might be delayed.

Conclusions and Interpretations

What is perhaps most evident from this historical overview, case study, and review of existing data is the complexity of the role played by a major research university in the process of state economic development. Iowa is certainly not alone in the drive to develop "high-tech" industries which follow the models of California's Silicon Valley, Massachusetts' Route 128, or North Carolina's Research Triangle. Iowa, in its efforts, has attempted to popularize the notion of a "Golden Circle" radiating out from the state capital, Des Moines, and encompassing major nearby research centers such as Iowa State University. Whether this or similar efforts will be effective depends in large part on the cooperation and talents of the university administrators, faculty, students, and staff, who will be required in many cases to redirect their professional efforts toward short-term ends.

Universities such as Iowa State University are well-situated in some respects to participate in economic development activities such as research parks. However, it and other major research universities are torn between commitments to their traditional functions and a newer set of sometimes worrisome and sometimes highly fruitful possibilities to expand the range and quality of institutional outputs. Whether this multidimensionality of the views that members of the academic community bring with them to their participation in economic development is on balance positive for the university and for the political and economic interests behind the push for economic development is yet to be determined. Part of the success potential will be realized through the internal dynamics of university procedures and professionalism, and through the external dynamics of elections, economic fluctuations, shifts in public opinion, and perceptions of the proper role of higher education for the remainder of this century.

Universities, as large, complex organizations, have traditionally had at least a threefold mission of teaching, research, and service. Academic institutions and units within those institutions exhibit various degrees of emphasis on these areas of their mission. As new areas of research open up, usually because of the funding to support such efforts, key decisionmakers within universities must consider whether and to what extent they wish the institution to invest itself in an attempt to capture external funding. They must also decide to what extent a redistribution of current and expected future resources within the institution is necessary in order to sustain the revised research agenda. There are potential consequences growing out of such decisions about resource allocation and research agendas within the university and for groups external but related to the university's decisions. The highly permeable nature of university agenda-setting decisions is particularly obvious with respect to the impact that private industry may have on university resources and research goals through offers of financial support and cooperative research. The other area of permeability is that of the feedback received through "constituent" reactions to pending decisions or decisions already made by university officials.

Land-grant universities are perhaps peculiarly sensitive among American universities to the interplay of pressures from internal groups, industry, and relevant external publics. They must be responsive to the needs and demands of state legislatures and state executives, to the wishes of their internal administrators, faculty, and students, to the private corporate sector on which they increasingly depend for research funding, and to the citizens for whom they provide extension services and other support. Political constituents, in particular, are inclined to insist on often overly precise measures of the job-creating outcomes of their investment of public funds in universities for economic development (Jaschik, 1987). The expectations, reactions, and attitudes, whether reasonable and well-informed or not, of all such groups must be taken into consideration in the process of formulating broad research agendas, calculating probable trade-offs among various choices, and monitoring the progress achieved from the decisions that have been made.

It is revealing that, despite the vociferous opinions that are expressed in the literature on UIR linkages, few research projects have focused on this area of endeavor. In one exception to this, Blumenthal et al. (1986a) found that there were some potential pitfalls in universities' past efforts to benefit from the commercial application of research findings by obtaining patents and granting licenses. The researchers concluded that universities should expect to be involved in lawsuits resulting from patenting and that university administrators may confront a choice of policies that overemphasize consulting, increase the share of royalties given to inventors and their departments at the possible expense of the overall needs of the university, and value applied research results in faculty personnel decisions, with attendant risks of conflict over traditional academic values favoring basic research. It seemed to the authors that more detailed, yet broad-based, research was needed.

In reviewing the results of these surveys and in attempting to make sense of their meaning for the ethics and practicality of university research in biotechnology, it is instructive to keep in mind that academic institutions have been said by two leading organizational theorists (Cohen and March, 1974) to be characterized by "organizational anarchy." Further, it is well to recall the views of March and Olson (1976: 176) that institutions of higher education are "complex 'garbage cans' into which a striking variety of problems, solutions, and participants may be dumped." Thus, our results should be seen in light of the normal creatively chaotic state of academia and the consequent lack of specific knowledge on the part of many of its institutional actors regarding policy.

The simple fact that internal disagreement is fairly minimal among the academic constituent groups regarding the "proper" direction for university biotechnology research does not and should not provide sufficient justification for such a direction. However, discussion regarding the basis for future university actions in this area are not likely, based on these empirical results, to be the source of intense internal battles over ethics. It is much more likely that debates will arise from questions such as: What will this research do to or for family farmers? What will this research mean for the farm economy? This potential focus of future debates is foreshadowed by discussions which have already been held in legislative bodies, within the university, and between citizens and university actors about the impact of biotechnology research on the family farm in the United States and on Third World economies in general. Beyond the consensus point that the family farm should not be harmed by the outcomes of biotechnology research lies the fundamental reality that not all rural residents are likely to benefit equally from university-based research in biotechnology. In fact, it is an article of faith among students of the process of technological innovations and diffusion that there will be differential benefits from any new technology. This is likely to provide the starting point for debate on ethical issues surrounding biotechnology.

Notes

The authors wish to express their thanks to the Survey Section of the Iowa State University Statistical Laboratory, to Kazi Ahmed for computer analysis, to Thomas Schliesman for assistance with coding and data collection, and to Kristi Hetland for secretarial assistance. This chapter represents a portion of the research being conducted by the Ethical Issues in Biotechnology Committee of Iowa State University, with financial support from the state of Iowa, the Iowa State University Graduate College, the Northwest Area Foundation, and the Joyce Foundation.

1. Each of the items presented in Table 12.1 was structured as a traditional Likert five-point, fixed-response question, with the responses including: "strongly agree" (coded as "1"), "agree," "uncertain," "disagree," and "strongly disagree." Table 12.1 shows the wording of each of these five items, together with the sample mean score averaged over all response values as coded above, the sample standard deviation of the responses (sd), and the number of valid responses (n) for each item. A larger mean value corresponds to a greater average tendency to disagree with a statement, while a smaller mean value indicates that respondents on average were more likely to be in agreement with a statement. Larger standard deviations show a greater degree of dispersion among the responses to a particular item.

13

Biotechnology Policy Knowledge: A Challenge to Congressional Policymakers and Policy Analysts

David J. Webber

Biotechnology is an emerging technology, industry, and policy issue that has the potential for radically transforming a number of American social, economic, legal, academic, and international institutions. An increased use of biotechnology practices and procedures has potential environmental risks, a wide range of economic repercussions, and implications for international trade and relations. It also raises important ethical and legal questions, such as the appropriateness of altering the genetic makeup of organisms or the stresses placed on existing patent protection of intellectual property.

Policymakers are just beginning to understand and keep abreast of the developments in biotechnology which might affect American society, therefore placing demands on the political system. Academic and professional analysts with varied backgrounds have examined numerous aspects of biotechnology and their potential implications for American society. The newness and complexity of the field of biotechnology provides policy analysts with an excellent case study with which to examine their ability to provide useful, and usable, information, and to study the ability of policymakers to stay informed and ask important questions relating to the operation of this policy arena.

Despite an impressive record of scientific advancement, the future of biotechnology is not clear. Both the direction and pace of biotechnology applications in the United States depend on public policy decisions. These decisions affect the legal, economic, and scientific support for further research, development, and, ultimately, application. Policy analysts can assist policymakers in the decisionmaking process by producing policy knowledge that covers diverse aspects of the impacts of biotechnology. They can contribute to the orderly development, control, and regulation of biotechnology by identifying the various political factors and events shaping biotechnology policy and by assessing regulatory schemes as they develop.

Additionally, because of the newness and uncertain future of biotechnology, analysts can offer research that is intended to inform discussions about future policies. A continuing challenge for policymakers and policy analysts alike is to keep up with changing policy conditions, expectations, and demands. In a "new" area like biotechnology this challenge is acute. If policy analysis is to be useful in the biotechnology policymaking arena, it must be analytical, evaluative, and speculative in that it anticipates future developments. It must address the concerns of policymakers in a timely and usable way. According to Lasswell (1968: 181), *"the policy sciences study the process of deciding or choosing and evaluate the relevance of available knowledge for the solution of particular problems"* (emphasis added). Producers of analysis intended to affect policymaking need to be interested in and to understand the distribution and use of their research in the policy process.

This chapter examines biotechnology policy knowledge by focusing on the perspectives of the intended users of such knowledge—congressional policymakers—and those of the producers of new knowledge about biotechnology. This chapter first identifies policy questions asked by members of Congress during congressional hearings, concerns expressed in members' speeches and writing, and those expressed in reports of the Office of Technology Assessment (OTA). Also presented are the domain and illustrative examples of biotechnology policy knowledge. In concluding this analysis a challenge is given to analysts and policymakers to produce and use a variety of types of policy knowledge which will enhance decisions affecting biotechnology and its impact on the United States.

Congressional Concerns and Questions Regarding Biotechnology

Biotechnology as a policy issue is new enough that it has not generated a widely agreed on set of congressional concerns. Because of a 1986 administrative order from the Office of Science and Technology Policy, the "Coordinated Framework for Regulation of Biotechnology" (*Federal Register*, 1986) has been the primary policy guideline and Congress has not been an active, direct participant in the design of biotechnology regulation. The congressional role in biotechnology policy has been primarily (1) oversight of agencies involved in the Coordinated Framework, (2) funding for biotechnology research, and (3) consideration of changes in related federal policies, for example, the patentability of genetically altered animals (see Plein and Webber, 1989).

The Coordinated Framework depends on existing agencies that, under present law, have concurrent jurisdiction. For example, a food product produced using a genetically altered microorganism might be viewed as a "chemical substance" and regulated by the Toxic Substance Control Act administered by the Environmental Protection Agency. It might also be viewed as a food additive normally regulated by the Food and Drug Administration according to the Food, Drug, and Cosmetic Act. Still yet, because of its responsibility to inspect meat and poultry products, the Department of Agriculture has a claim to jurisdiction. This approach to regulation requires no new legislation and, therefore, does not require formal congressional involvement.

Members of Congress view biotechnology from many perspectives; some members are primarily concerned with environmental aspects, some with agricultural and economic implications, and some with moral and ethical aspects of this new technology (see Plein and Webber, 1988, 1989). There has been a variety of congressional hearings and executive reports on diverse aspects of biotechnology. They range from specific concerns about support for recombinant DNA research to concerns about environmental release of genetically altered pesticides and even the impact of bovine somatotropin. A 1984 OTA report identified 10 factors of importance to biotechnology: financing and tax climate; health and environmental regulation; university-industry relations; government funding for research; availability of trained personnel for the emergent biotechnology industry; patent protection and rights; antitrust law; international market and trade arrangements; government policies relating to biotechnology; and public opinion.

As the biotechnology issue has evolved, the public's interest in biotechnology has also evolved. Plein (Chapter 10) presents a three-phased evolution of public interest in genetic engineering, arguing that public concern with the scientific development of biotechnology evolved from primarily a concern with ethics in the early 1970s, to an interest in health and environmental safety in the late 1970s, to the present focus on the economic dimensions of biotechnology.

Many members of Congress have expressed their concerns about biotechnology and its regulation through official remarks in committee or on the floor, in speeches, and in their writings. One of the earliest expressions of congressional concern was offered by Senator Adlai Stevenson (D-IL) in his statement opening three days of hearings by the Senate Subcommittee on Science, Technology, and Space in November 1977.

These hearings will attempt to cast some needed light on two [sic] questions that have been at the heart of the recombinant DNA controversy: how we can reap the benefits of recombinant DNA research while protecting humanity against unacceptable risks; how can we protect researchers, the public at large, and the environment from hazard while respecting the scientist's freedom to conduct research in a responsible manner; and finally, to what degree can this protection be accomplished by self-regulation and to what degree must we rely on public authority? (A. Stevenson, 1977)

In a 1984 conference organized by the Brookings Institution, Senator (then Representative) Albert Gore (D-TN) identified three broad areas of concern about biotechnology: the impact of new information on society, the impact of new products and substances on the environment, and the application of biotechnology to human beings. The first issue relates to the new genetic information that can be generated by biotechnological processes. Senator Gore asks (1985: 13-14) "What will biotechnology's impact be on the insurance industry when microcategories can be included in actuarial tables reflecting more accurate descriptions of risks due to individual genetic characteristics?" Gore summarized the major questions addressed as:

1. What are the risks of deliberate release?
2. What is the state of the art in the ability to predict the environmental consequences of such a release?
3. How well positioned are the federal agencies—the Environmental Protection Agency, the Department of Agriculture, and the National Institutes of Health—to make decisions regarding releases into the environment of new genetically altered organisms?
4. Are the laws adequate; is there a way to provide better coordination and more adequate scientific expertise?

While a representative, Gore served on the Subcommittee on Toxic Substances and Environmental Oversight, which held the first hearings on the environmental release of genetically altered organisms. The committee did not call for the creation of a new agency or new legislation (Gore, 1985: 17).

Representative John Dingell (D-MI), who chaired the Oversight and Investigations Subcommittee of the House Energy and Commerce Committee, stated in its May 1984 review of the scientific and commercial development of biotechnology that "the most urgent concern is the apparent inadequacy of the base of scientific knowledge used by the federal agencies to formulate judgements about new developments. . . When the committee looked at regulation to protect the public health and environment, the first thing discovered was the pressing need for research" (1985: 26). Additionally, Dingell posed eight specific questions concerning biotechnology (Dingell, 1985: 27-31):

1. Will the industrial domination of biotechnology research imperil basic research in the future?
2. Will the development strategies of the commercial interests be sufficiently broad to serve fully the public interest? For example, over 150 million people get malaria each year, but they are among the poorest people in the world. Will commercial incentives exist to invest development money if the potential consumers have no buying power?
3. Will biotechnology constitute a major escalation of the potential for biological warfare and terrorism?

4. Will public misunderstanding of human genetics and biotechnology mean the ghosts of the Scopes trial will haunt each new discovery and every new therapy?

5. Can the public debate about genetic engineering and biotechnology be improved?

6. Are there adequate preparations to deal with emergencies arising in the biotechnology industry?

7. Will the threat of tort liability owing to unforeseen consequences of the technology conspire to discourage established and conservative firms from entering the field, leaving the action to less risk-adverse buccaneers?

8. Will new interpretations and extension of patent law to life forms serve the public interest?

Senator Tom Harkin (D-IA), a member of the Senate Agriculture and Small Business Committees, in "Biotechnology in Agriculture and America's Competitiveness" (1988), suggests that Congress needs to address at least the following five issues:

1. We need to increase our funding support for research, both basic and applied.

2. We need to develop greater focus in our research and development efforts.

3. We need to streamline our regulatory efforts.

4. We need to work towards assuring that creativity is protected in the patent process both here and abroad.

5. We need to address public concerns by taking safety seriously and providing better information.

In 1988, Senator Patrick Leahy (D-VT), Chairman of the Agriculture Committee, identified eight issues that must be addressed in a national biotechnology policy:

1. Agricultural applications of biotechnology must be a national priority. We must ensure that farmers—big and small—benefit from new biotech tools.

2. The United States must support the world's premier biotechnology research program.

3. We must support small biotechnology firms, which frequently pioneer new discoveries.

4. We must use the tools of biotechnology to protect and enhance our environment.

5. We have a responsibility to resolve patenting issues.

6. We must reaffirm our commitment to the open exchange of scientific information.

7. We must untangle our regulatory system so that it provides adequate protection to the public and clear guidelines to industry.

8. We must establish international mechanisms that prevent runaway research and that aid developing nations in using the tools of biotechnology.

On February 29, 1988 (some 10 months after the first patent on a genetically

altered animal—a mouse—was granted), Senator Mark Hatfield (R-OR) introduced Senate Bill 2111: a bill to amend the patent law to prohibit the patenting
of genetically altered or modified animals. Senator Hatfield expressed his concerns about the ethical and moral dimensions of biotechnology developments,
noting that:

Congressional consideration of this matter must touch upon several areas, including the
ethical implications of the creation, and exclusive rights to, an animal never before existing in nature. . . . This revolutionary science may produce results nothing short of mirac-
ulous in their impact upon the health and well-being of mankind. But there is a dark side
to the knowledge we now hold. Man has tapped the power to create living things purely
for convenience and profit. To then confer patents to such creations could blur the line
between man's role as steward of the planet and man's exploitation of the Earth's riches
(Hatfield, 1988).

In addition to these specific concerns expressed by individual members of
Congress, OTA has issued several reports on biotechnology, including a five-part
series entitled "New Developments in Biotechnology." Because OTA is a research unit of Congress administered by a bipartisan, bicameral Congressional
Board (see Ellis and Hanna, 1989), the issues and concerns that are the focus of
OTA reports can be inferred as reflecting the concerns of members and congressional committees. Table 13.1 presents a summary of this five-part series and related OTA reports.

The Domain of Biotechnology Policy Knowledge

Policy knowledge (Webber, 1989) is the body of human knowledge available
to assist policymakers in their understanding of the causes and consequences of
government decisions, including their subsequent impact on society and the
world. Policymaking requires the linking of information and explanations from
various subfields of human knowledge and a combination of types of knowledge.
As defined here, policy knowledge is broader than, and subsumes, the fields of
policy research, policy analysis, and policy sciences. Webber (1989) has identified six types of policy knowledge, characterized by the extent to which they are
systematic and objectively verifiable:

1. Policymaker (personal) knowledge: popular accounts that explain how a policy works;
   this knowledge can be communicated by a policymaker to a citizen.
2. Journalistic knowledge: information and reports widely available that describe and explain a policy issue.
3. Practitioners' experience or clinical knowledge: comprehensive accounts by those involved about how a policy actually works.
4. Policy research: specific studies that attempt to systematically explain a specific
   policy.

Table 13.1
Summary of OTA Biotechnology Reports

Commercial Biotechnology: An International Analysis, 1984. Assesses the competitive position of the United States with respect to Japan and four European countries in terms of industrial use of recombinant DNA, cell fusion, and novel bioprocessing techniques.

Technology, Public Policy, and the Changing Structure of American Agriculture, 1986. Examines the relationship of technology to agricultural production, structural change, rural communities, environment and natural resource base, finance and credit, research and extension, and public policy.

Ownership of Human Tissues and Cells, 1987. Examines the economic, legal, and ethical rights of human sources of tissues and cells involved in the ownership and commercialization of products derived from three technologies (tissue and cell culture, cell fusion to produce monoclonal antibodies, and recombinant DNA).

Public Perceptions of Biotechnology, 1987. Reports the results of a nationwide survey of public knowledge and opinion about biotechnology and examines the willingness of the American people to accept risks in return for benefits of scientific innovation.

Field Testing Engineered Organisms, 1988. Examines a range of options for congressional consideration relating to criteria for review of planned release of genetically engineered organisms, the appropriate administrative mechanisms for applying such criteria, and the research base supporting the planned release.

U.S. Investment in Biotechnology, 1988. Describes the levels and types of investment in biotechnology currently being made by the federal, state, and private sectors and examines the following issues as they affect investments: levels of research and development funding, research priorities, interagency coordination, information requirements, training and education needs, monitoring of university-industry research, state efforts to promote biotechnology, the effects of tax law on commercial biotechnology, the adequacy of Federal assistance for start-ups, and the effect of export controls.

Patenting Life, 1989. Reviews patent laws as they relate to the patentability of microorganisms, cells, plants, and animals, as well as specific areas of concern, including deposit requirements and international considerations.

Source: Forewords of each report.

5. Policy-oriented research: disciplinary research that was not undertaken to study a specific problem but that has immediate application for explaining how a policy works.

6. Disciplinary research: academic books, articles, and reports undertaken to "contribute to an academic body of knowledge." They are helpful in understanding the basic background within which a policy must operate.

As is true in other areas of technical knowledge, the amount of policy-relevant literature concerning biotechnology is voluminous. Just as there is no unified, coordinated biotechnology policy, biotechnology policy knowledge includes a diverse body of books, journals, articles, reports, and periodicals produced by a wide variety of disciplines, professions, and organizations. Woodman et al. (1989) edited a 350-page guide, *Biotechnology and the Research Enterprise*, consisting of hundreds of citations. Their review is organized into eight major topics: federal research policy, university-industry relationships, conflicts of interest, university research, the biotechnology industry, international biotechnology research, related issues (public perceptions, ethical implications, economic impacts, and historical perspectives), and a directory of biotechnology organizations.

Table 13.2 provides illustrative examples of articles and books that comprise part of the body of "biotechnology policy knowledge" that is available to policymakers concerned with biotechnology policy. These examples are only a sample of the literature available to citizens, staffers, and official policymakers for their use and consideration while formulating policy in this area.

Policy knowledge, like political influence or resources, is not effective if retained in the hands of the producer. The knowledge utilization literature (see Webber, 1989) suggests that policymakers do not generally seek information and knowledge to assist them in understanding every decision they make. Policy knowledge must be distributed from the producer to the policymaker so that it can be used in making policy decisions. As Sabatier and Whiteman (1985) describe, in a decisionmaking body like a legislature, policy information seldom flows directly from outsiders to policymakers. Instead it follows a more complicated route from outsider to committee staff, committee staff to specialist legislator, and from specialist legislator to ordinary legislator. A full model of policy knowledge distribution must include a wide variety of participants in the policy process involved in distributing policy knowledge.

The Match between Congressional Concerns and Biotechnology Policy Knowledge Themes

While the availability of policy knowledge does not imply its use (see Webber, 1989), a necessary condition for policymakers' use of policy knowledge is that it must conform with policymakers' interests and concerns. Table 13.3 compares congressional concerns with the themes appearing in the biotechnology policy knowledge literature. Members of Congress have expressed a wide variety of concerns about biotechnology, including environmental release, research fund

Table 13.2

Illustrative Examples of Biotechnology Policy Knowledge by Type

Personal Knowledge   Congress Members' contact with scientists who explain the importance of their research or with dairy farmers who describe the potential impact of bST on small farms.

Journalistic Knowledge

Robert Weaver. 1984. "Beyond Supermouse: Changing Life's Genetic Blueprint." *National Geographic* 166: 818-47.

Amal Kumar Naj. 1989. "Clouds Gather over the Biotech Industry." *Wall Street Journal* January 30: B1, B5.

Claudia Wallis. 1987. "Should Animals Be Patented?" *Time* (May 4): 110.

David Wheeler. 1989. "Critics Sue to Halt Gene Experiment Involving Humans." *The Chronicle of Higher Education* February 8: A5, A8.

Sheldon Krimsky et al. 1989. "Controlling Risk in Biotech." *Technology Review* (July): 62-70.

Jack Doyle. 1985. *Altered Harvest* (New York: Vintage Press).

Sharon McAuliffe and Kathleen McAuliffe. 1981. *Life for Sale* (New York: Coward, McCann & Geoghegan).

Edward Yoxen. 1983. *The Gene Business* (New York: Harper and Row).

Bruce K. Zimmerman. 1984. *Biofuture* (New York: Plenum Press).

Edward Sylvester and Lynn C. Klotz. 1987. *The Gene Age* (New York: Charles Scribner's Sons).

Practitioners' Knowledge

Paul Berg et al. 1974. "Potential Biohazards of Recombinant DNA Molecules." *Science* (July 26): 303.

Policy Research

Richard Fallert et al. 1987. *bST and the Dairy Industry* (Economic Research Service, United States Department of Agriculture).

Robin K. Perso and Jon A. Brandt. 1988. "bST and the U.S. Dairy Industry: Impacts and Implications." *Policy Studies Journal* 17(1): 193-202.

Policy-Oriented Research

Symposium on "Biotechnology, Agriculture, and Public Policy." 1988. *Policy Studies Journal,* containing articles such as:

R. Steven Brown, "The State Role in Regulating Biotechnology."

Beverly Fleisher, "Forces Shaping the Agricultural Biotechnology Industry: Patents, Insurance, Regulation."

Daniel L. Kleinman and Jack R. Kloppenburg, Jr. "Biotechnology and University-Industrial Relations: Policy Issues in Research and the Ownership of Intellectual Property at a Land Grant University."

William H. Von Hosen. 1988. "The FDA's Regulation of Veterinary Biotechnology: Business as Usual or New Era of Environmental Protection?" *Food, Drug, and Cosmetic Law Journal* 43: 847-76.

Table 13.2 (continued)
Disciplinary Research

David Jackson and Stephen P. Stich (eds.). 1979. *The Recombinant DNA Debate* (Englewood Cliffs, N.J.: Prentice-Hall).

Sheldon Krimsky. 1982. *Genetic Alchemy: The Social History of the Recombinant DNA Controversy* (Cambridge: MIT Press).

J. D. Miller, 1985. *The Attitudes of Religious, Environmental, and Science Policy Leaders Toward Biotechnology* (DeKalb: Public Opinion Library, Northern Illinois University).

J. R. Fowle, III. 1987. *Application of Biotechnology: Environmental and Policy Issues* (Boulder, Colo.: Westview Press).

Werner Arber et al. (eds.). 1984. *Genetic Manipulation: Impact on Man and Society* (Cambridge: Cambridge University Press).

---

ing, patenting, and international competitiveness. With the exception of the adequacy and effectiveness of the current regulatory framework and the potential use of biotechnology in biological warfare, OTA appears to have responded to, or anticipated, congressional concerns. Additionally, OTA seems to have focused on the social and economic implications of biotechnology in a way that is broader than expressed congressional concerns.

Academic biotechnology policy knowledge is narrower than OTA reports and congressional concerns in its scope, focusing on research procedures, funding, and implications for universities, ethical considerations, and adverse impacts on particular segments of society (for example, small-scale farming). Little academic policy analysis is concerned with international economic issues and the ability of the United States to prepare personnel for the biotechnology industry. Two areas virtually absent from the social science-based policy analysis literature are the adequacy of current regulation and the estimation of environmental risks. Especially for political science-oriented policy analysts, the void of knowledge about the adequacy of regulation should be regarded as a major challenge to the ability of the policy sciences to stand ready to assist policymakers.

When comparing congressional concerns with policy knowledge topics, two issues emerge that need to be examined: first is the temporal relationship between the production of policy knowledge (especially the more systematic types) and the expression of congressional concern; second is the extent to which biotechnology policy knowledge is used in Congress. The first issue refers to the sequence of producing policy knowledge and its impact in the policy process. Specifically, the contribution, anticipation of policy problems, and production of diverse policy knowledge by analysts must be assessed. Currently, biotechnology policy knowledge, policy-oriented research, and disciplinary policy knowledge appear to be produced in reaction to congressional and OTA concerns rather than leading policy discussions by contributing pathbreaking analysis.[1] For example, OTA reports are cited in eight of the preceding 12 chapters of this volume.

Table 13.3
Comparison of Congressional Concerns with Themes in Available Biotechnology Policy Knowledge

---

Members' Concerns

Environmental risk of deliberate release; ability to predict consequences of release; regulatory effectiveness, adequacy, and coordination; funding and performance of basic research; priorities of biotechnology applications; protection from biological warfare and terrorism; public opinion, debate, and support; preparation for emergencies; patent protection and tort liability; international competitiveness; animal patenting.

Policy Themes Identified by OTA (1984)

Financing and tax climate; health and environmental regulation; university-industry relations; government funding for research; availability of trained personnel for the emergent biotechnology industry; patent protection and rights; antitrust law; international market and trade arrangements; government policies relating to biotechnology; public opinion.

Research Themes Identified by Woodman, Shelley, and Reichel (1989)

Federal research policy; university-industry relationships; conflicts of interest; university research; the biotechnology industry; international biotechnology research; public perceptions; ethical implications; economic impacts; historical perspectives.

Research Themes Examined in the Policy Studies Journal *(1988) Symposium and This Volume (1990)*

Risk and policymaking; university-industrial research relations; economic and legal aspects of the biotechnology industry; the role of states; environmental concerns; religious and other interest-group perspectives on biotechnology; implications for agriculture; food safety; government regulation.

The second issue raised by comparing congressional concerns with biotechnology themes involves the extent and fashion with which Congress "uses" biotechnology policy knowledge. A challenge for Congress, in other policy areas as well as in the biotechnology arena, is keeping up with, digesting, and using existing policy knowledge. While "knowledge use" has proven difficult to conceptualize and measure (see Webber, 1989), a better understanding has been gained of the impact policy knowledge can have in the congressional process. Whiteman focuses on the use of specific OTA reports within congressional committees, not individual users, and writes (1985: 307-308):

Those who take a narrow perspective on the role of policy analysis in decision making, focusing on the voting decision of individual members, are usually led to question whether analytic information is used to any significant degree and are always led to question whether this use produces any real change in the nature or quality of public policy. By adopting a broader perspective on the role of policy analysis, this study has found frequent use of analytic information in a variety of legislative activity. These findings carry clear implications regarding the effect on both legislative outputs and process.

Studies of the use of policy analysis find few unique and identifiable effects of that use on policy outputs, and this study is no exception. Certainly no fundamental changes in legislative outcomes can be attributed to the use of OTA [Office of Technology Assessment] information from the five projects examined. In a few cases, analytic information apparently led to technical revisions of pending legislation. . . . More commonly, some provisions of legislation . . . correspond to OTA findings, but the complexity of formulation activities in congressional committees prevents attribution of these provisions solely to OTA information.

Effects on the deliberative process are much more apparent. Without necessarily altering legislative outputs, the use of OTA information (particularly for strategic purposes) can alter the terms of debate. At a minimum, analytical information can increase the sophistication of arguments presented for and against legislative proposals. Further, if all participants come to regard an OTA analysis as authoritative, the findings can become a baseline for debate. Use of this information can then focus debate and even eliminate lines of argument entirely.

Biotechnology is still a young policy issue marked by the absence of major congressional action. One policymaking consequence of the executive establishment of the Coordinated Framework in 1986 is that it reduced the immediate need for legislative action, thereby allowing time for the production and accumulation of a body of biotechnology policy knowledge. Given the multiplicity of interests involved and multiple committees with jurisdiction (Plein and Webber, 1989), any major legislative proposal will almost certainly create a demand for, and the use of, this body of policy knowledge. In the meantime, producers of biotechnology policy knowledge should assess the accumulated literature, reproducing and refuting earlier work, anticipating the implications of future developments, and identifying knowledge gaps to be addressed before a more complete body of policy knowledge can be made available to congressional policymakers interested in biotechnology.

Notes

This review of biotechnology policy knowledge is limited to social science-oriented policy analysis, thus excluding at least two fields that should contribute heavily to creating better biotechnology policy: the life sciences and law. Several legal analyses that can serve as a point of entry into that literature are: Harlow (1986), Gibbs and Kahan (1986), and Jaffe (1987).

1. Producers of academic and policy-oriented biotechnology policy knowledge do have input into OTA's research projects through participation on advisory panels and contracted research. The Advisory Panel to the five volume, "New Developments in Biotechnology," has several academicians (including Professor Sheldon Krimsky of Tufts University who has written extensively on the social and ethical aspects of biotechnology).

Bibliography

Abbott, Russell. 1988. "Current Status of Computer Assisted NDAs." *Drug Information Journal* 22(1): 55.

Abelson, P. H. 1983. "High-Technology Jobs." *Science* 219: 243.

Abelson, P. H. 1986. "Evolving State-University-Industry Relations." *Science* 231: 317.

Abelson, P. H. 1988. Editorial. *Science* 701.

Abrahams, H., and B. J. Musgrave. 1982. "The DES Labyrinth." *South Carolina Law Review* 33: 663-711.

Abramson, S. H. 1986. "Confidential Business Information versus the Public's Right to Disclosure—Biotechnology Renews the Challenge." *Kansas Law Review* 34(3): 681-701.

Adams, N., and R. K. Dixon (eds.). 1986. *Forestry Networks* (Morrilton, Ark.: Winrock International).

Adler, R. 1984. "Biotechnology as Intellectual Property." *Science* 224: 357-63.

Alexander, M. 1985. "Environmental Release: Reducing the Uncertainties." *Issues in Science and Technology* 1(Spring): 57-68.

American Seed Trade Association. 1984. *Report of Public Research Advisory Committee: Subcommittee on Research Priorities* (Washington, D.C.).

Angus, F. 1981. "The Promise and Perils of Genetic Meddling." *Christianity Today* 25(May 8): 26-29.

Animal Health Institute BST Public Information Program. 1987. *Annual Report* (Alexandria, Va.: Animal Health Institute).

Annexstad, J. 1986. "Bovine Somatotropin Controversy and Impact." *Dairy Herd Management* 23: 22-25.

Balandrin, M. F., J. A. Klocke, E. S. Wurtele, and W. H. Bollinger. 1985. "Natural Plant Chemicals: Sources of Industrial and Medicinal Materials." *Science* 228: 1154-60.

Baldwin, R. L., and S. C. Middleton. 1987. "Biology of Bovine Somatotropin." In Bovine Somatotropin Education Work Group (eds.), *Proceedings of the National Invitational Workshop on Bovine Somatotropin* (Washington, D.C.: Extension Services, USDA), pp. 11-23.

Baum, Rudy. 1984. "Genetic Engineering Engulfed in New Environmental Debate." *Chemical & Engineering News* (August 13): 15-22.

Baum, Rudy. 1987. "Agricultural Biotechnology Advances Toward Commercialization." *Chemical Marketing Reporter* 65(August): 9-14.

Bauman, D. E., P. J. Eppard, M. J. DeGeeter, and G. M. Lanza. 1985. "Responses of High Producing Dairy Cows to Long Term Treatment with Pituitary and Recombinant Somatotropin." *Journal of Dairy Science* 68: 1352-62.

Baumgardt, B. R. 1988. "Biotechnology and the Animal Sciences." In W. B. Lacy and L. Busch (eds.), *Biotechnology and Agricultural Cooperatives: Opportunities and Challenges* (Lexington, Ky.: Kentucky Agricultural Experiment Station).

Bent, S. A., R. L. Schwaab, D. G. Gonlin, and D. D. Jeffery. 1987. *Intellectual Property Rights in Biotechnology Worldwide* (New York: Stockton Press).

Bentham, J. 1789, republished 1948. *The Principles of Morals and Legislation* (New York: Hafner Publishing Co.).

Berg, Paul, et al. 1974. "Potential Biohazards of Recombinant DNA Molecules." *Science* (26 July): 303.

Berry, Jeffrey M. 1977. *Lobbying for the People* (Princeton, N.J.: Princeton University Press).

Betz, F., M. Levin, and M. Rogul. 1983. "Safety Aspects of Genetically-Engineered Microbial Pesticides." *Recombinant DNA Technical Bulletin* 6(4): 135-41.

Bio/Technology. 1988. "The Federal Scene: Waiting Out the Eclipse." 6(12): 1379-1384.

Blank, R. H. 1981. *The Political Implications of Human Genetic Technology* (Boulder, Colo.: Westview Press).

Blumenthal, David, Sherrie Epstein, and James Maxwell. 1986a. "Commercializing University Research: Lessons from the Experience of the Wisconsin Alumni Research Foundation." *New England Journal of Medicine* 314: 1621-26.

Blumenthal, David, Michael Gluck, Karen Seashore Louis, Michael A. Stoto, and David Wise. 1986b. "University-Industry Research Relationships in Biotechnology: Implications for the University." *Science* 232(June 13): 1361-66.

Blumenthal, David, Michael Gluck, Karen Seashore Louis, and David Wise. 1986c. "Industrial Support of University Research in Biotechnology." *Science* 321(January 17): 242-46.

Boehlje, M., and G. Cole. 1985. "Economic Implications of Agricultural Biotechnology." Paper presented at the Iowa Academy of Science Annual Meeting, Pella, Iowa.

Bonga, J. M., and J. D. Durzan (eds.). 1987. *Cell and Tissue Culture Methods in Forestry* (The Hague: Martinus-Nijhoff).

Borcherding, J. R. 1987. "Growth Hormone Work Gets a Health Checkup." *Successful Farming* 85: 30.

Bosin, Morris R., and Wayne T. Matthews. 1988. "The Public Administrator Engages

Biotechnology: A Case of Multiple Roles." Paper presented at the Annual Meeting of the American Political Science Association, Washington, D.C.

Briggs, K. A. 1983. "Clerics Urge U.S. Curb on Gene Engineering." *New York Times* (June 9): A1, A19.

Brill, Winston. 1985. "Safety Concerns and Genetic Engineering in Agriculture." *Science* 227: 381-84.

Brill, Winston. 1987. " Genetic Engineering Applied to Agriculture: Opportunities and Concerns." *American Journal of Agricultural Economics* 68: 1081-87.

Brill, Winston. 1988. "Why Engineered Organisms Are Safe." *Issues in Science and Technology* 4(3): 44-50.

Brown, L. R., W. U. Chandler, C. Flavin, J. Jacobsen, C. Pollock, S. Postel, L. Starke, and E. C. Wolf. 1987. *State of the World* (Washington, D.C. : Worldwatch Institute).

Browne, William P. 1987a. "An Emerging Opposition? Agricultural Interests and Federal Research Policy." In Don F. Hadwiger and William P. Browne (eds.), *Public Policy and Agricultural Technology: Adversity Despite Achievement* (London: Macmillan Press), pp. 81-90.

Browne, William P. 1987b. "Bovine Growth Hormone and the Politics of Uncertainty: Fear and Loathing in a Transitional Agriculture." *Agriculture and Human Values* 4(1): 75-80.

Browne, William P. 1988. *Private Interests, Public Policy and American Agriculture* (Lawrence: University Press of Kansas).

Buchanan, J. M., and G. Tullock. 1962. *The Calculus of Consent* (Ann Arbor: University of Michigan Press).

Bullers, Finn. 1987. "Hansen: ISU Must Lead Development." *The Daily Tribune* (December 21): 1,6.

Bultena, Gordon, and Paul Lasley. Forthcoming. "The Dark Side of Agricultural Biotechnology: Farmers' Appraisal of the Benefits and Costs of Technological Innovation." In Michael Warren et al. (eds.), *Agricultural Bioethics* (Ames: Iowa State University Press).

Burke, E. 1789, republished 1987. *Reflections on the Revolution in France*, edited by J. G. A. Pocock (Indianapolis: Hackett Publishing Co.).

Burley, J., and L. A. Lockhart. 1985. "Chemical Extractives and Exudates from Trees." *Ann. Proc. Phytochem. Soc. Eur.* 26: 91-102.

Burros, Marian. 1977. "The Saccharin Ban: A Bittersweet Aftertaste." *Washington Post* (March 31): E1, E6, E7.

Burtness, J. H. 1986. *Genetic Manipulation* (New York: Lutheran Church in America).

Busch, L., and W. B. Lacy. 1988. "Biotechnology: Its Potential Impact on Interrelationships Among Agriculture, Industry, and Society." In Food and Nutrition Board, National Research Council (eds.), *Biotechnology and the Food Supply* (Washington, D.C.), pp. 75-105.

Bush, Vannevar. 1945. *Science: The Endless Frontier, A Report to the President* (Washington, D.C.: USGPO).

Business Week. 1984. "Biotech Comes of Age." (January 23): 84-91.

Buttel, F. H. 1985. "Biotechnology and Genetic Information: Implications for Rural People and the Institutions that Serve Them." *The Rural Sociologist* 5: 68-88.

Buttel, F. H. 1986a. "Agricultural Research and Farm Structural Change: Bovine Growth Hormone and Beyond." *Agriculture and Human Values* 3(4): 88-98.

Buttel, F. H. 1986b. "Biotechnology and Public Agricultural Research Policy: Emergent Issues." In K. A. Dahlberg (ed.), *New Directions for Agriculture and Agricultural Research* (Totowa, N.J.: Rowman and Allenheld).

Buttel, F. H., and J. Belsky. 1987. "Biotechnology, Plant Breeding and Intellectual Property: Social and Ethical Dimensions." *Science, Technology, and Human Values* 12(1): 31-49.

Buttel, F. H., and M. Kenney. 1987. "Biotechnology and International Development: Prospects for Overcoming Dependence in the Information Age." In Don F. Hadwiger and William P. Browne (eds.), *Public Policy and Agricultural Technology: Adversity Despite Achievement* (London: Macmillan Press), pp. 109-121.

Buttel, F. H., M. Kenney, and J. Kloppenburg. 1984. "Biotechnology and the Third World: Toward a Global Political-Economic Perspective." *Politics and the Life Sciences* 2: 160-64.

Buttel, F. H., M. Kenney, and J. Kloppenburg. 1985. "From Green Revolution to Biorevolution: Some Observations on the Changing Technological Bases of Economic Transformation in the Third World." *Economic Development and Cultural Change* 34: 31-52.

Bylinsky, G. 1985. "Test-Tube Plants." *Fortune* (September 2): 50-53.

Casey, W. L., and L. S. Moss. 1987. "Intellectual Property Rights and Biotechnology." *Idea* 27(4): 251-67.

Chassey, Bruce. 1987. "Prospects for Genetic Manipulation of Lactobacilli." *FEMS Microbiology Reviews* 46: 297-312.

Chermside, Herbert B. 1987. "The License to Transfer Technology." *Research in Action* 12(2): 9-11.

Cohen, Michael, and James G. March. 1974. *Leadership and Ambiguity: The American College President* (New York: McGraw-Hill, Carnegie Commission for the Future of Higher Education).

Cohen, S. N. 1977. "Recombinant DNA: Fact and Fiction." *Science* 195: 654-57.

Colwell, R. K., E. A. Norse, D. Pimentel, F. E. Sharples, and D. Simberloff. 1985. "Genetic Engineering in Agriculture." *Science* 229: 111-12.

Congressional Quarterly Almanac. 1978. (Washington, D.C.: Congressional Quarterly).

Congressional Quarterly Weekly Report. 1988. "House Panel Approves Biotechnology Bill." (September 10): 2553.

Congressional Quarterly Weekly Report. 1988. "Farmers Prevail on Biotech Patent Bill." (September 17): 2623.

Consumer Reports. 1987. "An Apple a Day Is O.K.—for Now." (October): 594.

Consumer Reports. 1989. "Alar: Not Gone, Not Forgotten." (May): 288-90.

Cornucopia Project. 1981. *Empty Breadbaskets?* (Emmaus, Pa.: Rodale Press).

Council for Agricultural Science and Technology. 1977. *Hormonally Active Substances in Foods: A Safety Evaluation.* Report No. 66. March.

Crawford, M. 1986. "Regulatory Tangle Snarls Agriculture Research in the Biotechnology Area." *Science* 234(4774): 275-77.

Cummings, L. C. 1986. "The Political Reality of Artificial Sweeteners." In Harvey M. Sapolsky (ed.), *Consuming Fears: The Politics of Product Risks* (New York: Basic Books).

Curry, Judith. 1986. "Biotechnology Policy—Public Perception, Participation, and the

Law." In *Research for Tomorrow* (Washington, D.C.: U.S. Department of Agriculture).

The Daily Tribune. 1987. "A Good Start." (December 21): 8.

Daus, Donald, and G. Winter. 1986. "Patents for Biotechnology." *Idea* 26: 263-82.

David, Edward E., Jr. 1983. "High Tech and the Economy: What Does It All Mean?" *Research Management* (September/October): 27-28, 30.

Davis, B. W. 1987a. "Bacterial Domestication: Underlying Assumptions." *Science* 235: 1329-35.

Davis, B. W. 1987b. "Is Deliberate Introduction Ecologically Any More Threatening than Accidental Release?" *Genetic Engineering News* (October): 4.

Day, K. 1985. "Biotechnology Companies Meet Insurer Reluctance." *Los Angeles Times* (May 28): IV.1, 14.

De Vos, W. M. 1986. "Gene Cloning in Lactic Streptococci." *Netherlands Milk Dairy Journal* 40: 141-54.

Dembo, D., C. Dias, and W. Morehouse. 1985. "Biotechnology and the Third World: Some Social Economic, Political and Legal Impacts and Concerns." *Rutgers Computer & Technology Law Journal* 11: 431-68.

Denny, Brewster C. 1982. "The High-Technology Fix." *Science* 217(August 27): 781.

Dexter, Lewis Anthony. 1970. *Elite and Specialized Interviewing* (Evanston, Ill.: Northwestern University Press).

Diamond v. Chakrabarty. 1980. 100 S. Ct. 2204, U.S. Reports 477: 303-322.

Dibner, M. D., and N. G. Bruce. 1987. "The Greening of Biotechnology: The Growth of the US Biotechnology Industry." *Trends in Biotechnology* 5: 270-72.

Dickson, David. 1984, 1988. *The New Politics of Science* (Chicago: University of Chicago Press).

Dingell, John. 1985. "Biotechnology: What Are the Problems Beyond Regulation?" In Susan Panem (ed.), *Biotechnology: Implications for Public Policy* (Washington, D.C.: Brookings), pp. 25-31.

Dixon, R. K. 1988. "Forest Biotechnology Networking in Developing Countries." *Journal of Developing Areas* 22: 207-218.

Dixon, R. K., and D. H. Marx. 1987. "Mycorrizae." In J. M. Bonga and D. J. Durzan (eds.), *Cell and Tissue Culture in Forestry, Volume 2* (The Hague: Martinus-Nijhoff), pp. 336-50.

Dorfman, Nancy S. 1983. "Route 128: The Development of Regional High Technology Economy." *Research Policy* 12: 299-316.

Doyle, J. 1985a. *Altered Harvest* (New York: Viking Press).

Doyle, J. 1985b. "Biotechnology Research and Agricultural Stability." *Issues in Science and Technology* 2(Fall): 111-24.

Eaton, Gordon P. 1987. "Agricultural Research is Still Vital to Iowa's Future." *Des Moines Register* (26 February): 11A.

The Economist. 1988. "DNA: Inherited Wealth." (April 30): 1-18.

Eibach, U. 1981. "Genetic Research and A Responsible Ethic." *Theology Digest* 29(2): 113-17.

Ellis, Gary G., and Kathi E. Hanna. 1989. "Evaluating Biomedical Technology for The U.S. Congress: Animal Experimentation, and Public Policy" *Policy Studies Review* 8: 357-68.

Encyclopedia of Education, Volume 5. 1971. (New York: Macmillan).

Engelhardt, H. T., Jr. 1984. "Persons and Humans: Refashioning Ourselves in a Better Image and Likeness." *Zygon* 19(3): 281-95.

Entwistle, P. F. 1983. "Viruses for Insect Pest Control." *Span* 16: 1-4.

Epstein, Michael A. 1983. *Modern Intellectual Property* (New York: Law and Business, Harcourt Brace; 1986 Supplement: Prentice Hall, Law & Business).

Epstein, R. A. 1980. *Modern Products Liability Law* (Westport, Conn.: Quorum Books).

Epstein, R. A. 1988. "The Political Economy of Product Liability Reform." *American Economic Review* 78(2): 311-15.

Fallert, R., T. McGukin, C. Betts, and G. Brunner. 1987. *bST and the Dairy Industry: A National, Regional, and Farm-Level Analysis* (AER-579, USDA, Economic Research Service).

FDA Today. 1988. (December).

Federal Register. 1977. 42: 19996.

Federal Register. 1979. 44: 44274.

Federal Register. 1983. 48: 31910.

Federal Register. 1984. 49: 29136-29141.

Federal Register. 1985. 50: 47174-47195.

Federal Register. 1986. 51: 23302-23350.

Federal Supplement. 1986. (see U.S. 637 *Federal Supplement* 25).

Financial Times. 1989. "Biotechnology." (May 31): 22.

Finer, Herman. 1966. "Administrative Responsibility in Democratic Government." In Peter Woll (ed.), *Public Administration and Policy* (New York: Harper and Row).

Fiskel, Joseph and Vincent T. Covello (eds.). 1986. *Biotechnology Risk Assessment: Issues and Methods for Environmental Introductions* (New York: Pergamon Press).

Fleisher, Beverly. 1988. "Forces Shaping the Agricultural Biotechnology Industry." *Policy Studies Journal* (Fall): 169-80.

Fleisher, Beverly. 1989. "Characterizing the Economic Risk Associated with Deliberately Released Genetically Engineered Microbial Agents." *American Journal of Agricultural Economics* 71(2): 480-84.

Food and Drug Administration (see U.S. Food and Drug Administration).

Forrester, Jay. 1982. "Planning in the Face of Power." *Journal of the American Planning Association* (Winter): 67-80.

Foundation on Economic Trends. 1988. *General Information Packet* (Washington, D.C.).

Fowler, R. B. 1985. *Religion and Politics in America* (Metuchen, N.J.: American Theological Library Association and Scarecrow Press).

Fox, Jeffrey. 1987. "The U.S. Regulatory Patchwork." *Bio/Technology* 5(12): 1273-77.

Friedrich, Carl J. 1966. "Public Policy and the Nature of Administrative Responsibility." In Peter Woll (ed.), *Public Administration and Policy* (New York: Harper and Row), pp. 221-46.

Fusfeld, Herbert I. 1980. "The Bridge Between University and Industry." *Science* 209(July 11): 221.

Fusonie, A. "Charles E. North: Pioneer Scientist in the Dairy Industry: His Contributions to the Passage of Milk Pasteurization Laws in Kansas City, Missouri" (National Agricultural Library, unpublished paper).

Gafo, J. 1980. "Biological Engineering and the Future of Man." *Theology Digest* 28(2): 125-28.

Geisler, C. C., and E. M. DuPuis. 1989. "From Green Revolution to Gene Revolution: Common Concerns about Agricultural Biotechnology in the First and Third Worlds." In J. J. Molnar and H. Kinnucan (eds.), *Biotechnology and the New Agricultural Revolution* (Boulder, Colo.: Westview Press).

General Accounting Office (see U.S. Congress. General Accounting Office).

General Synod United Church of Christ. 1987. "Public Policy Statement on the Church and Genetic Engineering for the Council for Health and Human Service Ministries Related to the United Church of Christ" (New York: United Church of Christ).

Gibbs, Jeffrey N., and Jonathan S. Kahan. 1986. "Federal Regulation of Food and Food Additive Biotechnology." *Administrative Law Review* 38: 1-32.

Gladwell, Malcolm. 1989. "Biotech Industry Trying to Cook Up a Comeback." *Washington Post* (March 6): 1, 24.

Glaser, Lawrence K. 1986. *Provisions of the Food Security Act of 1985* (Washington, D.C.: USDA, Economic Research Service).

Glass, D. J. 1988. "An Industry Representative's View of the System, Public Remarks" (The Keystone Environmental, Citizen, State, and Local Leadership Initiative Regional Workshop on Biotechnology, Austin, Texas, July 15).

Gold, M., and T. Wilson. 1981. "Depo-Provera: New Developments in Decade Old Controversy." *Family Planning Perspectives* 13: 35-37.

Goldberg, T. 1987. "Moving toward Public Participation in Biotechnology." In J. R. Fowle, III (ed.), *Application of Biotechnology: Environmental and Policy Issues* (Boulder, Colo.: Westview Press), pp. 165-73.

Goodfield, J. 1978. *Playing God* (New York: Harper and Row).

Goodman, R. M., H. Hauptli, A. Crossway, and V. C. Knauf. 1987. "Gene Transfer in Crop Improvement." *Science* 236: 48-54.

Gordon, J. C., C. T. Wheeler, and D. A. Perry (eds.). 1979. *Symbiotic Nitrogen Fixation in Management of Temperate Forests* (Corvallis: Oregon State University Press).

Gore, Albert, Jr. 1985. "A Congressional Perspective." In Susan Panem (ed.), *Biotechnology: Implications for Public Policy* (Washington, D.C.: Brookings), pp. 12-18.

Green, R. M. 1985. "Genetic Medicine in the Perspective of Orthodox Halakhah." *Judaism* 34 (Summer): 263-77.

Green, William. 1986. "The Politics of Pharmaceutical Regulation and Innovation: The F.D.A. and the Odyssey of Depo-Provera." Paper presented at the American Political Science Association Meeting.

Greenawalt, K. 1988. *Religious Convictions and Political Choice* (New York: Oxford University Press).

Grobstein, Clifford. 1983. "Who is Janus?" *Politics and the Life Sciences* 2(1): 55-59.

Gurwitz, Aaron S. 1982. "The New Faith in High Tech." *Wall Street Journal* (October 27): 32.

Guttman, Joel M. 1978. "Interest Groups and the Demand for Agricultural Research." *Journal of Political Economy* 86(2): 467-84.

Hadwiger, Don F. 1982. *The Politics of Agricultural Research* (Lincoln: University of Nebraska Press).

Hagstrom, Jerry. 1982. "High-Tech Leaders Have Their Own Ideas of What Government Can Do for Them." *National Journal* (May 15): 861-65.

Hall, Stephen. 1987. *Invisible Frontiers: The Race to Synthesize the Human Gene* (Redmond, Wash.: Tempus).

Halloran, Jean. 1986. "To Ban or Not to Ban: What are the Ethics of the Question." *Agriculture and Human Values* 3: 5-9.

Hamm, Larry G. 1981. "The Impact of Food Distributor Procurement Practices on Food System Structure and Coordination" (North Central Research Project 117, Working Paper 58).

Hamm, Larry G. 1987. "Dairy Policy Situation and Outlook." Paper presented at Outlook '88: United States Department of Agriculture's 64th Agricultural Outlook Conference, Washington, D.C.

Hansen, M., L. Busch, J. Burkhardt, W. B. Lacy, and L. R. Lacy. 1986. "Plant Breeding and Biotechnology: New Technologies Raise Important Social Questions." *BioScience* 36(1): 29-39.

Hardy, R. W. 1988. "Current and Future Research Priorities, Public Remarks" (The Keystone Environmental, Citizen, State, and Local Leadership Initiative Regional Workshop on Biotechnology, Austin, Texas, July 14).

Hardy, R. W. F., and D. J. Glass. "Our Investment: What Is at Stake?" *Issues in Science and Technology* 1(Spring 1985): 69-82.

Harkin, Tom. 1988. "Biotechnology in Agriculture and America's Competitiveness." *Policy Studies Journal* 17(1)(Fall): 68-72.

Harl, N. 1984. "Economic and Environmental Effects of Development in Biotechnology." Paper presented at the Annual Meetings of the Western Agricultural Economics Association, San Diego.

Harlander, S. 1988. "Biotechnology and Food Processing." In W. B. Lacy and L. Busch (eds.), *Biotechnology and Agricultural Cooperatives: Opportunities and Challenges* (Lexington: Kentucky Agricultural Experiment Station).

Harlow, Ruth E. 1986. "The EPA and Biotechnology Regulation: Coping with Scientific Uncertainty." *Yale Law Journal* 95: 553-76.

Harmon, Michael M. 1981. *Action Theory for Public Administration* (New York: Longman).

Hatfield, Mark. 1988. *Congressional Record*, p. S 1620. February 29.

Hebblethwaite, J. F. 1988. "The Future of Plant Biotechnology in Agriculture: A Corporate Strategy." In W. B. Lacy and L. Busch (eds.), *Biotechnology and Agricultural Cooperatives: Opportunities and Challenges* (Lexington: Kentucky Agricultural Experiment Station).

Henderson, J., and R. Quandt. 1958. *Microeconomic Theory: A Mathematical Approach* (New York: McGraw-Hill Book Company).

H.E.W. News. 1977. (March): 1-6 (Washington, D.C.: Department of Health, Education, and Welfare).

Hinman, C. W. 1984. "New Crops for Arid Lands." *Science* 225: 1445-48.

Hoffman, G., and G. Karney. 1988. "Can Justice Keep Pace with Science?" *Washington Post* (April 10): B10.

House of Bishops, Message #112. 1985. "Final Text of Resolution (A090a)." Journal of the 68th General Convention of the Episcopal Church, Anaheim Meeting.

Huber, P. W. 1987. "Biotechnology and the Regulation Hydra." *Technology Review* (November/December): 57-65.

Huggins, A. R. 1984. "Progress in Dairy Starter Technology." *Food Technology* 38: 41-50.

Hunter, Beatrice. 1975. *Food Additives and Federal Policy* (New York: Scribners).

Hutton, Richard. 1978. *Bio-Revolution: DNA and the Ethics of Man Made Life* (New York: Mentor).

IBA Reports. 1989. "Industrial Leaders and Analysts Gather for Annual IBA Meeting." (April): 1, 2, 5.

Industrial Biotechnology Association. 1989. *U.S. Biotechnology: Meeting the Global Challenge* (Washington, D.C.).

Ingalsbe, G. 1984. "Cooperative Facts." *Cooperative Information Report 2* (Washington, D.C.: USDA/ACS).

International Rice Research Institute. 1985. *Biotechnology in International Agricultural Research* (Manila).

Iowa, State of. 1986. *Laws of the Seventy-first General Assembly.* 1986 Session, Chapter 1207, 295-96.

Jaffe, Gregory A. 1987. "Inadequacies in the Federal Regulation of Biotechnology." *Harvard Environmental Law Review* 11: 491-550.

Jaschik, Scott. 1987. "States Trying to Assess the Effectiveness of Highly Touted Economic Programs." *The Chronicle of Higher Education* (June 3): 19, 26.

Johansen, Elaine, and Marian Steinberg. 1986. "Science and Democracy: The Limits of Managing Risk." Paper presented at the annual meeting of the American Political Science Association.

John, Kenneth, and Robin Henig. 1988. "No-Excuses Genes." *The Washington Post National Weekly Edition* (February 22-28): 37.

Johnson, Deborah. 1986. "The Ethical Dimensions of Acceptable Risk in Food Safety." *Agriculture and Human Values* 3: 171-79.

Jones, D. 1983. "Genetic Engineering in Domestic Food Animals: Legal and Regulatory Considerations." *Food, Drug, and Cosmetic Law Journal* 38: 273-87.

Jones, D. 1985. "Commercialization of Gene Transfer in Food Organisms: A Science Based Regulatory Model." *Food, Drug, and Cosmetic Law Journal* 40: 477-93.

Kaiser, R. B. 1980. "Three Clerics Urge President and Congress to Set Up Controls on Genetic Engineers." *New York Times* (July 15): A16.

Kalter, R. R. 1985. "The New Biotech Agriculture: Unforeseen Economic Consequences." *Issues in Science and Technology* 2(Fall): 122-33.

Kalter, R. J., R. Milligan, W. Lesser, W. Magrath, and D. Bauman. 1984. "Biotechnology and the Dairy Industry: Production Costs and Commercial Potential of the Bovine Growth Hormone. Prepared for Cornell University Center for Biotechnology" (Cornell University, Department of Agricultural Economics). *A.E. Research* 84 (December): 22.

Kawar, Amal, and Richard Sherlock. 1989. "Theoretical Issues in the Regulation of Genetically-Engineered Organisms: The Case Of Deliberate Release" *Politics and the Life Sciences* (January).

Kelman, Steven. 1983. "Regulation and Paternalism." In T. Machan and Bruce Johnson (eds.), *Rights and Regulation* (San Francisco: Pacific Institute Press).

Kenney, Martin. 1986. *Biotechnology: The University-Industry Complex* (New Haven: Yale University Press).

Kenney, Martin, and F. H. Buttel. 1985. "Biotechnology: Prospects and Dilemmas for Third World Development." *Development and Change* 16: 61-91.

Khan, A. G. 1972. "The Effect of Vesicular-Arbuscular Mycorrhizal Associations on Growth of Cereals: I. Effects on Maize Growth." *New Phytologist* 71: 613-19.

Kintner, Earl W., and Jack Lahr. 1982. *An Intellectual Property Law Primer*, 2nd ed. (New York: Clark Boardman Co.).

Kirk, R. 1982. *The Portable Conservative Reader* (New York: Penguin Books).

Kirk, T. K., J. W. Jeffries, and G. F. Letham. 1983. "Biotechnology: Applications and Implications for the Pulp and Paper Industry." *Tappi* 66: 45-51.

Kirkman, C. H. 1980. "Cooperative Member Responsibilities and Control." *Cooperative Information Report 1, Section 7* (Washington, D.C.: USDA/ACS).

Klaenhammer, T. R. 1987. "Plasmid-directed Mechanisms for Bacteriophage Defense in Lactic Streptococci." *FEMS Microbiology Review* 46: 313-25.

Klausner, A. 1988. "AGS-DNAP Merger Signals Ag Biotech Shakeup." *Bio/Technology* 6(2): 113-14.

Klausner, A., and J. Fox. 1988. "Some Bird's-Eye Views of AGBIOTECH '88." *Bio/Technology* 6(3): 243-44.

Klausner, A., and J. Van Brunt. 1987. "Regional Development: Striving for an Edge." *Bio/Technology* 5 (February): 134-36.

Kloppenburg, J. 1984. "The Social Impacts of Biogenetic Technology in Agriculture: Past and Future." In Gigi M. Berardi and Charles C. Geisler (eds.), *The Social Consequences and Challenges of New Agricultural Technologies* (Boulder, Colo.: Westview Press).

Kloppenburg, J. 1988. *First the Seed: The Political Economy of Plant Biotechnology, 1492-2000* (New York: Cambridge University Press).

Kondo, J. K., and L. L. McKay. 1985. "Gene Transfer Systems and Molecular Cloning in Group N Streptococci: A Review." *Journal of Dairy Science* 68: 2143-59.

Krimsky, Sheldon. 1982. *Genetic Alchemy: The Social History of the Recombinant DNA Controversy* (Cambridge: MIT Press).

Lacy, W. B., and L. Busch. 1988a. "Changing Division of Labor Between the University and Industry: The Case of Agricultural Biotechnology." In J. Molnar and H. Kinnucan (eds.), *Biotechnology and the New Agricultural Revolution*. American Association for the Advancement of Science Symposium Series. (Boulder, Colo.: Westview Press), pp. 21-50.

Lacy, W. B., and L. Busch. 1988b. "Biotechnology: Consequences and Strategies for Cooperatives." In W. B. Lacy and L. Busch (eds.), *Biotechnology and Agricultural Cooperatives: Opportunities and Challenges* (Lexington: Kentucky Agricultural Experiment Station).

Larrabee, John. 1989. "New Milk-Production Drug Runs into Strong Opposition." *USA Today* (July 21): 3A.

Larson, B., and F. Kuchler. 1989. "The Simple Analytics of Technology Adoption: Bovine Growth Hormone and the Dairy Industry." Paper presented at the Southern Agricultural Economics Association Annual Meetings, Nashville, Tennessee.

Lasley, Paul, and Gordon Bultena. 1987. "Farmers' Opinions on the Relationship Between Land Grant Colleges and Private Industry." Paper presented at the 1987 meeting of the Rural Sociological Society, Madison, Wisconsin.

Lasswell, Harold. 1968 "Policy Science" in *International Encyclopedia of the Social Sciences* (New York: Macmillan and Free Press) 12: 181-88.

Leahy, Patrick J. 1988. "Toward a National Biotechnology Policy." *Issues in Science and Technology* (Fall): 26-29.

Lee, J. R. 1983. "Choice and Harms." In T. Machan and Bruce Johnson (eds.), *Rights and Regulation* (San Francisco: Pacific Institute Press).

Lewin, T. 1986. "The Liability Insurance Spiral." *New York Times* (March 8): 35, 37.

Lilla, Mark. 1981. "Ethos, Ethics, and Public Service." *The Public Interest* (Spring): 3-17.

Lindsey, Quentin W. 1985. "Industry/University Research Cooperation: The State Government Role." *Journal of the Society of Research Administrators* (Fall): 85-90.

Linnell, Robert H. 1982. "Government Research Support: Impact on Ethical and Economic Issues." In Robert H. Linnell (ed.), *Dollars and Scholars* (Los Angeles: University of Southern California Press).

Lipman-Blumen, Jean, and Susan Schrom. 1984. *The Paradox of Success: The Impact of Priority Setting in Agricultural Research and Extension* (Washington, D.C.: Science and Education, Office of the Assistant Secretary, USDA).

Longworth, John W. 1987. "Biotechnology: Scientific Potential and Socioeconomic Implications for Agriculture." *Review of Marketing and Agricultural Economics* 55(4): 187-99.

Makulowich, J. S. 1988a. "Agbio Suddenly Captures Industry Attention." *Genetic Engineering News* 8(4): 1, 28.

Makulowich, J. S. 1988b. "Merger of DNAP & AGS Weds Experience in Plant Tissue Culture to Recombinant DNA Skills." *Genetic Engineering News* 8(2): 1, 33.

March, James G., and Johan P. Olson. 1976. *Ambiguity and Choice in Organizations* (Oslo: Universitetsforlaget).

Marcus, Alan. 1985. *Agricultural Science and the Quest for Legitimacy* (Ames: Iowa State University Press).

Markle, G. E., and S. S. Robin. 1989. "Biotechnology and the Social Reconstruction of Molecular Biology." In D. E. Chubin and E. W. Chu (eds.), *Science Off the Pedestal* (Belmont, Calif.: Wadsworth Publishing Co.).

Marraro, C. H. 1982. "Regulating Food Additives and Contaminants." In Lester B. Lave (ed.), *Quantitative Risk Assessment in Regulation* (Washington, D.C.: Brookings).

McAuliffe, Sharon, and Kathleen McAuliffe. 1981. *Life for Sale* (New York: Coward, McCann & Geoghegan).

McCormick, R. A. 1985. "Genetic Technology and Our Common Future." *America* 152(April 27): 337-42.

McCurdy, Patrick P. 1985. "To Patent or Not to Patent?" *Chemical Week* (July 17): 3.

Melloan, George. 1988. "Learning Political Science at Crop Genetics." *The Wall Street Journal* (May 10): 39.

Mellon, Margaret. 1987. "Biotechnology." In S. Novick, D. Stever, and M. Mellon (eds.), *Law of Environmental Protection, Volume 2* (New York: Clark Boardman Co.).

Meltzer, M. I. 1987. "Repartitioning Agents in Livestock: Economic Impact of Porcine Growth Hormone" (unpublished Master's Thesis, Cornell University).

Merrill, R., and P. Hutt. 1980. *Food and Drug Law: Cases and Materials* (Minneapolis: West Publishing Co).

Merrill, R., and M. Taylor. 1985. "Saccharin: A Case Study of Government Regulation of Environmental Carcinogens." *Virginia Journal of Natural Resource Law* 5: 33-73.

Mill, John Stewart. 1912. *On Liberty* (London: Oxford University Press).

Miller, H. I. 1987. "The Case for Qualifying Case by Case." *Science* 236: 133.

Miller, J. A. 1984. "The Clergy Ponder the New Genetics." *Science News* 25 (March 24): 188-90.

Miller, J. D. 1985. *The Attitudes of Religious, Environmental, and Science Policy Leaders Toward Biotechnology* (DeKalb: Public Opinion Laboratory, Northern Illinois University).

Miller, L. I. 1985. "Biotechnology Mergers Signal Industry Consolidation." *Genetic Engineering News* 5(2): 6-7.

Moe, Ronald C. 1987. "Exploring the Limits of Privatization." *Public Administration Review* 47: 453-60.

Molnar, J. J., and Kinnucan, H. (eds.). 1989. *Biotechnology and the New Agricultural Revolution* (Boulder, Colo.: Westview Press).

Monsanto. 1988. "Farming: A Picture of the Future." *Science* 240(4858): 1384.

Moses, P., and C. Hess. 1987. "Getting Biotech into the Field." *Issues in Science and Technology* 4(1): 35-40.

Moses, P., J. Tavares, and C. Hess. 1988. "Funding Agricultural Biotechnology Research." *Bio/Technology* 6(Feb): 144-48.

Nader, L., and C. Nader. 1981. "A Wide Angle on Regulation: An Anthropological Analysis." In R. G. Noll (ed.), *Regulatory Policy and the Social Sciences* (Berkeley: University of California Press), pp. 141-60.

Naj, Amal Kumar. 1989. "Clouds Gather over the Biotech Industry." *Wall Street Journal* (January 30): B1, B5.

Nash, N. 1986. "Calculating Risk Is a Riskier Business Now." *New York Times* (May 25): D1.

NASULGC (see National Association of State Universities and Land Grant Colleges).

National Academy of Sciences. 1970. *Safety of Saccharin for Use in Foods* (Washington, D.C.: N.A.S. Press).

National Academy of Sciences. 1974. *Safety of Saccharin and Sodium Saccharin in the Human Diet* (Washington, D.C.: N.A.S. Press).

National Academy of Sciences. 1979. *Microbial Processes: Promising Technologies for Developing Countries* (Washington, D.C.: N.A.S. Press).

National Academy of Sciences. 1987. *Introduction of Recombinant DNA-engineered Organisms into the Environment: Key Issues*. Committee on the Introduction of Genetically Engineered Organisms into the Environment (Washington, D.C.: N.A.S. Press).

National Association of College and University Business Officers (NACUBO). 1978. *Patent and Copyright Policies at Selected Universities* (Washington, D.C.: NACUBO).

National Association of State Universities and Land Grant Colleges. 1983. *Emerging Biotechnologies in Agriculture: Issues and Policies*. Progress Report II.

———. 1985. *Emerging Biotechnologies in Agriculture: Issues and Policies*. Progress Report IV.

_____. 1987. *Emerging Biotechnologies in Agriculture: Issues and Policies.* Progress Report VI.

National Council of Churches, Panel on Bioethical Concerns. 1984. *Genetic Engineering: Social and Ethical Consequences* (New York: Pilgrim Press).

National Council of the Churches of Christ in the U.S.A. 1986. "Genetic Science for Human Benefit." Document adopted by the Governing Board, May.

National Council of University Research Administrators (NACURA). 1984. *Intellectual Property Series* (Washington, D.C.: NACURA).

National Public Radio. 1988. *All Things Considered* (March 29).

National Science Foundation. 1985a. *Academic Science/Engineering: R&D Funds, Fiscal Year 1983.* Detailed Statistical Tables, NSF 85-308 (Washington, D.C.: USGPO).

National Science Foundation. 1985b. *Federal Support to Universities, Colleges, and Selected Nonprofit Institutions, Fiscal Year 1983.* Detailed Statistical Tables, NSF 85-381 (Washington, D.C.: USGPO).

Nelkin, Dorothy. 1987. *Selling Science* (New York: W. H. Freeman and Co.).

New York Times. 1987. "Patents Disputed in Biotechnology." (March 9): D1, D5.

Newmark, P. 1983. "International Biotechnology: UN Center to Be Based in India." *Nature* 302: 100.

Norman, Colin. 1983. "Clerics Urge Ban on Altering Germline Cells." *Science* 220 (June 24): 1360-61.

Norman, Colin. 1983. "Legal Threat, Cold Delay UC Experiment." *Science* 222: 309.

Office of Technology Assessment (see U.S. Congress. Office of Technology Assessment)

Olson, Mancur. 1982. *The Rise and Decline of Nations* (New Haven: Yale University Press).

Omenn, Gilbert S. 1983. "University-Corporate Relations in Science and Technology: An Analysis of Specific Models." In Thomas W. Langfitt, Sheldon Hackney, Alfred P. Fishman, and Albert V. Glowasky (eds.), *Partners in the Research Enterprise: Corporate Relations in Science and Technology* (Philadelphia: University of Pennsylvania Press).

Orton, T. 1988. "Biotechnology and the Plant Sciences." In W. B. Lacy and L. Busch (eds.), *Biotechnology and Agricultural Cooperatives: Opportunities and Challenges* (Lexington: Kentucky Agricultural Experiment Station).

Palmer, Archie M. 1948. *Survey of University Patent Policies: Preliminary Report* (Washington, D.C.: National Research Council).

Payne, R. 1988. "The Emergence of Trade Secret Protection in Biotechnology." *Bio/Technology* 6(2): 130-31.

Phillips, C. S. 1988. "The Alleged Laws of Cultural Change." Paper presented at the meeting of the American Political Science Association, Washington, D.C., September 1-4.

Plein, L. Christopher. 1989. "The Emergence of the Pro-Biotechnology Coalition: Issue Development and the Agenda Setting Process." Paper delivered at the Annual Meeting of the American Political Science Association, Atlanta, Georgia, August 31.

Plein, L. Christopher, and David J. Webber. 1988. "Congressional Consideration of Biotechnology." *Policy Studies Journal* 17(1): 136-47.

Plein, L. Christopher, and David J. Webber. 1989. "Biotechnology and Agriculture: An

Evolving Congressional Policy Arena." In Carol Kramer (ed.), *The Political Economy of U.S. Agriculture* (Washington, D.C.: Resources for the Future Foundation).

Plucknett, D. L., and N. J. H. Smith. 1982. "Agricultural Research and Third World Food Production." *Science* 217: 215-20.

Plucknett, D. L., N. J. H. Smith, J. T. Williams, and N. M. Anishetty. 1983. "Crop Germplasm Conservation and Developing Countries." *Science* 220: 163-69.

Pollack, A. 1987. "Gene Splicing Payoff is Near." *The New York Times* (June 10): D1, D5.

Posner, Richard. 1979. "The Federal Trade Commission's Mandated Disclosure Program." In Harvey Goldschmid (ed.), *Business Disclosure* (New York: McGraw-Hill).

Pray, C., K. Neumeyer, and S. Upadhyaya. 1988. "Private Sector Food and Agriculture Research in the United States: Data Sources and Determinants of R&D Expenditure" (Working Paper, Rutgers University Department of Agricultural Economics and Marketing).

President's Commission for the Study of Ethical Problems in Medicine and Biomedical and Behavioral Research. 1982. *Splicing Life: A Report on the Social and Ethical Issues of Genetic Engineering with Human Beings* (Washington, D.C.: USGPO).

Price, Don K. 1965. *The Scientific Estate* (Cambridge: Harvard University Press).

Price, Don K. 1969. "Conclusion: Knowledge and Power." In Paul J. Piccard (ed.), *Science and Policy Issues: Lectures in Government and Science* (Itasca, Ill.: Peacock Publishers), pp. 135-42.

Princeton Synergetics, Inc. 1985. *Federal Government Provision of Third-Party Liability Insurance to Space Vehicle Users.*

Raines, L. 1988. "The Mouse That Roared." *Issues in Science and Technology* (Summer): 64-70.

Randall, C., B. Mandelbaum, and T. Kelly. 1980. "Letters from Three General Secretaries to President Carter." In *Genetic Engineering: Social and Ethical Consequences.* A report of the National Council of Churches, 1984 (New York: Plenum Press), pp. 47-49.

Rauch, Jonathon. 1987. "Drug on the Market." *National Journal* 19(14): 818-21.

Regal, P. 1987. "Models of Genetically Engineered Organisms and Their Ecological Impact." *Recombinant DNA Technical Bulletin* 10(3): 67-85.

Reichel, Brian J. 1988. "Public Policy and University-Industry Research Relationships in Biotechnology: Organizational Kudos and Caveats" (unpublished Masters Thesis, Iowa State University).

Reichel, Brian J., Paul Lasley, William F. Woodman, and Mack C. Shelley, II. 1989. "Economic Development and Biotechnology: Public Policy Response to the Farm Crisis in Iowa" (unpublished paper, Iowa State University).

Reiter, J. 1986. "Genetic Therapy and Ethics." *Theology Digest* 33(2): 245-50.

"Report of the Standing Commission on Human Affairs of Health, 1985." *The Blue Book* (General Convention of the Episcopal Church).

Richards, Bill. 1989. "Sour Reception Greets Milk Hormone." *Wall Street Journal* (September 15): B1.

Richardson, R. 1984. "Cooperative Statistics: Current and Historical." In M. K. Overholt (ed.), *American Cooperation* (Washington, D.C.: American Institute of Cooperation).

Riche, R. W., D. E. Hecker, and J. U. Burgan. 1983. "High Technology Today and To-morrow: A Small Slice of the Employment Pie." *Monthly Labor Review* (November): 50-58.

Rifkin, J. 1983. *Algeny* (New York: Viking Press).

Rifkin, J. 1985. *Declaration of a Heretic* (Boston: Routledge and Kegan Paul).

Rifkin, J. 1987. *Time Wars: The Primary Conflict in Human History* (New York: Henry Holt and Co.).

Rifkin, J., and T. Howard. 1977. *Who Should Play God?* (New York: Dell).

Rockefeller Foundation. 1982. *Science for Agriculture* (New York: Rockefeller Foundation).

Rogoff, M., and S. L. Rawlins. 1986. "Food Security: A Technological Alternative" (unpublished paper).

Roman Catholic Church. 1987. "Instruction on Respect for Human Life in Its Origins and on the Dignity of Procreation: Replies to Ascertain Questions of the Day." Rome, March 10. Reprinted in the *New York Times* (March 11, 1987): A14-A17.

Rose, Carol. 1987. "Iowa Pursues High-Tech Research Glory." *Des Moines Register* (March 22): 1C, 3C.

Rosenfeld, A. 1979. "Judaism and Gene Design." In F. Rosner and J. Bleich (eds.), *Jewish Bioethics* (New York: Hebrew Publishing Co.).

Rosenfeld, S. 1983. "The F.D.A. and Medroxyprogesterone Acetate: What Are the Issues?" *Journal of the American Medical Association* 249: 2922-24.

Rosner, F. 1979. "Genetic Engineering and Judaism." In F. Rosner and J. Bleich (eds.), *Jewish Bioethics* (New York: Hebrew Publishing, Co.).

Rosner, F. 1981. "Test Tube Babies, Host Mothers, and Genetic Engineering in Judaism." *Tradition* 19(2): 141-48.

Ruehle, J. L., and D. H. Marx. 1979. "Fiber, Food, Fuel and Fungal Symbionts." *Science* 206: 419-22.

Ruttan, Vernon. 1982a. "Changing Role of Public and Private Sectors in Agricultural Research." *Science* 216: 23-29.

Ruttan, Vernon. 1982b. *Agricultural Research Policy* (Minneapolis: University of Minnesota Press).

Sabatier, Paul, and David Whiteman. 1985. "Legislative Decision Making and Substantive Policy Information: Models of Information Flows." *Legislative Studies Quarterly* 10: 395-421.

Saliwanchik, Roman. 1982. *Legal Protection for Microbiological and Genetic Engineering Inventions* (Reading, Mass.: Addison-Wesley).

Sanders, M. E., P. J. Leonard, W. D. Sing, and T. R. Klaenhammer. 1986. "Conjugal Strategy for Construction of Fast Acid-producing, Bacteriophage-resistant Lactic Streptococci for Use in Dairy Fermentations." *Applied Environmental Microbiology* 52: 1000-1007.

Sandine, William. 1985. "The Streptococci in Milk Products." In S. E. Gilliland (ed.), *Bacterial Starter Cultures for Foods* (Boca Raton, Fla.: CRC Press), pp. 5-23.

Sandine, William. 1987. "Looking Backward and Forward at the Practical Applications of Genetic Researches on Lactic Acid Bacteria." *FEMS Microbiology Reviews* 46: 203-20.

Schattschneider, E. E. 1960. *The Semi-Sovereign People* (New York: Holt, Rinehart and Winston).

Schell, 0. 1984. *Modern Meat: The Pharmaceutical Farm* (New York: Random House).

Schlein, Edgar H. 1984. "Coming to a New Awareness of Organizational Culture." *Sloan Management Review* (Winter): 3.

Schmid, A. Allen. 1985. "Biotechnology, Plant Variety Protection, and Changing Property Institutions in Agriculture." *North Central Journal of Agricultural Economics* 7(2): 129-38.

Schneider, Keith. 1987. "Morass of Gene Regulations Leads to Dismay on All Sides." *New York Times* (September 29): C1, C5.

Schneider, Keith. 1988. "Biotechnology's Cash Cow." *New York Times* (June 12):47, 49, 52.

Schrage, M., and N. Henderson. 1984. "Biotech Becomes a Global Priority." *Washington Post* (December 17).

Schuck, P. H. 1986. *Agent Orange on Trial: Mass Toxic Disaster in the Courts* (Cambridge: Belknap Press of Harvard University Press).

Scott, Jim, and L. Christopher Plein. 1988. "BGH and the Dairy Industry: Agenda-Setting for Adoption and Acceptance." Paper presented at the annual meetings of the Midwest Sociological Society, Minneapolis, Minnesota, March 23-26.

Shales, Tom. 1977. "Tears & Fears: Threat to Saccharin Spurs New Hoarding." *Washington Post* (March 15): B1, B7.

Sharples, F. E. 1987. "Regulation of Products from Biotechnology." *Science* 235: 1329-32.

Sheiner, N. 1978. "DES and a Proposed Theory of Enterprise Liability." *Fordham Law Review* 46(5): 963-1007.

Shelley, Mack C., II, Brian J. Reichel, William F. Woodman, and Paul Lasley. 1989. "Perceptions of the Role of University Research in Biotechnology: Town, Gown, and Industry." *Proceedings of the 1987 Iowa State University Agricultural Bioethics Symposium* (Ames: Iowa State University Press).

Sherwin, Douglas S. 1983. "The Ethical Roots of the Business System." *Harvard Business Review* (November-December): 183-92.

Shue, Henry. 1986. "Food Additives and Minority Rights: Carcinogens and Children." *Agriculture and Human Values* 3: 191-200.

Simberloff, D., and R. K. Colwell. 1984. "Release of Engineered Organisms: A Call for Ecological and Evolutionary Assessment of Risks." *Genetic Engineering News* 4(8): 4.

Singer, M. F. 1985. "Genetics and the Law: A Scientist's View." *Yale Law and Policy Review* 3: 315-35.

Smircich, Linda, and Charles Stubbart. 1985. "Strategic Management in an Enacted World." *Academy of Management Review* 10(4): 724-36.

Smith, D. E. 1970. *Religion and Political Development* (Boston: Little, Brown and Co).

Smith, D. E. 1974. *Religion and Political Modernization* (New Haven: Yale University Press).

Snow, C. P. 1961. *Science and Government* (Cambridge: Harvard University Press).

Solomon, Bart. 1987. "Measuring Clout." *National Journal* 19(27): 17.

Spitler, Amanda. 1987. "Controversy Over Animal Patents." *Bioscience* 37(9): 652.

Staba, J. 1985. "Milestones in Plant Tissue Culture Systems for the Production of Secondary Products." *Journal of Natural Products* 48(2): 203-209.

Stallmann, J., and A. Schmid. 1987. "Property Rights in Plants: Implications for Biotechnology Research and Extension." *American Journal of Agricultural Economics* 69(2): 432-37.

Stanfield, Rochelle L. 1987. "Screened Genes." *National Journal* 19(39): 2420-22.

Steiner, Peter O. 1977. "The Public Sector and the Public Interest." In *Public Expenditure and Policy Analysis* (Chicago: Rand McNally).

Sterling, J. 1988. "Agbio Products Edge Closer to Marketplace." *Genetic Engineering News* 8(5): 1,15,16.

Stevenson, Adlai. 1977. "Opening Statement." Hearings of Senate Committee on Commerce, Science, and Transportation (Subcommittee on Science, Technology, and Space) on "Regulation of Recombinant DNA Research."

Strobel, G. 1987. "Strobel: 'I Have Acted in Good Faith.'" *The Scientist* (October 19): 11-12.

Sun, M. 1986. "Local Opposition Halts Biotechnology Test." *Science* 231: 667-68.

Swaminathan, M. S. 1982. "Biotechnology Research and Third World Agriculture." *Science* 218: 967-72.

Sylvester, Edward, and Lynn C. Klotz. 1987. *The Gene Age* (New York: Charles Scribner's Sons).

Taylor, Sarah. 1988. "Patenting Life" (Issue Brief, Congressional Research Service, Washington, D.C.).

Teske, Richard H. 1987. "Milk from BST-Treated Cows: Its Safety for Human Consumption." In *Proceedings of the National Invitational Workshop on Bovine Somatotropin* (Washington, D.C.: Extension Services, USDA), pp. 31-33.

Thompson, Paul B. 1984. "Need and Safety: The Nuclear Power Debate." *Environmental Ethics* 6(1): 57-68.

Thompson, Paul B. 1987. "Agricultural Biotechnology and the Rhetoric of Risk: Some Conceptual Issues." *The Environmental Professional* 9: 316-26.

Thompson, Paul B. 1988. "Agriculture, Biotechnology, and the Political Evaluation of Risk." *Policy Studies Journal* 17(1): 98-108.

Torrey, J. G. 1985. "The Development of Plant Biotechnology." *American Scientist* 73: 354-63.

Tort Policy Working Group. 1987. *An Update on the Liability Crisis* (Washington, D.C.: USGPO).

Trewhitt, Jeff. 1985. "U.S. Midwest Makes Pitch for Biotech-Research Firms." *Chemical Engineering* (April 15): 27, 29.

Troster, L. 1984. "Therapy or Engineering: Jewish Responses to Genetic Research." *Reconstructionist* (April-May)49: 21-25.

Trubatch, Janet. 1988. Presentation on organizational incentives at workshop entitled "... And So the Poor Dog Had None," at the annual meeting of the Society of University Patent Administrators.

Twentieth Century Fund Task Force on the Commercialization of Scientific Research. 1984. *The Science Business* (New York: Priority Press).

U.S. Congress. General Accounting Office. 1986. *Biotechnology: Analysis of Federally Funded Research* (USGPO).

U.S. Congress. House. 1972. Committee on Science and Astronautics. *Genetic Engineer-*

ing: *Evolution of a Technological Issue. Report to the Subcommittee on Science, Research, and Development.* 92nd Cong., 2nd sess. November.

————. 1977. Committee on Interstate and Foreign Commerce. Subcommittee on Health and the Environment. *The Recombinant DNA Research Act of 1977.* 95th Cong., 1st sess. March 15, 16, 17.

————. 1978. *The Depo-Provera Debate: Hearings Before the House Select Committee on Population.* 95th Cong., 2nd sess.

————. 1983. Committee on Science and Technology, Subcommittee on Investigations and Oversight Hearings. *Human Genetic Engineering.*

————. 1986. Committee on Agriculture. *Review of the Status of the Potential Impact of Bovine Growth Hormone: Hearings Before the Subcommittee on Livestock, Dairy, and Poultry.* 99th Cong., 2nd sess. June 11.

U.S. Congress. Office of Technology Assessment. 1979. *Drugs in Livestock Feed, Volume 1: Technical Report* (USGPO).

————. 1981. *Assessment Impacts of Applied Genetics: Micro-Organisms, Plants and Animals* (USGPO).

————. 1984a. *Commercial Biotechnology: An International Analysis* (USGPO).

————. 1984b. *Technologies to Sustain Tropical Forest Resources* (USGPO).

————. 1986. *Technology, Public Policy, and the Changing Structure of American Agriculture* (USGPO).

————. 1987a. *New Developments in Biotechnology: Volume 2, Public Perceptions of Biotechnology* (USGPO).

————. 1987b. *Technologies to Maintain Biological Diversity* (USGPO).

————. 1988. *New Developments in Biotechnology: U.S. Investment in Biotechnology* (USGPO).

————. 1989. *New Developments in Biotechnology: Volume 5, Patenting Life* (USGPO).

U.S. Congress. Senate. 1968. Committee on Government Operations. *National Commission on Health, Science, and Society: Hearings Before the Subcommittee on Government Research.* March 7, 22, 27, and 28; April 2.

————. 1976. Committee on Labor and Public Welfare and Committee on Judiciary. *Oversight Hearings on the Implementation of NIH Guidelines Governing Recombinant DNA Research: Joint Oversight Hearing of the Subcommittee on Health and Subcommittee on Administrative Practices and Procedures.* 94th Cong., 2nd sess. September 22.

————. 1977. Committee on Commerce, Science, and Transportation. Subcommittee on Science, Technology, and Space. *Regulation of Recombinant DNA Research.* 95th Cong., 1st sess. November 2,8, 10.

————. 1984. Committee on Environment and Public Works. *Potential Environmental Consequences of Genetic Engineering. Hearings Before the Subcommittee on Toxic Substances and Environmental Oversight.* 98th Cong., 2nd sess. September 25, 27.

U.S. Department of Agriculture. 1950-1987. *Milk Production* (Washington, D.C.: USDA, National Agricultural Statistics Service).

————. 1984. *Marketing Operations of Dairy Cooperatives* (Washington, D.C.: USDA, Agricultural Cooperatives Services).

————. 1986. *Yearbook of Agriculture: Research for Tomorrow* (USGPO).

————. 1987a. *BST and the Dairy Industry: A National, Regional, and Farm-Level Analysis* (USGPO).

———. 1987b. *Biotechnology: The Challenge. Proceedings of the USDA Biotechnology Forum* (USGPO).

U.S. Department of Commerce. International Trade Administration. 1988. "Biotechnology" In *1988 U.S. Industrial Outlook* (USGPO).

U.S. Department of Health and Human Services. Public Health Service. National Institutes of Health. 1984. *DES Task Force Summary Report* (Reprinted as NIH Publication No. 84-1688, Bethesda, Md.) August.

U.S. Food and Drug Administration. 1986. *FDA Veterinarian* 1(2): 3-5.

U.S. Food and Drug Administration. 1986. *New Developments in Veterinary Biotechnology*.

———. 1988. *Food Biotechnology: Present and Future* (USGPO).

U.S. 637 *Federal Supplement* 25 Foundation on Economic Trends v. Thomas (D.D.C, 1986).

United States Code. Title 35-Patents. 1982 Edition.

University of North Carolina (UNC). Patent Task Group of the University Council on Biotechnology. 1983. "UNC Council on Biotechnology Patent Task Group Report." *Journal of College and University Law* 9(4): 541-53.

Unkovic, Dennis. 1985. *The Trade Secrets Handbook: Strategies and Techniques for Safeguarding Corporate Information* (Englewood Cliffs, N.J.: Prentice-Hall).

Van Ravenswaay, E., M. E. Smith, and S. R. Thompson. 1986. "The Effects of Heptachlor Contamination on Dairy Sales in Oahu." In E. C. Mather and J. B. Kaneene (eds.), *Economics of Animal Diseases* (Michigan State University: W. K. Kellogg Foundation).

Vobejda, Barbara. 1987. "Report Sees No Special Risk in Genetic Engineering." *Washington Post* (August 19): A3.

Von Oehsen, William H. 1988. "The FDA's Regulation of Veterinary Biotechnology: Business as Usual or New Era of Environmental Protection?" *Food, Drug, and Cosmetic Law Journal* 43: 847-76.

Wald, K. D., D. E. Owen, and Samuel S. Hill, Jr. 1988. "Churches as Political Communities." *American Political Science Review* 82(2): 531-48.

Webber, D. 1984. "New Industry Enters Era of Increased Public Scrutiny." *Chemical and Engineering News* (August 13): 23-33.

Webber, David J. 1986. "Analyzing Political Feasibility: Political Scientists' Unique Contribution to Policy Analysis." *Policy Studies Journal* 14: 545-53.

Webber, David J. 1989. "The Distribution and Use of Policy Knowledge in the Policy Process." Paper prepared for delivery at the Policy Studies Organization Conference on "Advances in Policy Studies, 1950-1990," at the Annual Meeting of the American Political Science Association, Atlanta, August 30-September 3.

Wehr, Elizabeth. 1984. "Slow Move from Laboratory to Market." *Congressional Quarterly Weekly Report* (December 15): 3094.

Wehr, Elizabeth. 1988. "Senate Clears Trade Bill by Lopsided Vote." *Congressional Quarterly Weekly Report* (August 6): 2215.

Weiss, C. 1985. "The World Bank's Support for Science and Technology." *Science* 227: 261-65.

Westphal, David. 1987. "ISU and U of I Tie Research, New Industry." *Des Moines Times Register* (February 22): 1A, 5A.

Wheeler, David. 1988. "Harvard University Receives First U.S. Patent Issued on Animals." *The Chronicle of Higher Education* (April 20): 1,8.

Wheeler, David. 1989. "Critics Sue to Halt Gene Experiment Involving Humans." *The Chronicle of Higher Education* (February 8): A5, A8.

Whiteman, David. 1985. "The Fate of Policy Analysis in Congressional Decision Making: Three Types of Use in Committees." *Western Political Quarterly* 38: 294-311.

Wildavsky, Aaron. 1987. *Searching for Safety* (New Brunswick, N.J.: Transaction Books).

Winterfeldt, Detlof, and Ward Edwards. 1984. "Patterns of Conflict about Risky Technologies." *Risk Analysis* 4: 55-68.

Woodman, William F., Brian J. Reichel, and Mack C. Shelley, II. 1989. "University-Industry Relationships in Biotechnology: Convergence and Divergence in Goals and Expectations." *Proceedings of the 1987 Iowa State University Agricultural Bioethics Symposium* (Ames: Iowa State University Press).

Woodman, William E., Mack C. Shelley, II, and Brain J. Reichel.1989. *Biotechnology and the Research Enterprise: A Guide to the Literature* (Ames: Iowa State University Press).

World Council of Churches. 1982. *Manipulating Life: Ethical Issues in Genetic Engineering* (Geneva, Switzerland: World Council of Churches).

Wynder, A., and M. Stillman. 1980. "Artificial Sweetener Use and Bladder Cancer." *Science* 207: 1214-17.

Wysocki, B., Jr. 1987. "Japanese Now Target Another Field the U.S. Leads: Biotechnology." *The Wall Street Journal* (December 17): 1,18.

Young, Arthur, and G. Steven Burril. 1988. *Biotechnology 89: Commercialization* (New York: Maryann Liebert).

Young, F. E., and H. I. Miller. 1987. "The NAS Report on 'Deliberate Release': Toppling the Tower of Bio-Babble." *Bio/Technology* 5: 1010.

Yoxen, E. 1983. *The Gene Business: Who Should Control Biotechnology* (New York: Harper and Row).

Zilinskas, Raymond. 1983. "New Biotechnology: Potential Problems Likely Promises." *Politics and the Life Sciences* 2(1): 42-52.

Index

About the Contributors

MORRIS BOSIN is a member of the Office of Planning and Evaluation, Planning and Management Communications Staff, of the Food and Drug Administration. His work on the topic of bureaucratic responses to biotechnology has appeared in the *Policy Studies Review.*

WILLIAM P. BROWNE is a Professor of Political Science at Central Michigan University. In addition to numerous articles and book chapters, his publications include several books on public policy problems, the most recent of which is *Private Interests, Public Policy, and American Agriculture* (Kansas, 1988).

LAWRENCE BUSCH is a Professor of Sociology at Michigan State University. Along with William Lacy he has authored *Science, Agriculture, and the Politics of Research* and edited *The Agricultural Scientific Enterprise*. He has written extensively in the field of society and agriculture.

WILLIAM D. COLE is a graduate student in the Department of Sociology at the University of Kentucky.

ROBERT K. DIXON is currently with the Environmental Protection Agency in Corvallis, Oregon, and formerly was an Associate Professor in the School of Forestry at Auburn University. His work has appeared in such journals as the *Journal of Developing Areas.*

BEVERLY FLEISHER is an agricultural economist with the Government Studies Group, Division of Science Resources Studies, of the National Science Foundation. She formerly served with the Economic Research Service of the USDA. Her work has appeared in the *American Journal of Agricultural Economics* and other publications.

LARRY G. HAMM is an Associate Professor of Agricultural Economics at Michigan State University. He has also served as an economist for the USDA's Economic Research Service. His monographs and journal articles result from research done in these areas.

CHARLES JOHNSON is Professor of Political Science and Associate Dean of the College of Liberal Arts at Texas A&M University. His work has appeared in such journals as *Western Political Science Quarterly*, *Social Science Quarterly*, and *Law and Policy*.

AMAL KAWAR is an Associate Professor of Political Science at Utah State University. Her work has appeared in *Politics and the Life Sciences*.

FRED KUCHLER is an economist with the USDA's Economic Research Service. He has worked in the areas of agricultural and environmental policies at the USDA since 1981, when he received a Ph.D. in economics from Virginia Polytechnic Institute.

WILLIAM B. LACY is a Professor of Rural Sociology and Assistant Dean of Research, College of Agriculture, Pennsylvania State University. He has written widely in the field of society and agriculture. Among his works are *Science, Agriculture, and the Politics of Research* (coauthored with Lawrence Busch) and *The Agricultural Scientific Enterprise* (which he coedited with Lawrence Busch).

PAUL LASLEY is an Associate Professor of Sociology at Iowa State University, where he specializes in rural sociology and conducts an annual opinion poll of Iowa farm operators.

JOHN McCLELLAND is an agricultural economist with the USDA's Economic Research Service. He has a Ph.D. in agricultural economics from the University of Georgia. His research has focused on the dynamics of investment decisions and impacts of new agricultural technologies.

ROBIN MOORE has a Masters in Public Administration from Texas A&M University. She is currently working as a hospital administrator in Texas.

SUSAN E. OFFUTT is an economist with the Office of Management and Budget. She has worked as an economist at the USDA and taught agricultural economics at the University of Illinois. She received a Ph.D. in agricultural economics from Cornell University.

L. CHRISTOPHER PLEIN is a Ph.D. candidate in Political Science at the University of Missouri-Columbia. His research interests focus on the policy dimensions of science and technology issues and rural economic development issues.

BRIAN J. REICHEL is a doctoral student in Sociology at Iowa State University, and is simultaneously pursuing graduate studies in public administration at Iowa State University and the juris doctor degree from the Drake University Law School.

MACK C. SHELLEY, II is an Associate Professor of Political Science and Statistics at Iowa State University, where he specializes in public policy, social statistics, and American politics.

RICHARD SHERLOCK is a Professor of Languages and Philosophy at Utah State University. His work has appeared in *Politics and the Life Sciences*.

PAUL B. THOMPSON is an Associate Professor of Philosophy and Agricultural Economics at Texas A&M University. He has published numerous articles on biotechnology and public policy. He has been an International Affairs Fellow of the Council on Foreign Relations, and a Resident Fellow at Resources for the Future in the National Center for Food and Agricultural Policy.

DAVID J. WEBBER is an Associate Professor of Political Science at the University of Missouri-Columbia and has published articles concerning both environmental policy and the use of policy information in the policy process.

THOMAS C. WIEGELE is a Professor of Political Science and Director of the Program for Biosocial Research/Social Science Research Institute at Northern Illinois University.

WILLIAM F. WOODMAN is a Professor of Sociology at Iowa State University, where he specializes in complex organizations and public policy.